Travel and Description Series · Volume XII

Rølvaag enjoying the back yard of his home at 311 Manitou in Northfield, May 1917. Photo courtesy Ella Valborg Tweet.

Concerning Our Heritage

by

OLE E. RØLVAAG

Translated with an Introduction by

SOLVEIG ZEMPEL

1998
The Norwegian-American Historical Association
Northfield · Minnesota

COVER:

The design is the one on the original Norwegian edition
published by the St. Olaf College Press in 1922.

PREFACE

A reader in the 1990s might find some of the arguments in *Concerning Our Heritage* quaint and even self-evident. It is well to remember, however, that they were written in a climate of intolerance and hysterical agitation for abandoning all vestiges of immigrant cultures. Many Norwegian Americans were heeding the call of Americanization. In the intolerant historical context of the 1920s, Ole E. Rølvaag's admonition to his fellow Norwegian Americans to honor their heritage consequently becomes an eloquent protest against the injustice suffered by all Americans not of Anglo-Saxon background as well as a personal testament to the value of an ancestral heritage. In the years that followed, Rølvaag gave artistic expression to these same ideas in superbly crafted fictional depictions of immigrant life.

The Norwegian-American Historical Association is pleased to make available under its imprint this carefully annotated and thoughtfully introduced translation of Rølvaag's concerns about preserving the Norwegian-American heritage. As Rølvaag's granddaughter, Solveig Zempel has both a personal and a professional attachment to the topic and the clear advantage of a family Rølvaag tradition; as professor of Norwegian at St. Olaf College she has given insightful scholarly attention to Rølvaag's literary career. Her earlier translations of Rølvaag's works include *The Third Life of Per Smevik* in 1971, translated together with Ella Valborg Tweet, and in 1984 *When the Wind is in the South and Other Stories by O.E. Rolvaag*. In 1991 Zempel edited and translated *In Their Own Words: Letters from Norwegian Immigrants*. She has lectured extensively on Rølvaag's authorship to general and academic audiences both in the United States and in Norway.

Finally, I wish to acknowledge with much gratitude the contributions of my capable and dedicated editorial assistant Mary R. Hove in preparing the manuscript for publication. She is also responsible for the index.

ODD S. LOVOLL
St. Olaf College
University of Oslo

ACKNOWLEDGMENTS

I am thankful to the Norwegian-American Historical Association whose archives at St. Olaf College in Northfield, Minnesota, are a treasure trove of materials on Rølvaag and the context in which he lived and worked. Forrest Brown, Ruth Crane, Lloyd Hustvedt, and Odd Lovoll of NAHA all provided invaluable support and assistance, as well as a congenial working atmosphere. Odd Lovoll deserves special thanks for suggesting that I take on this project, encouraging me as I proceeded with it, and for thorough and helpful editing, ably assisted by Mary Hove.

I wish to thank my family for their support, and especially my husband Elden Zempel and my sister Torild Homstad for their willingness to read and critique drafts of the manuscript, and my mother Ella Valborg Tweet for answering numerous questions and sharing her personal knowledge and insight.

Ingeborg Kongslien and Dagfinn Worren provided generous hospitality as well as assistance in tracking down citations and help with the meaning of difficult passages. Brynhild Rowberg graciously shared with me the draft translation she had prepared under the direction of Kenneth Bjork.

Finally, I am grateful to St. Olaf College for providing me with a sabbatical leave, as well as the necessary facilities to carry out this work.

SOLVEIG ZEMPEL
St. Olaf College

CONTENTS

Concerning Our Heritage

INTRODUCTION

"Well, good luck with your book, whether you find a market or not. We can comfort ourselves with the thought that in 100 years learned people will be writing with great understanding about us and our contributions to American culture."[1]

O.E. Rølvaag formulated the ideas presented here during the first two decades of this century, then collected and published them in book form in 1922. His intended audience was "his people"—Norwegian Americans living primarily in the Upper Midwest. Why translate these essays by, about, and for a small group of early twentieth-century immigrants now? One reason of course is to allow English-speaking scholars to gain insight into the thinking of a major American writer. But perhaps more important, the issues Rølvaag struggled with reflect the timeless tensions between immigrant pasts and assimilated futures that are the circumstances of all Americans. Furthermore, immigration is a world phenomenon, and it is my hope and belief that the message Rølvaag wrote for "his people"—the message that men and women need to understand the history of the people they came from and to know their literature, music, and arts in order to know themselves—will through this translation resonate with a new generation of readers.

In the year 1896, Ole Edvart Rølvaag was one of nearly seven thousand Norwegians who emigrated to the United States. There he joined close to half a million of his countrymen who had come before him and he would be followed by almost a quarter of a million more, who together formed the community of Norwegian Americans. These were the people Rølvaag came to call "his people" or in the terms of the time "his race"—what we today would call his ethnic group.

According to his own account, written in a letter to his fiancée, Jennie Berdahl, Rølvaag left his beloved home in Norway to fulfill his ambition to become something great in the world. Already at an early age he had developed a sense of calling and a desire to become something more than a fisherman. He was looking for opportunity—opportunity to gain an education, to develop his intellect, and to find an outlet for his desire to write.[2]

Rølvaag was born and grew to young adulthood on the island of Dønna, lying off the coast of Helgeland in northern Norway. His father Peder Benjamin Jakobsen Rølvaag was a fisherman and his mother Ellerine Pedersdotter took care of the home and the family of seven children. In spite of poverty and limited formal education, the family were all voracious readers, making extensive use of the local library and keeping up with national and international trends by subscribing to a Christiania newspaper. Lively discussions of the issues of the day were a source of entertainment for the family. Ole was especially close to his gifted older brother Johan, who set a high standard for the younger brother to live up to. Yet Johan, in spite of his intellectual ability, remained an impoverished fisherman. Toward the end of his life, he wrote a series of beautifully written philosophical letters to his brother in America. In one of these letters, Johan praises Rølvaag's talent and urges him to become a prophet for his people.[3]

The Rølvaag children ended their formal schooling of nine weeks a year for seven years as soon as they were confirmed at the age of fourteen. Ole, like the other boys in his community, sailed to the Lofoten fishing banks for the first time as a fourteen-year-old, and continued as a fisherman there for the next six years. He nearly lost his life in a terrible storm in 1893, and shortly thereafter he wrote to an uncle in South Dakota asking him for the loan of enough money for a ticket to America. In 1896 he finally received the precious ticket and set out later that summer to join his uncle Jakob Jakobsen in Elk Point, South Dakota. He worked for three years as a farmhand near Elk Point; the events and experiences of these years he described with both drama and humor in his first published novel, *Amerika-Breve* (Letters from America, translated as *The Third Life of Per Smevik*).

Working as a farmhand, however, was not the kind of opportunity Rølvaag had dreamt about when he gave up an offer to captain his own fishing boat in order to leave for America. Encouraged by a local pastor, he enrolled in Augustana Academy, a Norwegian-American Lutheran preparatory school in Canton, South Dakota. It was here that he first became acquainted with the Berdahls, a family of pioneer immigrants who had come to South Dakota in the 1870s. Rølvaag became good friends with John Berdahl at Augustana Academy, and he later married John's sister, Jennie, who also attended school there. He learned much factual information about the pioneer period from Jennie's father and uncles. During his student days at Augustana Rølvaag was influenced by the first of several important teachers, and he not only began a serious study of literature but also made his first attempts at writing for an audience. He graduated with honors in 1901, and his commencement address was reported in the local newspaper. According to the newspaper account, he laid out in this speech his fundamental belief that immigrants can become good citizens and contribute to their adopted country only by drawing on their own language, culture, and national heritage.

Following his graduation from Augustana Academy, Rølvaag decided to continue his education at St. Olaf College in Northfield, Minnesota. Again, he chose a school with strong Norwegian-American and Lutheran ties where he could acquire a well-rounded classical education. Here too, he was fortunate to meet excellent teachers who encouraged his love for and understanding of Norwegian language and literature. He took a heavy load of coursework, wishing to make the most of this opportunity and also to make up for lost time. Among other subjects, he studied Latin, Greek, German, English, history, church history, mathematics, and psychology. In addition to coursework and participation in many activities, he continued writing, and a number of his short pieces appeared in college publications. During this time and until their marriage in 1908, he carried on an extensive correspondence with his fiancée, Jennie Berdahl. In these charming letters he reveals his ambition and his sense of mission to serve "his" Norwegian-American people.

Already older than most of his fellow students, Rølvaag was eager to begin a career so he could get married and settle in a home of his own. When President J.N. Kildahl offered him a teaching post at St. Olaf contingent on spending a year doing graduate work at the university in Christiania, Norway, he accepted enthusiastically. He borrowed money from Kildahl, and in 1905, less than ten years after he had left his homeland as a poor fisherman, he returned to Norway as a graduate student.

While at the university in Christiania, Rølvaag learned several very important lessons. One was how much he had changed, how much he had been influenced by his years in America. He was different from the other students, not only older but bolder. He spoke up, asked questions, and as always was ambitious to gain the maximum possible knowledge from his courses. Just as at St. Olaf, he took the heaviest load allowed, and it was a bitter pill for him when illness forced him to miss many lectures. During this time he also came to understand that he was no longer a Norwegian, but had become an American, or at least a Norwegian American. Extensive notebooks show how hard he worked, and also what great teachers he studied under.[4] He studied the history of Norwegian literature under Gerhard Gran, psychology with Arne Löchen, *landsmaal*[5] under Marius Hægstad, Norwegian ballads under Moltke Moe, Norwegian history under Ernst Sars, and philology with Hjalmar Falk. All these men were important scholars of the time, and certainly influenced Rølvaag's views on Norwegian history, literature, and culture. While he was in Norway, Rølvaag read Norwegian literature extensively, and deepened his understanding of Ibsen, Bjørnson, Garborg, Lie, and other Norwegian authors. In addition to his concentration on Norwegian literature and history, Rølvaag was especially interested in the study of psychology, and he found that he was the only student in his psychology class who had read William James. In a telling description of his final examination, we see that Rølvaag desperately wanted to do well, particularly, as he wrote to his fiancée Jennie, "because I was an American, and the big fellows in Christiania have not much faith in us. Perhaps my *examen* may do a little to strengthen it."[6] And indeed, it must have, for he received the highest grade possible.

Rølvaag's education—from his boyhood schooling in Norway through his academy and college work in Norwegian-American institutions to his graduate work at the university in Norway—was steeped in the notions of romantic nationalism. Norway had become free from Denmark in 1814, only to be united with Sweden under a common king until 1905. During this entire period Norway was struggling to define a separate national identity. Artists, intellectuals, and political leaders did this through a cultivation of the common "folk" heritage in art, music, folktales, and language, and by emphasizing historical connections to Norway's heroic, independent past.[7] Rølvaag, like many other immigrants, brought these national romantic ideas with him when he crossed the ocean.

Upon returning to Northfield, Rølvaag started teaching in both the academy and the college. In addition to Norwegian, which was his main subject, he taught geometry, physiology, geography, Greek, and Bible history. He was also head resident in the dormitory. After their marriage in 1908, Rølvaag and his wife founded a new home in Northfield. Four children were born to the family, but both the eldest and the youngest died in early childhood.

As time went on, Rølvaag gradually came to concentrate on Norwegian language and literature. He became chairman of the Department of Norwegian in 1916, a post which he held until shortly before his death. In 1920, he added courses on Ibsen and on immigration history, both taught in English. The course on immigration history was one of his favorites, giving him the opportunity to present to his students his ideas on national identity, preservation of heritage, and Norwegian culture. The lecture notes for this course form the core of the first section of *Concerning Our Heritage*.

Rølvaag was very close to President Lars Boe, and became part of an inner circle of advisers to the president. He willingly stepped in to help whenever necessary, and even served briefly as college registrar. He went on fund-raising missions and donated regularly to college fund drives. Perhaps his biggest sacrifice on behalf of the college was to give up part of his first sabbatical, when he was in the midst of writing his famous novel of Norwegian-American pioneer life, in order to travel around the Midwest raising funds to replace the chapel that burned down in 1923. Even with this interruption, he had completed nearly half the manuscript for *I de dage*, the first half of what would become *Giants in the Earth*, before sailing for Norway in the spring of 1924. There he finished the manuscript and it was accepted for publication by Aschehoug. It was a tremendous coup for Rølvaag, as an obscure Norwegian-American writer, to have a novel published by one of the leading Norwegian publishers.

Though Rølvaag was unknown in America outside the Norwegian-American community, within that community he was a leading figure. By the time *I de dage* was published in Norway, he had already published four novels, several textbooks, and numerous short stories, as well as editorials and newspaper columns, occasional poetry, and essays. All were written in Norwegian and published by Norwegian-American presses, journals, and newspapers in America. Not everything Rølvaag wrote was equally well received by his Norwegian-American audience and he became a controversial figure, with both defenders and detractors. Some detractors objected to his ideas on heritage and preservation,[8] others were concerned with the negative portrayal of Norwegian Americans in some of his books, or they had a more general objection to what they considered indecent in his literary works.[9] On more than one occasion there were calls for his removal from St. Olaf College. However, President Boe, though he disagreed with Rølvaag in some of his ideas, always supported him and these calls came to nothing.[10]

Rølvaag helped organize the Nordlandslag (society for people from the district of Nordland in northern Norway) in 1909. He was an officer for many years, and helped arrange meetings as well as contributing regularly to its publication, *Nord-Norge*. In 1910, he was elected secretary of Samfundet for Norsk Sprog og Kultur (Society for Norwegian Language and Culture), which also generated an enormous volume of correspondence. This society consisted of a group of Norwegian-American educators, and was devoted to the promotion of the teaching of Norwegian and to providing adequate textbooks and teaching materials. During the height of the anti-foreign hysteria during and after World War I, and partly as a reaction to the controversy over attempts to drop the word "Norwegian" from the name of the Norwegian Lutheran Church in America, Rølvaag helped found the society For Fædrearven (For the Ancestral Heritage). He accepted the post of secretary and wrote many of the columns which appeared under the masthead of the society in the weekly newspaper *Visergutten*. Rewritten excerpts from these editorials appear in the essays in *Concerning Our Heritage*. In 1925, Rølvaag helped found the Norwegian American Historical Association (NAHA), and was the first secretary of this organization.[11] He devoted countless hours to collecting and organizing books, pamphlets, and other materials for the NAHA archives. In a letter to a friend, he wrote that he and his wife had addressed 500 letters for NAHA that week. Rølvaag not only helped organize these societies and carried on an enormous correspondence on their behalf, he also attended numerous meetings throughout the Upper Midwest and was frequently one of the main speakers.

Rølvaag's family may not always have appreciated his extensive travel and frequent absences from home, but for the contemporary researcher into his life and thought these absences have created a treasure trove of materials in the form of the many letters he wrote to friends and acquaintances, and especially to his wife and children. He traveled to Norway four times, and on these trips he would often start a letter on the train and continue it while on the boat, adding many pages each day of observation, philosophizing, and loving words. By the time he mailed the letter at his destination, it might be twenty or more pages long. The family letters are warm and intimate, revealing much of Rølvaag's personality and temperament. Rølvaag was an inveterate correspondent, and it is fascinating to see how he varied his style in accord with the personality and the type of relationship he had with each recipient.[12]

Rølvaag was a man with many irons in the fire all his life, combining teaching, organizational work, support for the college, and his writing. He was often plagued by ill health, which sapped his energy, and in his private letters he sometimes wrote that he was discouraged because he could not accomplish all that he wanted to do. He escaped the Minnesota winters for two years, residing for several months in the South during 1929 and 1930. His heart finally failed him, and he died in his home in Northfield at the age of 55, in November of 1931.

During the last years of his life, Rølvaag found himself catapulted into literary fame on two continents. He was courted by Norwegian authors who solicited his help in finding translators and publishers in America, and he gained new friends among the literary and intellectual establishment in the United States.[13] The poor fisherman from Norway had fulfilled his calling, been faithful to his mission in life, and it had led him down a remarkable path.

In his literary works Rølvaag expressed his views on immigration, culture, and heritage through his fictional characters and their fates. Augsburg Press in Minneapolis published his first novel in 1912. The Norwegian title, *Amerika-Breve* (Letters from America), indicates its form, and the English title, *The Third Life of Per Smevik,* hints at its content.[14] The English title comes from a statement made by the protagonist in one of his first letters home. His first life, he explains, was lived in his old home in Smeviken, Norway. His second life, which seemed like an eternity to him, was lived on the three-week journey by sea, railroad, and foot to his new home in Clarkfield, South Dakota. He is now about to embark on his third life, that of an immigrant in a new land. The letters that make up the remainder of the book describe this third life and his reactions to it. Although cast as fiction, there is no doubt that many of the incidents and certainly the feelings expressed in the book are based on Rølvaag's own experiences and emotional reactions. His brother Johan, in commenting on the novel, claimed that it was based on Rølvaag's own letters to his family in Norway. And Rølvaag had the temerity to insert one of his own speeches into the novel by having his protagonist copy it out for his father and brother, purportedly to help them decide whether or not to emigrate. The message of the speech, that of gains and losses, seems to weigh most heavily on the losses. "We lost our Fatherland . . . we lost spiritual contact with our own people and our own nation . . . we lost the inexpressible!"[15] In this speech, the balance falls on the negative, on the tragic side of immigration; however, in the novel as a whole that is less clear. The young Per Smevik has left his first and second lives behind, and is embarking on the third. This life, like Rølvaag's own, allowed him to pursue an intellectual and spiritual occupation that would have been denied to him had he remained in Norway. The gains are not merely material, and the question of whether or not they are worth the price is left open. Per Smevik's father and brother do, after all, decide to join him in America.

Rølvaag's next novel, *Paa glemte veie* (On Forgotten Paths), was also published by Augsburg Press just two years later. This book has never been translated into English, and consequently has not been as much discussed in the critical literature. In this apprentice work Rølvaag is fumbling his way toward the development of his literary themes and characters. Chris Larsen is wholly materialistic and cares nothing for spiritual values or national heritage. He stands in sharp contrast to his wife Magdalena and even more so to his daughter Mabel, whose life work becomes the salvation of her father's soul. Rølvaag himself summed up this novel in a letter, saying: "It is about a girl who is herself a Christian, but who has an unbeliever for a father. She sacrifices her life for him, in order to bring him to God; but the farther she goes on the path of duty, the more thorny the path becomes. She comes to be the diametric opposite of our 'better' youth who gather in meetings and at Luther League and brag and talk about 'the greatness of Service.' That is the main idea in a nutshell."[16]

It is not hard to see foreshadowing of Beret and Per Hansa in Chris and Mabel Larsen. The prairie personified also plays a large role in this novel, just as it does in so many of Rølvaag's works. Einar Haugen argues that *Paa glemte veie* is Rølvaag's attempt to portray the implacable ideal, the notion of an irrevocable call, of Kierkegaard and Ibsen put into practice on the South Dakota prairie. The attempt was noble, even if it failed as literature.[17]

Rølvaag's third published novel, *To tullinger* (Two fools), appeared in 1920, again under the Augsburg imprint, after a long period in which he concentrated on teaching, organizational work, and preparation of textbooks and teaching materials. This novel reflects not only the bitterness and disillusionment of the World War I period, but also the personal tragedies in Rølvaag's own life. First his beloved brother Johan died in 1913, then his mother and his oldest

son in 1915, and his youngest son in the spring of 1920. In this novel
Rølvaag gives his most pessimistic portrayal of what can happen
when people reject their traditions. In the end, the two main characters pursue purely materialistic goals, and, having forsaken everything for the sake of gold, freeze to death. Distrusting banks, they
carry their fortune in money belts, which are burned as trash by
those who find their bodies, leaving nothing. Rølvaag takes the opportunity in this novel to caricature those Norwegian Americans
who tried to deny their national heritage, as well as the American
society that demanded 100% Americanism. In a personal letter, Rølvaag described *To tullinger* as "my nastiest book."[18] And in general,
both the critics and the public agreed with that assessment. Years
later, after having achieved fame among the American reading public with *Giants in the Earth*, Rølvaag hired a translator to turn *To
tullinger* into English. However, he was very dissatisfied with the
translation, and finally rewrote the whole thing himself. The English version, called *Pure Gold*, was published in 1930. Rølvaag's Norwegian publishers took that version, had it retranslated, and
brought it out in Norway under the title *Rent Guld*.

Just one year after publishing his "nastiest" book, Rølvaag presented the Norwegian-American reading public with an entirely
different novel, *Længselens baat*, (*The Boat of Longing*), which he described as "my most beautiful book."[19] *The Boat of Longing* was re-
putedly Rølvaag's favorite of all his novels, and the one into which
he said he put more of himself than any other. This is also the only
one of his books in which significant portions of the action take
place in Norway and, specifically, in his home area of Nordland. As
Einar Haugen says, "Nordland, with its glory of summer and gloom
of winter, is more than a setting, it is a character in the tale."[20] The
sub-title "film pictures" seems apt, as the book has little plot, and
is rather a series of vignettes. The novel focuses on the soul of the
immigrant and emphasizes the dangers of rootlessness. Rølvaag la-
beled the novel "Book One," evidently intending to continue the
story. However, other writing intervened and, in spite of frequent
calls from friends and critics for the sequel, "Book Two" was never
written. *The Boat of Longing* gives the most poetic presentation of
Rølvaag's themes; here he is no longer as grimly pessimistic as in his

previous novel, as he emphasizes the relation between creative art and cultural inheritance. Rølvaag depicts the fate of the sensitive soul who cannot find a new culture to replace the one left behind, because there is no sub-culture, no established group in which to find a home. Just as the sensitive soul cannot thrive, neither can art thrive in a society of rootless and insecure people. While he was finishing this novel, Rølvaag said he was writing it to prove that "the damned foreigner" also has a soul.[21]

Finally, in 1923, Rølvaag got the sabbatical he had been longing for, and, in spite of the interruption caused by fund-raising trips for the college, he finished the manuscript for *I de dage* and *Riket grundlægges*, which together became in English *Giants in the Earth*. These were published by Aschehoug in Norway as two separate novels in 1924 and 1925, and were received by the Norwegian public and critics with great enthusiasm. Rølvaag became famous in Norway, and when the English translation appeared in 1927, he went overnight from being an obscure professor to an eminent American writer. Even before the English translation had been started, Rølvaag was convinced that this was "as American as anything can be of that sort. The language is dress—simply dress—and nothing more. Norway will never lay claim to these two novels. The subject matter as well as the treatment is American."[22] Today Rølvaag is in the position of belonging to two national literatures, for Norway does lay claim to these novels. In Norwegian literary histories Rølvaag is often classified as a regional writer, representing "Vesterheim" or Norwegian America.

Giants in the Earth is an epic novel about Norwegian immigrant pioneers with protagonists Per Hansa and his wife Beret providing a psychologically realistic portrait of the immigrant's struggle, a portrait which becomes universal in its artistic greatness. The American critic Joseph Baker maintains that "the pioneer struggle with the untamed universe may serve as a symbol for the condition of man himself against inhuman destiny."[23] While Per Hansa and other pioneers in the group are concerned with physical survival and establishing their new homes, Beret worries about what will become of their souls. She feels most keenly the spiritual and cultural loss that results from being cut off from the homeland and ties of family and tradition. Though Beret is presented sympathetically, there is also much to be said for the optimistic, forward-looking Per Hansa. He is seen as using his heritage, rather than losing it, when he applies his knowledge of sailing and fishing to new situations in the new culture. We may see this as a form of healthy adaptation in contrast to Beret's sometimes sick longing for a perhaps idealized past.[24] In this novel, Rølvaag turns the American dream on its head, and reiterates the same question he had raised in many speeches and essays throughout his career: At what cost has this greatness been won? To the American reading public, this was a new idea, and it won him a wide and enthusiastic audience. *Giants in the Earth* was both a popular and a critical success. It has been in print continuously to this day, and has been translated into a myriad of languages.

Rølvaag continued the story of Beret and her children in the two novels which followed *Giants in the Earth*. Both were published by Aschehoug in Norway, followed by English translations by his American publisher, Harper's. *Peder Seier (Peder Victorious)* opens with an image reminiscent of *The Third Life of Per Smevik*. As a young child, Peder feels that he moves in three different rooms. These three rooms include the one in English, where he is happiest and most himself, the one with his mother and family, where everything is in Norwegian, and a third room where he is alone with God, which is also in Norwegian. During the course of the novel, Peder is never able to fully integrate these various strands of his personality. The novel gives an insightful portrait of the psychology of an adolescent, and also continues Beret's story, relating how she carries on the work of Per Hansa and becomes the best farmer in the settlement. Rølvaag again circles around his familiar themes of the importance of maintaining the ancestral heritage, faith, and language. Rølvaag himself said that he was "afraid of this book. Our people will scarcely understand it. I have attempted to draw in pictures the reasons why one of the 99 lambs goes away from us, and most readers will not understand this. However, I believe I have written more beautifully about life this time than ever before."[25] Rølvaag wrote to the American critic Percy Boynton that "*Peder* deals more with the inner side of the problem."[26]

In this same letter to Boynton, Rølvaag says that he cannot discuss Peder objectively, since he is not half done with him yet. The final novel from Rølvaag's pen, *Den signede dag* (That blessed day), published in English as *Their Fathers' God*, continues with the story of Peder's young adulthood, his marriage to the Irish-American Susie Doheny, his burgeoning political ambition, and the desert his life becomes when he chooses to reject his heritage. Because Peder rejects his own culture, language, religion, and heritage, he cannot accept Susie's right to hers. This—combined with the ill effects of Beret's interference in his blossoming relationship with Susie before their marriage and the difficulties the young couple face in reconciling their differences while sharing a household with Beret—results in the collapse of their marriage.

Peder's problem is not that he has married an Irish-American Catholic, but that he has rejected his own religion and heritage. After all, Per Hansa and Beret were also in some ways incompatible personalities, just as Peder and Susie are. Stirring different cultural and religious backgrounds into the mix surely does not make things easier. However, if Peder could only have understood and accepted his own cultural heritage then he might have understood and accepted Susie's as well, but because he has locked up two of the rooms in his heart, he is not a whole person. If he can only unlock those other rooms in his heart and accept himself for what he really is, then there may be hope for him in the future.

Of contemporary American critics, only the *New York Times* appears to have understood the message of Rølvaag's final novel: "If Rølvaag is right—and he convinces one that he is—then that fond dream of the 'melting pot' went into the discard during those very years when it was most vigorously being talked. . . . Those interested in American evolution have much to ponder in this frank study."[27]

In both *Peder Victorious* and *Their Fathers' God* Beret continues to assert the value, even the absolute necessity, of maintaining the ancestral language and cultural traditions. Pastor Kaldahl, who sometimes functions as Rølvaag's spokesperson in the novel, reminds Peder that "you have been entrusted with a rich inheritance built up through the ages. . . Is it not your irrevocable duty to see how much of it you can preserve and hand on to those coming after you? A people that has lost its traditions is doomed." However, Peder rejects his arguments: "We're Americans here." To which Kaldahl, using a somewhat mixed metaphor, replies: "Does the leopard change his spots by coming into new pastures?" Peder sees America as a new foundation where "the whole structure must be new." But Kaldahl reminds him that many of its timbers have been brought from far away, some even from Norway.

Some literary historians have criticized Rølvaag for his biological metaphors, and even characterized Beret's words "We don't mix potatoes and wheat in the same bin" as "almost disgusting."[28] Orm Øverland counters this by saying that "one needs to look at this question with greater nuance. It is one thing when a strong group uses an exclusive racial ideology to hold down a weaker group. It is another matter altogether when a vulnerable group attempts to preserve its own distinctive qualities." He goes on to remind us that "encouraging one's own ethnic group to preserve its own [culture, language, etc.] does not imply anything of lesser worth or value in that which other groups have."[29] We might note in this context that Beret does not talk about mixing potatoes with dirt or wheat with chaff. Rølvaag himself wrote to Percy Boynton that he intended his novels to "be true for all racial groups, more or less, and endure the acid test of time."[30] Rølvaag was not alone in ascribing cultural characteristics to various national groups. Thinkers such as American philosopher Horace Kallen and many others held similar views. This "vague identification of culture with ancestry served mainly to emphasize the antiquity, the uniqueness, and the permanence of nationality. It suggested the inner vitality of one's own culture, rather than the menace of another race."[31]

Rølvaag planned at least one more novel about Peder Victorious, and it may well be that he intended to bring about a final synthesis. This we will never know. St. Olaf President Lars Boe claimed so, based on his many conversations with Rølvaag. Boe wrote: "We [Norwegian Americans] are notoriously ugly under pressure, and Peder is ugly. As a Norwegian or alien people, we have been married to 'Susie.' Rølvaag was firmly convinced that we would not necessarily have to separate from Susie permanently. But the day would come when Beret would 'come back in her boy.' That is what I am fighting for. In what form and manner shall Beret come back among the Norwegian-American people? It is up to a school like St. Olaf to point the way. It is up to us to make it possible to save those cultural and religious values which our fathers brought with them. Rølvaag had an abiding faith that it would be done, though he was often very *mismodig* [discouraged]."[32]

Rølvaag left home himself, and had his literary characters leave home, for complex reasons, with ambivalent feelings and complicated results. He struggled constantly with balancing the issues of gain and loss. Rølvaag showed through the psychological realism of his literary works the necessity for individuals and groups to respect their cultural traditions, language, and heritage. The same themes that Rølvaag presents in his fiction form the core ideas in the essays in *Concerning Our Heritage*.

Norwegian Americans in the first half of the twentieth century were living in a time of rapid change and a period of fierce demands for assimilation. Rølvaag felt very strongly that maintaining their ethnic identity was important for their self-respect and for their ability to function positively in the greater American society. Not only were Norwegian Americans under intense pressure of "Americanization" from the greater society, they were at the same time in a period of debate and disagreement among themselves over their identity and their role in society. Leaders and members of the community disagreed, sometimes violently, over what constituted, or should constitute, their place in American society. Defending the cultural values of Norwegian Americans and advancing their claims as valuable members of American society became the life work of Rølvaag and other Norwegian-American leaders.

Rølvaag was what we might today call a "cultural pluralist." His vision of America was of a mosaic of ethnic communities, each preserving and promoting its own language, culture, and traditions, which could be united around American political ideals. Philosopher and professor Horace Kallen, himself a German Jewish immigrant, held the view that tolerance of cultural persistence was integral to the philosophy of the United States. Kallen is generally recognized as the first exponent of cultural pluralism; his major work on this theme, *Culture and Democracy in the United States*, came out in 1924. He rejected both assimilation and amalgamation and advocated the right and duty of each immigrant group to preserve its own language, institutions, and cultural heritage. Members of minority groups would of course learn English and participate in American institutions, but his vision of the United States was of a "cooperation of diversities."[33] Rølvaag would have substantially agreed with Kallen's oft-quoted statement that "What is inalienable in the life of mankind is its intrinsic positive quality—its psycho-social inheritance. Men may change their clothes, their politics, their wives, their religions, their philosophies, to a greater or lesser extent; they cannot change their grandfathers. Jews or Poles or Anglo-Saxons, in order to cease being Jews or Poles or Anglo-Saxons, would have to cease to be, while they could cease to be citizens or church members or carpenters or lawyers without ceasing to be. The self-hood which is inalienable in them . . . is ancestrally determined, and the happiness which they pursue has its form implied in ancestral endowments."[34]

In the concluding words of *Concerning our Heritage*, which was published two years before Kallen's book, Rølvaag wrote: ". . . as citizens we are Americans and only Americans. But in ancestry, in descent, in kinship we are Norwegians and can never be anything else no matter how desperately some of us try. I for my part can only believe that it is an eternal truth that our people came here originally from Norway. Therefore we are Norwegians by descent. . . . As I understand it, there are riches and possibilities here which we have scarcely tapped."

Not only the exaggerated form of the melting pot was wrong, according to Kallen, but so was any kind of policy which had as its goal assimilation of the immigrant. Instead of assimilation, Kallen proposed recognition and deliberate fostering of the enduring quality of ethnic differences so that America should become a federation of distinct nationalities.[35] Kallen suggested visualizing America as an orchestra rather than as a melting pot because in an orchestra individuals and small groups work together to produce a harmony of sound from a variety of different instruments.[36] Though he also rejected the melting pot, Rølvaag's views were not entirely in accordance with Kallen's, especially the notion of a federation of distinct nationalities. Rølvaag stated frequently that he was opposed to the formation of a "little Norway in America." He acknowledged that the Norwegian language would disappear, and he understood that contact and assimilation had positive as well as negative sides. Rølvaag was, however, well acquainted with Kallen's ideas, and in a letter to Waldemar Ager he warmly recommended Kallen's book, *Culture and Democracy in the United States*, adding that he found it "amusing to see that other folks are thinking just the same thoughts that you and I have been chewing over for nearly a generation."[37]

By 1920, Rølvaag had developed a course in immigration history, which he taught in English. Notes for this course outline its purpose from Rølvaag's point of view: "I would like to have every young man and woman of Norwegian descent to feel proud of the part which our race has played in the development of this country. I would like to instill the deepest veneration and strongest love of the homes which our own parents and grandparents have built on this side of the Atlantic. . . . So I am giving this course in the boyish hope that I thereby may lead a few of our own young people to think more of their own fathers and mothers and the work they have done in this country, to appreciate their own race more. . . . Hence, I am giving this course in the hope that those who take it may become better Americans. . . . And lastly, I am giving this course in order that those who take it may see that our people have done their full share in the building up of the Northwest in a material way."

Rølvaag then proceeded to challenge his students to do their full share in a spiritual way also. This, he said, will depend entirely upon the younger generation, who must press onward into the future with all possible energy, and, he went on, who must do this by showing "the greatest faithfulness to your race, to the cultural and spiritual heritage which you have received . . . You must not erase your racial characteristics in order to become better Americans. . . . *So I want to repeat it.* If we, as an element in American society, shall be able to accomplish the greatest possible, we must see to it that we preserve our racial trait. Otherwise we have nothing whatever to contribute to the future greatness of America."[38]

Rølvaag was an idealist, and he believed that the legacy, or "racial trait" as he called it, that all immigrants must carry with them included their religion, language, stories, songs, poetry, values, and customs. He firmly believed that there was room for all ethnic heritages within the American society. In a manuscript titled "Is there a Place for the Ancestral Heritage within the American Society?" he wrote that "we are our heritage" He went on to insist that "we need the French ethnic heritage, and the Scotch and the English, certainly the German too, and all the others as well." He asked rhetorically, "But what do we want with the Norwegian respect for the law and love of home, our inborn reverence for all that is holy?" We all agree that "we need the smoothness and elegance of the French. German industry and thoroughness is useful and we can take that, the might of the British is indispensable, and we must praise and protect the great natural sense for art of the southern European." He went on to try to convince his Norwegian-American audience that "we need the Norwegian heritage on this side of the Atlantic" along with all these others.[39] Rølvaag constantly stressed the importance of understanding one's own culture and both the abilities and the flaws in one's own people. For how else, he asked, "can one learn to *use* the abilities and avoid the flaws?" Rølvaag added that "we can only get to know our people through knowing their history and their literature. This knowledge of our own past we *must* have, otherwise we become rootless."[40]

Einar Haugen explains that when Rølvaag spoke of his "people" or his "kin" he meant his "ethnic group in America," and by "ancestral heritage" he meant what we today might call this group's "Norwegian ethnicity." To Rølvaag "the preservation of that ethnicity as intact as possible and its infusion into the developing American culture was an ethical duty laid down by divine fiat in every ethnic group."[41] Scholars such as Philip Gleason and John Higham have commented on these terms. Gleason says that: "We must remember that the term and concept ethnicity had not yet been introduced in the 1930s. People spoke much more inclusively in those days of 'racial groups' and 'race feeling,' or of immigrant 'nationalities.'"[42] According to John Higham: "The very concept of race had not yet attained its later fixity and definiteness. Racial nationalism, having arisen out of political and literary speculation, not out of scientific inquiry, displayed a characteristic vagueness. In the sense in which nationalists used the word, 'race' often meant little more than national character. It usually suggested some sort of innate impulse, but, despite the growing biological interests of the nineteenth century, this was understood as an ongoing spirit more than a physiological actuality."[43] Though the terms "ethnic group" and "ethnicity" had not been invented at the time Rølvaag wrote, it is clear that these are the terms we would use today for the concepts he was talking and writing about.

It is important to note that though Rølvaag maintained a core belief in the value of understanding and preserving the ethnic heritage, his thinking matured and developed through the years. Rølvaag realized early—and accepted the fact—that the English language would eventually replace Norwegian as a means of communication among Norwegian Americans, and that important aspects of the heritage could and must be passed to a new generation through the medium of English.[44] By 1931, less than 10 years after *Concerning Our Heritage* came out, Rølvaag could write to Andreas Ueland (author of *The Minor Melting Pot*): "On the language problem you are wrong. If you will take the trouble to study the official reports, you will find that the Norwegian language has disappeared, almost, from the city churches, and is fast disappearing in the rural districts as well. In this matter too, 'the law of necessity' is operating. That's why your 'Minor Melting Pot' looks like an old anachronism—like a Sancho Panza fighting old women, windmills, and what nots instead of knights in armor."[45]

Rølvaag fought, however, to promote the importance to Norwegian Americans of learning Norwegian. Knowing both Norwegian and English, he said, allows us to drink from the wells of three great cultures: the American, the English, and our own. Though Rølvaag did not wish to preserve the Norwegian language at all costs, he wanted the transition to come gradually, and he believed that young people of Norwegian descent were well served to learn Norwegian as a foreign language. After all, his professional life was tied to the teaching of Norwegian to American youth. Rølvaag argued that from a cultural standpoint there is no foreign language study that will bring greater benefit to an American of Norwegian descent than the study of what he called "our racial language."[46]

In attempting to understand the context in which Rølvaag developed his ideas we must first consider that he arrived in the United States near the end of a period of anti-foreign agitation which lasted from the late 1880s and into the mid-1890s. Though he may not have encountered much of this out on the thoroughly Norwegian South Dakota prairies, he could hardly have failed to be aware of it.[47] The hysteria and violence died down for a time, only to flare up again in 1914.[48] According to the American historian John Higham, the agitation of the period was directed at the whole category of "hyphenated Americans." "By threat and rhetoric 100 per cent Americanizers opened a frontal assault on foreign influence in American life. They set about to stampede immigrants into . . . adoption of the English language, and into an unquestioning reverence for existing American institutions. They bade them abandon entirely their Old World loyalties, customs, and memories. They used high-pressure, steamroller tactics."[49] One of the most blatant examples of this was Governor William L. Harding of Iowa, who issued a proclamation banning the use of any language but English in public places, over the telephone, in public speeches, and at church services.

In reaction to the many forces of anti-foreign agitation, in 1918 the annual convention of the Norwegian Lutheran Church in America resolved to drop the word "Norwegian" from the name of the church. This action in turn was perceived by some as a "true war of extermination against everything Norwegian."[50] Rølvaag and other leaders in the Norwegian-American community reacted strongly, and in fact the resolution was reversed at the next convention.

The teaching of foreign languages in the schools also came under attack. Bills were put forth in several state legislatures to prohibit the teaching of any language but English in the schools.[51] Rølvaag wrote a note in his pocket calendar for 1918 listing as debate or essay topics: "What can Scandinavian language teachers do to counteract the depressing influence upon the study of Swedish and Norwegian resulting from the propaganda against the study of German? And what place in the educational life of our state should the Scandinavian languages rightfully have?"[52] Attacks on the Norwegian language came from within the Norwegian-American community as well. In 1920 Rølvaag received a letter requesting speakers who would talk about the ancestral heritage and would help "get rid of" those Norwegian Americans who hated the Norwegian language and "who got attacks of hysteria during the war." "Now," the letter continues in deliberately exaggerated language, "it is the fashion to chatter in English both at school and in church, whether one understands the language or not, but when it comes to business, well, there it isn't shameful to use one's mother tongue for there the dollar is worshipped, and then it's not so bad to use Norwegian, but to worship God in one's mother tongue is considered a shame in a Norwegian settlement."[53]

Immigrant parents were intimidated by organized campaigns based on the slogan, "Speak English."[54] Carl Chrislock maintains that "millions of second-, third-, and fourth-generation Americans were deprived of meaningful contact with the world of their fathers and mothers. . . . Many Norwegians found themselves in an obsessive search for acceptance—and most upwardly mobile parents did not perceive the maintenance of Norwegianness as one of the keys to their children's future. . . . Whether such an environment reinforced national unity is questionable. That it narrowed cultural horizons is more certain."[55]

In Rølvaag's words: "Everything that is not of Anglo-American origin has been rendered suspect to an ominous degree. . . . In some places ill will and suspicion turned into the most rancorous persecution. . . . All that was strange was dangerous; so it had to be extirpated. They were not particular about the means, and woe to anyone who tried to object!"[56] In Rølvaag's pocket calendar for 1920, he wrote notes for "Different Views of Our Heritage." He wrote of the need to differentiate those descendants of Norwegian people who are "interested in their Norwegian culture" from those who are "promoting the national interests of Norway." "We are good Americans!" he notes. "Why are people so hateful toward us? They don't like to be reminded that they are doing wrong. What must we do? We must be willing to tolerate being misunderstood, we must tolerate ridicule, slights, even persecution. We have to speak up even if it costs us our friends. We must practice [Norwegian culture] in our family life, and use our earthly means to support the cause."[57]

Historian Elliott Barkan maintains that the 1920s was quite possibly one of the worst decades in American history for "outsiders." And in this context it is important to remember that Norwegian Americans were most definitely considered to be outsiders. Barkan goes on: "In that era of Prohibition, Americans wanted to prohibit far more than just the consumption of alcohol. Immigrants and their children confronted racism, nativism, and exclusion, while continuing their efforts to build communities and contribute to America. . . . Even white European immigrants were not exempt from bigoted treatment."[58]

It is no wonder that Norwegian Americans felt themselves to be under attack. They were under attack—and not only from this anti-foreign sentiment from the larger American, Yankee-dominated society, but also from the forces of materialism, from the intense pressure for assimilation, from the surrounding English language, and from the younger generation who rejected the heritage of their parents and grandparents. Rølvaag responded fiercely to this attack, and counterattacked in both speeches and essays. As a man waging a desperate battle, Rølvaag needed to use the strongest possible words. He was fighting indifference from his own people, as well as antagonism from the main culture. Rølvaag had a two-fold purpose with his preaching about the Norwegian cultural heritage. First he was trying to foster a sense of self-knowledge and self-worth among Norwegian Americans in the face of the negative attitudes of American society. In addition, it was his firm belief that preservation of the best in the heritage of each immigrant group would lead to a stronger and finer America. In order to do this, he needed to articulate for the Norwegian Americans their values and their heritage and to convince them to hold on to these. His speeches and essays on these topics were directed entirely at his own people.

Rølvaag was certainly not alone in this work. Rasmus B. Anderson, as early as the 1860s, wrote about the necessity for doing missionary work among the Norwegian immigrants in order to arouse enthusiasm for their ancestors and their language and literature. He wanted the Norwegian immigrants to be good Norwegians and loyal Americans at the same time.[59] Norwegian-American journalist and author Waldemar Ager, Rølvaag's friend and ally in this battle, wrote many editorials and articles as well as novels on this theme.[60] Much later, esteemed historians such as Norwegian-American Theodore C. Blegen and Norwegian Ingrid Semmingsen concurred with Rølvaag's notion of Norwegian national characteristics. Blegen mentioned as typically Norwegian many of the same characteristics that Rølvaag described in his work.[61] Semmingsen wrote that "the rural Norwegian emigrant . . . was accustomed to toil and struggle against the forces of nature, while local self-government and egalitarian democracy conformed to the patterns of culture and aspirations he brought with him from home. He could to a certain extent build on his own foundations."[62] Dorothy Skårdal, however, reminds us that many of the traits pointed out by Rølvaag (and others) as typically Norwegian are in fact characteristic of all peasant cultures and are also claimed by many other ethnic groups.[63]

Norwegian historian Sigmund Skard compares Rølvaag's thoughts on nationality and the "folk soul" as well as the "civilized and humane" in the literary and linguistic heritage to those of Norwegian philosopher Christopher Bruun and the ideas of the folk high-school movement.[64] Skard goes on to remark that the problems Rølvaag struggled with have, in the succeeding generation, become world problems, and that today his works seem "frighteningly current." Rølvaag did not write for and about "only a small group of Norwegian Americans" in their struggle against a society which demanded conformity." No, Skard says, "The bell tolls for us too. The pioneers on the prairie are as distant from contemporary Americans as the Vikings are from Norwegians of today, but the power in Rølvaag's message has not faded away along with the society he described."[65] The message Skard refers to is Rolvaag's idea of the importance of self-knowledge and of an identity bound to the culture of one's ancestry. Culture, for Rølvaag, included political ideals, social organization, attitudes toward nature, as well as literature, music, and the arts. It did not focus particularly on the idea of "ethnic culture" widely promulgated at the time, which consisted of colorful costumes, folk dances, and a few exotic foods.

Rølvaag's ideas on ethnic preservation and his rejection of the excesses of Americanization were hardly new or unique to Norwegian Americans. Leaders of Jewish, Irish, and other immigrant groups held similar views. Victor S. Greene has pointed out the fact that Jewish leaders stressed that "some of the ancient religious values found in the Torah and the Talmudic law closely resembled, and thus reinforced, American humanistic, democratic principles." Leaders in the Jewish community also emphasized the importance of the folk culture, and of maintaining the Yiddish language both as a means of adjustment and to help newcomers understand the history and values of their adopted country.[66] Irish Americans also declared that the Irish were not strangers to America, that the Irish immigrants were *by nature* good Americans, just as Rølvaag maintained was true for the Norwegian immigrants. Irish-American leaders also insisted on maintaining their identity as Irish.[67] These issues of the conflict between ethnic identity and preservation as opposed to assimilation continue to be discussed today. For example, in 1997, Hmong immigrants in Minneapolis and St. Paul worried about what will happen if their children fail to learn the Hmong language. They fear that much of their traditions and folklore will be lost. "We're Americans, yes. But it's important to keep our language, our culture."[68] Richard Rodriguez wrote in 1995 that "we . . . Latin American immigrants . . . have turned into fools. We argue among ourselves, criticize one another for becoming too much the gringo or maybe not gringo enough. We criticize each other for speaking too much Spanish or not enough Spanish."[69] These are just a few examples of how the issues and problems Rølvaag struggled with continue to be relevant today.

In 1922, Rølvaag interrupted his stream of fiction to collect his thoughts on immigration, culture, and heritage into a 200-page book, which he called *Omkring Fædrearven*, or *Concerning Our Heritage*. *Concerning Our Heritage*, as Rølvaag conceived it, was intended to counter arguments and forces from the larger society, but the sword is pointed at the enemy within, at those within the Norwegian-American community who bought into the assimilationist arguments and wanted to abandon the cultural values that Rølvaag and his allies held dear.

Rølvaag wrote to a friend that "*Concerning Our Heritage* is my *best* book."[70] Today we might say that it is his most forgotten book. Partly, of course, that is because it has never before been published in English.[71] And in terms of style or literary merit, surely Rølvaag was wrong in his evaluation. In both structure and style, *Concerning Our Heritage* is a strange creature. It was assembled out of three very different pieces, all of which circle around Rølvaag's central ideas of culture and heritage, but which were originally written in very different styles and for very different audiences. This makes for a book with little stylistic consistency and no clear sense of audience. The entire book shows the effect of having been written hurriedly and without the benefit of an outside editor. With all the stylistic and compositional problems in *Concerning Our Heritage*, why then did Rølvaag claim that it was his best book? It surely must be because in this book he was able to lay out most clearly and explicitly his program for what he calls "his people." In this book he openly speaks to his people and admonishes them as to what they must do if they are to make a genuine contribution to America and at the same time themselves be whole and true individuals. This book was not intended for anyone other than Norwegian Americans; nonetheless, the message in it is vitally relevant for other people and for other times.

Section One, "Reflections on Our Heritage," takes up over half the book and is based largely on lectures written for Rølvaag's course in immigration history at St. Olaf, although it also includes bits and pieces from speeches he had given and from the newspaper column he wrote on behalf of the organization For Fædrearven. The style is oral, and is obviously directed at a youthful audience. This section later formed the basis for his address at the Norwegian-American Centennial in 1925.[72] As Kenneth Bjork rightly points out, Rølvaag was not a historian, and his theories concerning history and its role in contemporary life stem from the romantic nationalism of the nineteenth century. "But instinctively—one might almost say emotionally—he sensed the importance of his people's migration to the New World." Bjork goes on to point out that

"American life has been enriched by the immigration of the nineteenth and twentieth centuries." Though Rølvaag's concern was chiefly for the Norwegian element, "the ramifications of his interest reach out to include all the races that today comprise the American population."[73]

Rølvaag opens *Concerning Our Heritage* with a ringing call to "will the impossible." He cites the Norwegian explorer Roald Amundsen, Ibsen's *Brand*, and Norwegian folk literature, as well as the Bible to challenge his youthful audience to a high standard of idealism. He claims this attitude of idealism as a characteristic of the Norwegian people and criticizes Norwegian Americans for not living up to it. Reflecting the concepts of romantic nationalism, Rølvaag then develops the notion of differences between individuals and common characteristics among individuals from the same nation. He attributes national characteristics to three factors: conditions of nature, way of life, and values. He mentions language as another, but unproven, factor. He illustrates his point by describing the differences in temperament between Danes, Swedes, and Norwegians, and then states that each nation in the world has contributed its own characteristic traits to form what we call world civilization. Rølvaag claims that Norwegian Americans, as children of the Norwegian people, have inherited certain attitudes and predispositions to a greater degree than the children of other nations. He first mentions physical characteristics, but dismisses them as unimportant. Those who promote the ancestral heritage are idealists, and as such are more interested in matters of the spirit, in inner family traits. America needs this heritage, and smoothing away all distinct national characteristics will only impoverish the country.

Rølvaag defines "ancestral heritage" by enumerating those elements of the Norwegian national character that he believes are worthy of preservation among Norwegian immigrants and their descendants. He develops these ideas at some length, giving historical, literary, and anecdotal evidence for each characteristic. Though his point here is to show what he believes to be positive traits, he is careful to indicate that when carried to excess they can be negative as well. He does not claim these as exclusively Norwegian, and sometimes gives examples of these traits in other folk-groups, especially citing the Jews of the Old Testament. Further, Rølvaag does not discount the value of contact with other cultures. In discussing the Viking period, he maintains that in travelling to other lands the Vikings not only robbed and plundered but also learned foreign customs, languages, and all kinds of useful things. "And the new things they learned, they took back with them to their home communities. In this way there was a blending of cultures in that time. They sowed of their own, and reaped of others to sow again in their home soil."

Rølvaag says of Norwegians that they are deeply rooted to a place, but also have a restless desire for travel and adventure. They have a profound feeling for nature, which he attributes partly to the magnificence of the Norwegian landscape. Love of home and of the memories and traditions belonging to it are also part of the Norwegian heritage. Equality under the common law—a kind of democratic-aristocratic attitude—springs from the Norwegian rural society. Norwegians place a high value on hospitality. They show obedience and respect for the law of the land. Norwegians have a keen desire for knowledge, and a highly developed aesthetic sensitivity—a feeling for art and beauty. Another characteristic Norwegian trait, he says, is a deeply religious feeling with an emphasis on a personal relationship to God. However, he is careful to add that this does not mean that Norwegians are angels, that they never sin, that they all go to church, or know the Bible by heart. The strongest and most important characteristic of the Norwegian people, according to Rølvaag, is their love of freedom, which leads them to set their highest priority on individual rights under a common law. Since this last trait is the essence of the American ideal, it means that the Norwegian immigrant is already a good American before he even leaves home.

The commandment "love your neighbor as yourself" implies a need to love yourself first before you can love your neighbor. Likewise modern psychology understands the importance of self-esteem, and most ethnic minority groups suffered from rather low self-esteem. Much of Rølvaag's writing for his own Norwegian Americans, in this book and elsewhere, therefore deals with the positive values of their cultural heritage in an effort to build their group self-image. In an argument that sounds up-to-date in the America of today, Rølvaag criticized society for "leaving so much of the bringing up of children to the schools. . . . If the school system had any understanding of folk-psychology, it would put top priority on fostering the feeling of ethnic identity in the children, instead of trying to break it down. In this way, youngsters would begin to feel their own human worth." He went on later to add that "if everything foreign is trash, and these youth are the close descendants of foreigners . . . then they, with all the inexorability of logic, must also be trash. . . . It is not possible to turn your back on your heritage and still continue to be a people. The person who acts in this way must perish." The question of identity is also important, and Rølvaag challenged his readers to "Know thyself!—Knowledge of ourselves, yes, even more important, of our people, our kin—the race we belong to, all its characteristics, good as well as bad, is invaluable for the individual, precisely because it enables one to become a true human being."

Rølvaag ends his discourse on the Norwegian heritage by posing a question: Can a person with a distinctly Norwegian view of life—with a "Norwegian soul"—be a good American citizen? He answers this question with a resounding "yes!" "Let us promote the Norwegian ancestral heritage, and our attachment to America will be all right."

With the understanding we have today of the importance of culture and society in forming a person's identity, lifestyle, and ideas, some of the notions in *Concerning Our Heritage* about the innate nature of cultural traits seem quaint at best. In fact, Rølvaag's understanding was more nuanced, and in one of his notebooks he has sketched a triangle with heredity at the base and environment and training forming the sides. Arrows from all three sides point to a circle in the center. Clearly, he understood that strictly biological heredity was not the sole determining factor in the make-up of an individual.[74] In any case, if ethnic characteristics were truly hereditary, he would not have to castigate the Norwegian Americans for losing them nor exhort them to preservation. Obviously he is not thinking of "heritage" in a strictly genetic fashion, but rather in the sense of an inheritance which can be squandered. However, at the time Rølvaag was writing, the notion that national characteristics were a part of an individual's hereditary makeup was widespread. He simply used the accepted notions and the terminology of his time to explicate his own ideas about the importance of preservation of culture and heritage, and, as Orm Øverland has pointed out, "The line between national pride and prejudice is not easily drawn."[75] Rølvaag's thinking on these issues was in line with the philosophy of Horace Kallen, and substantially in agreement with the ideas of prominent American thinkers such as Randolph Bourne and John Dewey.[76]

In the second section of *Concerning Our Heritage*, "Reflections on Our Literature," Rølvaag turns to a discussion of Norwegian-American literature. Much of the material in this essay was rewritten from a series of newspaper articles originally published in the Norwegian-American newspaper *Duluth Skandinav* in response to a series of anonymous attacks on Norwegian-American literature. The highly polemical style reflects the audience and the venue in which these articles originally appeared.

Rølvaag begins his essay by citing an article by his friend and fellow author, poet and pastor D.G. Ristad, calling for a discussion of which language, Norwegian or English, should be used by Norwegian-American writers. Rølvaag agrees that Ristad's question is worthy of discussion, but adds his own belief that someday a Norwegian-American literature written in English will blossom.

Then Rølvaag turns to a more controversial article by the Norwegian-American journalist N.N. Rønning. Rønning maintains that Norwegian-American literature is impoverished, and challenges authors by claiming that "they have nothing to say, they don't dare to say it, they can't say it forcefully enough, and they don't get anything for saying it."[77] In early 1922, Rønning wrote to Rølvaag inviting him to attack his "four points," saying they were written with the intention of starting a battle. He offers to send clippings of the piece to other literary men, and claims that "our society would benefit by some strife. If we have something to say, we ought to dare to say it, and we ought to say it in such a way that people will sit up and take notice." "We can all agree," he adds, "that we don't earn anything by saying it. So the strife need only rage on three of the four points." Rølvaag takes up the challenge and disagrees with Rønning on all of his points except the last. In his reply to Rønning, Rølvaag defends Norwegian-American literature and uses the occasion to explicate his ideas about what literature is and what value it has for the reader.

After this initial discussion, Rølvaag goes on to cite material edited from the newspaper feud that was carried on in the pages of *Duluth Skandinav* in early 1922. Rølvaag is replying to an anonymous attacker, supposedly a Lutheran pastor, who signs himself only as "S." No one has so far discovered who "S" really was, or even if he was actually a pastor. Rølvaag himself concluded, rightly or not, that "S" could not have been a pastor. It has even been hinted that "S" might have been Rølvaag's friend, John Heitmann, who had a financial interest in the newspaper and frequently wrote controversial articles under the pen name Bjarne Blehr in order to sell more newspapers. In any case, the attack was nasty, and Rølvaag replied forcefully and with satirical polemic. However, this essay also contains Rølvaag's thoughtful and profound interpretation of what literary art is and what it accomplishes. This exposition of the nature and function of art is, according to his biographers Jorgenson and Solum, "one of the most important statements of theory in the artist's entire production."[78]

In this essay, Rølvaag criticizes Norwegian Americans for their cultural and spiritual poverty, which is demonstrated by their lack of appreciation for art and literature. Literature, according to Rølvaag, carries the message of life, gives birth to thoughts, and sets minds on fire. Authors must have power over language in order to interpret the human soul and give insight into the secrets of life, to express "the inexpressible". Literature, he says, reflects life and explains life, it is the mirror of humanity. Its greatest value is the understanding it gives us of human psychology. To write is to see, and to see with understanding. If Norwegian-American literature is to be criticized, it would be on this point, that it has lacked vision, and the pictures drawn have therefore been unclear.

In describing what makes literature great, what gives it such a strong influence on life, Rølvaag claims that all great literature inspires the reader. Great literature must also either awaken a sense of beauty in the reader or ignite the reader's ethical consciousness to enthusiasm or indignation. Rølvaag concludes that literature is necessary for society to progress precisely because it provides true understanding of human psychology. Though he is defending Norwegian-American literature in this essay, many of his examples are drawn from Norwegian and world literature.

Though Rølvaag argued for the value of a Norwegian-American literature and for the necessity for the community to support such literary efforts, it is clear, as Orm Øverland points out, that the "literary culture of Vesterheimen [the Norwegian-American sub-culture] was marginal from most points of view." It was marginal in the greater community because it was written in Norwegian. And even those pieces written in English were of little interest to the rest of American society. As a literature primarily of the Midwest it was also marginal in a national literary culture centered in the urban East. And it was marginal even within the Norwegian-American community because "Norwegians did not emigrate to America in order to create a new culture and a new literature on American soil but to create a better living for themselves and their descendants. Their motives for emigration as well as their goals as immigrants were material rather than idealistic."[79] Of Norwegian-American literature, only Rølvaag's *Giants in the Earth* has gained any lasting place in the American literary canon, and even that place is sometimes shaky.[80]

The third, and shortest, section of *Concerning Our Heritage*, "Reflections on the Name Change," is based on a series of articles originally published in the church periodical, *Lutheraneren*.[81] Rølvaag was invited by the editors to present the arguments of those opposed to eliminating the word "Norwegian" from the name of the Norwegian Lutheran Church in America. The counter-arguments were presented by his former teacher and mentor, J.N. Kildahl. The quite different audience and original place of publication are of course reflected in the style and content of this section.[82]

Rølvaag makes use of the opportunity to communicate once more his views on the necessity of preserving language, culture, and heritage. He criticizes the church for ignoring the needs of immigrants and older members, and discusses how problems in the relationship between the generations and differences between urban and rural life affect the church. He acknowledges that English will eventually be the language of the church, but argues fiercely that the transition must come neither too soon nor too fast. He ends the essay with the ringing assertion that Norwegian Americans as citizens are Americans, and nothing but Americans, but they are Norwegians by descent, and the church, he maintains, has an absolute duty to make use of all the riches and possibilities inherent in their Norwegian heritage.

Rølvaag first approached Augsburg Press—which had published all his previous books—with these essays, but was turned down. However, President Boe agreed to allow the book to be published under the imprint of the St. Olaf College Press. Rølvaag described the process and results in the following words: "In 1922 I published at my own expense and at my own risk the book *Concerning Our Heritage*. I am still convinced, as I was at the time, that this is the most Norwegian book which has been published in America. I was young then, and full of belief; therefore I printed 2000 copies . . . . . My word, how many nights I sat up that fall and winter writing letters to people begging for help in selling that book! But it didn't work. If I hadn't been published by Aschehoug in 1924, I think I would have given up writing."[83]

Rølvaag was mightily discouraged over the sale and reception of *Concerning Our Heritage*. He complained to Simon Johnson about the lack of reviews and added that those reviews that had come out were not honest. "And the book is not selling.[84] We printed 2000 copies. That was wrong. And if I hadn't let St. Olaf College publish it! Maybe then the opposition would have dared to let loose; but now they are keeping quiet."[85] In another letter to Simon Johnson, Rølvaag maintains that he is likely to be crucified for this book. He reports that his old teacher Dr. J. Boraas wrote to him "if you aren't crucified for that book, then our people are stone dead." Well, he adds, crucifixion he can handle, "if only people will read the book!" It was indifference that he feared the most.

The files in the NAHA archives contain many letters about *Concerning Our Heritage*. Some writers are willing to sell the book on commission, others give excuses why they can't or won't sell it. Numerous orders and bills indicate that the sales were nearly all made by mail order and by individual salespeople around the country, mostly in the rural Midwest. In 1923 Rølvaag wrote to one of his contacts, a pastor, trying to get copies of the book sold. He said that he would like the book "smuggled into every home where Norwegian is still read. I think of it as a kind of missionary work." The pastor replied on the bottom of the letter that his "congregation is English and there are very few who read Norwegian." It must have been a great burden on an already busy man to have to manage all the bookkeeping involved in this enterprise. And it was discouraging to meet with the apathy or even downright hostility evident in some of this correspondence.

There are, however, also many letters praising the book and expressing sympathy with Rølvaag's ideas about preservation of language and heritage. One woman wrote saying she liked the reflections on literature, "all except the part about smoking," as she hated tobacco. A man from Grand Forks wrote that "The younger pastors, as I understand it, hate *Concerning Our Heritage* . . . . But the older ones on the other hand, praise it to the skies. . . . Desperate diseases take desperate remedies." Journalist and reviewer Torkel Oftelie called the book a "wake-up call" and wanted it read by every Norwegian man and woman in this country, though he didn't have much hope this would happen.

One letter in particular captures the spirit of Rølvaag's essays: "We have just finished reading [your book] and I want to express my appreciation . . . I consider it a masterly exposition of the subject dealt with and I agree thoroughly with all of it. I sincerely wish that very many of our people, and especially of the educated and the leaders, will read the book. It would even be well if the subject of 'Heritage,' considered with respect to any foreign nationality, could be expounded for general American consumption, as it would be a wholesome effect upon the attitudes some Americans assume towards foreigners and the descendants of foreign stock. It would also aid America to absorb many things of cultural value that immigrants can transmit to us. I wish that some organization would undertake to give this book a wide circulation."[86]

Several people wrote to President Boe about the book; one of these, a college classmate of Rølvaag's and a pastor, congratulated him on sponsoring the book, and added "I consider this one of the greatest forward steps in the history of our Alma Mater. . . . for it is not only money that St. Olaf needs, but a larger vision. . . As Americans of Norwegian descent we should remain loyal to the Nordic ideals in order to be true to ourselves."[87] Rølvaag's friend D.G. Ristad, also a pastor, thanked President Boe for daring to publish the book, which he says is not altogether an act of "sprinkling sugar on the porridge." St. Olaf College, he adds, "can afford to back him; and the rest of us are cheered on to back St. Olaf."[88] Boe replied by saying that "It may be that I am getting myself into trouble by doing what I have done with Prof. Rølvaag's book. However . . . I do not have any regrets." Boe says that Rølvaag has been doing excellent work at St. Olaf College in maintaining an interest in our heritage, and "he is entitled to every bit of encouragement we can give. In addition, I disagree with him in so many of the things he says that it affords me a good opportunity to do something to establish the spirit of 'free thinking' which is needed so much among our people." Boe acknowledges that he no doubt will be criticized for this act, but adds that "it may be fate that has started us out on Rølvaag's book. It concerns a matter which has been, is, and will be of importance to us at St. Olaf."[89]

In a separate note to Rølvaag, Ristad adds, "Well, good luck with your book, whether you find a market or not. We can comfort ourselves with the thought that in 100 years learned people will be writing with great understanding about us and our contributions to American culture."[90] Not quite 100 years have passed, so we cannot judge the accuracy of Ristad's prediction, but we do see that today "learned people" are still discussing these ideas.

The translation of this book has presented many challenges. These challenges have been not only linguistic but conceptual and contextual. These essays were written for a very different audience than will read this translation. The original audience had a knowledge base and context for understanding Rølvaag's ideas which is quite different from that of a contemporary reader. In order to help remedy this, I have supplied an extensive introduction and copious footnotes.

I have had many discussions with colleagues and done much thinking about how to translate accurately certain terms. In particular, the word "race" has been troublesome. The usage and meaning of this word in both English and Norwegian is different now than it was in the 1920s. I considered using the term "ethnicity" or "ethnic group," for this seems to most closely reflect the intended meaning to a contemporary audience. This solution, however, is anachronistic, and on the advice of the editor the term "race" has most often been rendered as "nationality" or "national."[91]

The rather significant shifts in style between the three sections have also created difficulties, and I have attempted to maintain these differences in style and tone as much as possible. In addition, Rølvaag has a tendency to use both irony and sarcasm, often writing the opposite of what he means. In translation, sometimes the irony has to be lost in order that the meaning can be understood. As one might expect, Rølvaag makes frequent use of folk sayings and references to folklore and tales. These are also difficult to convey to a non-Norwegian audience. In some cases I have let footnotes do the work, in other cases I have expanded on the information in the text.

Rølvaag himself admonished his translators to "translate the mood and let the story take care of itself." He was seldom satisfied with the translations made by others, and found working on them himself very difficult. When Rølvaag translated his own work he tended to substantially rewrite it, which is a luxury accorded only to the original author. Toward the end of his life he declared that translating was so troublesome that he intended to write his next book in English. I can only hope that this translation would have met with his approval and trust that it will serve to present Rølvaag's ideas as clearly and authentically as possible to an English-reading audience.

The design on the cover of Omkring Fædrearven *illustrates some of Røl-vaag's ideas of cultural tradition. The decoration around the picture is reminiscent of Viking and peasant art. In the picture is the hearth, the center of the home; sitting in front of it we see a young man (reminiscent of the Ash Lad of Norwegian folk literature), and next to him a grandfatherly figure, reminding us that traditions are handed down from one generation to another. The interior shown with its corner fireplace and log walls is typical of Norwegian rural architecture, and the grandfather is sitting in a carved* kubbestol, *a chair that reminds us of the beauty and utility of Norwegian folk art. That, as well as the skis stacked against the wall, tells us that traditions could be from the material culture as well as the spiritual and intellectual. The skis might indicate the desire for travel and adventure. The whole picture is infused with a cozy warm glow from the fireplace.*

SIMPLE REFLECTIONS ON
Our Heritage

1

An amusing anecdote is told about the famous Norwegian explorer Roald Amundsen. He had just finished preparations for his first expedition to the North Pole. The day of departure had come, the crew was assembled, everything was ready to go. Amundsen gathered everyone on deck and made the following speech: "Well, boys," he said. "We are off to the North Pole, but we'll just take a little trip down to the South Pole first and see how things are there." So they sailed south instead of north, and on this famous journey Amundsen discovered the South Pole.

This story illustrates a characteristic feature of the Norwegian people. Our people are a restless folk. They are strongly rooted, and yet they are restless. Their spirit ranges far and wide. The call of the unknown and the lure of adventure are stronger in our kin than they are in most other peoples. We are easily captivated by risk-taking. The Norwegian people can stand gazing at the impossible until they can't resist the challenge any longer; they simply have to try. The attempt is often brilliant and frequently it succeeds.

Many Norwegians have become national heroes just by wanting to accomplish the impossible and staking their lives on it. Henrik Ibsen entered the ranks of the great prophets precisely because in one of his greatest literary works he demanded the impossible.

> But help is useless to a man
> Who does not will more than he can.[1]

Thus Ibsen has Pastor Brand speak to a farmer who is willing enough to give up his farm to save his child but, when it gets to the sticking point, pulls back from paying for his son's salvation with his own life.

But help is useless to a man
Who does not will more than he can.

This is a remarkable sermon about help! And yet, perhaps it is not so strange. What kind of help should one give such a person? Food and clothing? The ability to earn more money? Greater earthly comforts? But what good do these things do for a person spiritually?

Ibsen has repeated the same thought in other works, using different words. He was a great thinker with a profound knowledge of human nature, and he really meant what he lets Pastor Brand say, that it is useless to try to help the person who does not will the impossible, for the good reason that this person will never accomplish anything out of the ordinary, anything more than Per and Paul in the Norwegian folktale could manage. Helping such a person does not advance mankind. Such a person is merely a part of the great gray masses. After the spark of life has been extinguished, no more is heard about them, their "place knows them no more."[2]

Per and Paul don't want anything beyond the ordinary, the everyday. Their minds never ring with longing for great and wonderful deeds. They have never felt compelled to fulfill all that is true and great about being human. They are too satisfied with the ordinary to be interested in the great mystery of existence. They have never sensed the beauty of the incomprehensible wonder of life. They have taken the sum of talents given to them, wrapped them in a cloth, and buried them in the ground. They think they can just dig up the original sum and present that on the day of reckoning. The Son of Man, the greatest of all judges of human nature, has, in this parable of the talents, pronounced a terrible judgment on such people.[3] Has this parable helped us? Oh, no, not at all. The ever-practical Per and Paul don't care one bit about the strict law of the soul expressed in this lively parable. They make their own calculations, keep their eyes firmly fixed on the possible—and calculate with the greatest shrewdness. And then they go out and do what is possible. After a while they disappear from the earth, and "their place knows them no more."

The Norwegian people have extolled the determination to accomplish the impossible, have glorified those who lived their lives with the intention of making the impossible possible. The Norwegian people have made this idea clear by personifying it, that is, by clothing it in a figure given flesh and blood in the folktales of our people.

The Ash Lad—as he is called in folklore—appears in many of our folktales. Let us just take a little look at him, and at his two brothers.

Per and Paul and Espen Ash Lad set out along the road. They are off to the palace to win the princess and half the kingdom—sometimes even the whole kingdom is at stake. In other words, they are out to accomplish the impossible. None of these three is a prince, and least of all Espen Ash Lad!—If they are to succeed, they must accomplish the impossible. In any case, being princes by birth wouldn't help them. In the competition that is about to take place, all are equal; the prince takes no precedence over the cotter's son.

They have a supply of provisions with them from home. It is remarkable that the folktales seldom neglect to mention those provisions. Whether Espen Ash Lad sets off alone or together with his brothers, they always carry some food from home. Even if home is the poorest of the poor, they still have something to bring with them on their journey.——How simple and beautiful this picture is!—It shows us that people always have something to sustain them when they leave their home!—Sometimes the provisions are delicious, cheese and meat and other good food. Other times they have only a dry crust of bread.

The task they have set out to accomplish is no easy one. The competition is fierce. The contest has been announced throughout the land. Anyone who wants to can compete. There is just one bright spot; the terms are the same for all.

But, to be sure, it is not such an easy task to win a princess and half the kingdom. Here is what has to be done in one version of the tale:—In the palace yard stands a huge tree; it is a monster of an oak. Not only that, the tree has magical properties, for no sooner is one chip chopped from the tree than two grow in its place. Whoever is to win the princess and half the kingdom must fell the oak in spite of the magic spell. And that is not all! Where the tree stands, the winner must dig a well that has water in it all the year around,—"for the king of England had a well like that." This spot, however, is nothing but hard granite. In all probability it is impossible to dig a well in such a place. Even if you managed to dig a hole in the rock, where would the water come from?

The whole thing seems so hopeless.

All the Pers and Pauls in the world have already been there and made the attempt. The trunk of the oak has become fearfully huge on account of it, and the rock hasn't got any softer either.

Finally these three brothers arrive. Per is the eldest, so he shall be the first to try. It doesn't take long before he's out of the running. And then he gets both ears cut off and is put out on an island just for making the attempt. The king thought he should have learned from the others and had sense enough not to try.—Paul's turn comes next. Exactly the same thing happens to him. The only difference is that his ears are cut off even closer to his head. Both Per and Paul become laughingstocks to the whole world. Isn't this what always happens when an ignorant fool puts his hands in his pockets and thinks he can whistle his way to life's riches and beauty?

When Espen Ash Lad steps forward the crowd begins to shout. "What are you doing here—you fool! Don't you see how the others have fared? Just look at Per and Paul!"

But Espen Ash Lad doesn't pay any attention to them. He is familiar with laughter and teasing, so this doesn't bother him in the least.—Just look at him now!—Calmly and confidently he goes to work. With an enigmatic, comfortable ease, he tackles the task. He grows with each passing moment, not in size, but in deep insight and intense strength. He has enticed their secrets out of the hidden powers; now he puts these secrets to use. One, two, three, the tree is felled, the well dug, and the water flows.

And so he wins the princess and half the kingdom. What seemed completely impossible for any human being to do he does as easily as one-two-three. Of course there is more to it than that. While his brothers were busy eating up the food, he went up in the hills and found himself an ax and a hoe that had been standing there for many a year waiting for him. And while Per and Paul hung around making fun of him, he went off and discovered the source of the stream. He unlocked the secrets of things that are so ordinary that most people scarcely notice them and thereby discovered the most unbelievable things. He managed perfectly well without food; he cared nothing for rest in order to concentrate on learning to *understand* things. Espen Ash Lad goes through life with an insatiable sense of wonder!

Espen Ash Lad appears in any number of folktales,—we meet him in almost every second tale. The folk imagination has embraced him as its favorite character; he appears time and time again, always the same, yet always just as fresh and interesting, always just as secretly gifted, just as good and great-hearted, just as untiring in his journey toward his goal.

Yes, that Ash Lad, that Ash Lad! He always accomplishes the impossible; he wills it and he does it. He rides up steep, slippery glass mountains. He herds the king's hares—the ones no one else can take care of. He tells lies so that the great brewing vat in the palace yard runs over, while he stands there telling the purest truth. He makes obstinate princesses laugh; others he teases until they become so angry they accuse him of lying. He kills trolls—whether they have one, or three, or seven heads, he cuts them right off. He rescues princes and beautiful princesses who have had magic spells cast over them and cannot become human again. In terrible storms and violent seas he sails to the outermost island and returns with great riches. He lies in front of the fireplace and sees beautiful visions in the glowing coals, then he goes out into the world to make these visions into reality. He doesn't give up until he reaches Soria Moria, the golden castle in the air. Most remarkable of all, he enters the home of the trolls, associates with them, coaxes their secrets from them, acquires their riches, and yet he remains human. Their magic doesn't harm him in the least.

Espen Ash Lad performs these and many other great deeds.

With what characteristics has the imagination of the Norwegian people endowed this lad, its favorite child? I would like to point out some of the Ash Lad's special qualities, because by looking at them we can learn to understand the Norwegian national character.

The first thing we notice is that the Ash Lad is a mama's boy. If there are several brothers, he is always the last to leave home, unless they all set out at once. At first glance, there is nothing special about this boy who lies in front of the fireplace or hangs around, hiding behind his mother's skirts. He doesn't show any promise for the future; nonetheless he is mother's favorite child; she senses what lies within him.———Imagination is in that boy, that is certain. He stares into the fire and sees visions; his second sight makes him unusual.———And he was born with an insatiable hunger for knowledge. He simply has to know about everything.———His good nature, his genuine kindheartedness, is just as boundless as his curiosity. Beasts of prey come and beg him for something to eat, and he feeds them as long as there is a single crumb in his bag; he is good to everyone who is suffering. He doesn't ask if they are "the deserving poor." For him, suffering is suffering, whether it is self-inflicted or undeserved.———He sneaks past the trolls whenever he can. On the other hand, when he does have to enter the home of the trolls, in he goes. He is able to associate with them, learn from them, wheedle their secrets out of them, without any of their magic sticking to him.———Of course he is frightened, but his fear does not stop him. He lies there hidden inside the chest and hears such a fearful noise from the trolls that he nearly jumps up under the ceiling, "but," he comforts himself, "if it doesn't get any worse, we'll just get used to it." Something in him is stronger than fear; that is his desire to get to the bottom of things. He never loses sight of his goal. No matter how far beyond the horizon, no matter how impossible it is, he will go forward; he must reach his goal in order to live. Wherever he turns, whatever fate befalls him, his most striking characteristics—his goodheartedness, his broad outlook, his fascination with the impossible, and finally his secret brilliant knowledge—yes, these characteristics save him every time.

In passing I want to remind you that other people also have their Ash Lad: the German folktales tell about "Der Dumling," the Swedes have their "Pinkel"; but both these figures are different from the Ash Lad. And the characteristic that sets him apart and raises him to a higher level is his hidden genius. As we listen to tales about him we notice this feature underneath the words, feel it so strongly that we are convinced of it. We sense that when it comes to a contest of strength, when it counts the most, this hidden genius will come out in manly deeds and unstoppable power. That is what is characteristically Norwegian about him.

Perhaps I have carried on unnecessarily long with this thought. But there is good reason. The Ash Lad figure plays such a large role in Norwegian history, in world history for that matter. Harald Fairhair, Olav Tryggvason, Olav Haraldson, Leif Erikson, King Sverre, Haakon Haakonson, and many others from medieval Norwegian history—they were Espen Ash Lads all of them. And Hans Nielsen Hauge, Henrik Wergeland, Svend Foyn, Fridtjof Nansen, Roald Amundsen, Christian Skredsvig, Stephan Sinding,[4] and a whole crew from more recent history—yes, what are they if not Espen Ash Lads?—They have all accomplished what the great masses, the great, stupid, gaping masses swore could never be done.

When we look at the progress of humankind over the earth, at what we call world history, is it not primarily about Espen and his deeds that we hear? All the others, the countless multitudes, are present simply as a mass—a dull, sluggish mass. This mass only opposes, laughs, and taunts, stands there with "practical experience" and swears that this venture of Espen's is impossible. We hear the derisive laughter following him as he sets out on his way. And it is always the clever ones—the big shots—who take the lead in scoffing at him!

We shouldn't really be surprised at this. Basically, it was really stupid of Moses to set out into the desert with the people of Israel, a people who had been slaves for hundreds of years. He must have known that no such thing had ever been done before, that the people lacked moral strength, that the thing was simply impossible. There were surely plenty of sensible people standing around laughing at this 80-year-old fool. No doubt well-meaning individuals advised him against this, showed him how foolhardy it was. It was clear to everyone—and especially to the intelligent people—that the man was crazy.

But he became famous for all time for this foolish act. The people he led became the mightiest people in the world. He himself never made it into the Promised Land; that was punishment for not having been foolish enough in the eyes of the world!

It was totally absurd of the twelve disciples to set out to found a new religion! And here they were, just ordinary men—fishermen, workers, uneducated everyday people with an unknown carpenter as their leader and master. What experience did these people have to prepare them to go out in the world and found a new religion? They didn't have any qualifications at all! If they had at least been college presidents, or powerful churchmen, or great generals, or shrewd businessmen, the kind with a talent for Big Business, with an understanding of organization, of public relations, and advertising,— well, then there might have been some hope for them. A great multitude of Pers and Pauls stood around and laughed. And that multitude included the elite, too, those who had a good education and held high offices.——They didn't just laugh either. They got terribly angry. And in their holy zeal they went out and nailed the carpenter's son to a cross. They wanted to put an end to the craziness, and they succeeded, but it wasn't quite the end they had in mind.

And what about Martin Luther? Well, wasn't he a crackpot? Why in the world should this weak, impoverished, unknown monk get into a fight with the strongest power in the world? It was stupid of him, there's no denying it. But look at the result of his stupidity!

When St. Olaf returned to Norway to attempt once again to convert his people, he committed an act of incredible folly. Common sense should have kept him away. He had already been chased out of the country by his own people; he was living in comfort at the Russian court. Why should he go back to Norway, where he knew that hatred awaited him? And look at the army that he had with him! Oh yes, let us admit that he acted foolishly.

But what were the results of this reckless act? Let me point out one of them: Here I sit writing this almost 900 years later in another part of the world, at a school which bears his name and has his battle cry as its motto. This seat of learning would scarcely have stood here on the Minnesota prairie if Olaf had not acted so foolishly back then.

It is remarkable how history treasures and carefully preserves the stories of these foolish acts and these idiots. It is precisely these people who are the great figures of history, towering through the ages like the tallest peaks in a mountain range.

We Norwegian Americans have so deplorably many Pers and Pauls among us. They have had the final say-so and have laid down the law. They have crawled up into high positions and have exercised power, often with a strong hand. Our great sin is our constant concern for propriety and our careful calculation of what is possible. We are clever accountants; but our calculations have choked out our ability to perform great deeds ever since pioneer times. In those days, there were giants among us. And now we sin by looking back on them with the greatest indifference. We calculate and calculate what is possible; we figure and we count the costs. Time and again when someone among us shows signs of becoming an Espen Ash Lad we simply chase him home again with gloomy faces and harsh words. "Hey you! No, stop!" we shout. We don't want anything to do with such magicians. We aren't like the king in the fairy tales, who always gave Espen a chance.

"It is impossible to get our children to learn Norwegian in America." This has been repeated thousands of times. Per and Paul nearly always say it. Of course, what else would they say? And as a result, they have never won the princess or the kingdom in the world of ideas and culture. Their ears have been cut off, so they can't hear how well it is going with Espen Ash Lad's children. Per and Paul have been whipped across their backs and had salt poured in their wounds rather often, for even they feel the sting when their own children scorn them.

"A Norwegian Youth Association in America—an organization where young people use the Norwegian language in their programs? Oh no, you know something like that would never work!" This was the calculation over a year ago. And people believed it, ignoring completely the needs of newcomers. But now such an organization has been formed; and young as it is, already the brotherhood stretches from coast to coast. Do you think Espen has been working among us?

"Norwegian heritage in America? What kind of nonsense is that?"—Many a Per and Paul among us has asked this question and reasoned this way. And yet an organization promoting the Norwegian heritage in America has come into being. Last summer at its annual meeting there were about 2,500 interested people in attendance. Admittedly, this organization has not yet won the princess and half the kingdom, but who knows? Espen might reach his goal.[5]

"It's impossible to get American youth to attend a program that is held in the Norwegian language. You can just kiss that thought good-bye." Who hasn't encountered this point of view? Who hasn't heard similar words? And yet there has never been such widespread interest in our Norwegian declamation contests as there was last winter. It is remarkable the way these things go. Last winter some students at St. Olaf put on Ibsen's play *Pillars of Society* in Norwegian. Only one of the seventeen students who participated was born in Norway. The leading roles were played by young people who had never even seen Norway. In the audience we had a man of very good taste who had seen the play performed on three different occasions in Kristiania. He told us afterward that one of the roles was played better than he had ever seen it performed in Norway. The boy who played that role was born and raised in America; he has never been to Norway. Thus we see that astonishing things can happen in our midst.

"Norwegian-American literature in the Norwegian language? Impossible! It simply won't work. If we Norwegian Americans ever become so literary that we begin to create literature, then it will be written in English." The Pers and the Pauls have made this statement into an article of faith. In spite of this, though I can't explain how it has come about, I know that we do have our own literature written in Norwegian. I have a nice bookcase standing here full of this kind of reading material. Just come and look!

I don't have the faintest idea how we are going to manage to get the Pers and the Pauls to sample these dishes. But I am absolutely convinced that when Espen comes along, he will figure out how to persuade our people to read Norwegian-American literature. Then our books will "go like hot cakes." And I am convinced that Espen will come. If only he would appear soon! I feel a bit like the old lady in the fairy tale who stood for a hundred years with her nose stuck in the tree trunk waiting for Espen to come. And at last he came. And if she could endure the wait, then our writers will have to manage it too.

> Help is useless for the man
> Who does not will more than he can.

A toast to the impossible! That is the only thing worth wanting. That alone will carry us forward. Willing the impossible may lead to ruin, but we all end up there anyway! Those who will the impossible shall not be lost, they shall prevail. A toast to the impossible!

If only we Norwegian Americans could learn to will the impossible as much as our ancestors have done! If only we could stop being so concerned with propriety and making our clever calculations! If only we could start to will great deeds; if only we reached and stretched just a little bit! Then the Norwegian people in America would be a greater blessing for this country than they are right now.—A toast to Espen Ash Land and the impossible!

2

About the only thing that all people have in common is the fact that they are different. For differences between people can always be found.

Only with identical twins do we find so much similarity that one individual cannot be distinguished from another. But such instances are so rare that they seem quite exceptional. And even when outward appearances are similar, it is even more rare that the mind and soul are alike in two individuals.

The differences are readily apparent between children in the same family who are not twins. Any one of you could name families where the children are so different in appearance that strangers couldn't guess that they were siblings.

The wider the circle of kinship becomes, the more the marks of similarity disappear. This should not surprise us. We are all members of the human race, and yet each of us is a unique individual, equipped with certain characteristic features that differentiate us from all others. Our Lord intended this and created us thus from the very beginning.

Nevertheless, in spite of these individual differences, people from the same nation have certain characteristics in common—inner and outer traits which bind them together as a group and differentiate one nation from others. One doesn't even need to take outward appearances into account in order to see these differences. One does not need to look at extremes such as the Negro and the Norwegian, the Indian and the Englishman to see this. The alert person who has traveled in other countries will easily recognize that this is true. Even among close neighbors, such as Norwegians and Swedes or Germans and French, one will quickly notice similarities within each group and differences between them. Even a common ancestry doesn't help much if neighboring nations have experienced a long separate history. The centuries tend to erase original similarities.

Similarities on the one hand and differences on the other come primarily from three sources: natural environment, way of life, and system of values. (Some researchers maintain that language is also a factor. This theory is no more than a hypothesis, yet it seems quite probable that language might play a role.)

Let's take a look at the Scandinavians. Originally, the Danes, the Swedes, and the Norwegians were brothers, and even today there are more similarities between these three peoples than between any one of them and any other European nation. And yet there are many differences between a Dane, a Swede, and a Norwegian. The Dane is the liveliest of the three, the most lighthearted. The Norwegian is the most melancholy; he is the brooding one, the doubter in this group of siblings. The Swede, on the other hand, has the most even temperament. He is certainly as gifted as the other two; his talents are just different.

If one crosses the North Sea from Norway to England, both inner and outer differences become more noticeable at once. And if one sails across the Baltic from Sweden and into Russia, the differences are striking.——And so it goes throughout the world.

It is these likenesses within groups and differences between them that have created what we call civilization or world culture. Each nation has contributed to this world civilization on the basis of its own uniqueness.

3

When we in the heritage movement talk about our heritage, we mean that as children of the Norwegian people we have been endowed since birth with certain aptitudes and predispositions to a greater degree than the children of other nations in this country. We have inherited them. Since they are a part of our very nature, we can't do anything about them; that is to say, we can neither brag nor complain that we have them. It is simply a fact.

We have acquired certain outward features in the same way, though as a rule we don't think about these when we talk about our heritage. But they are there too. One year recently some statistics were gathered at a number of our institutions of higher education. The physical education teachers measured all the boys—height, chest, etc. This was also done at St. Olaf College; and it turned out that our boys were on average larger than the boys at any of the other colleges in the country that participated in the study.

We don't talk much about this aspect of our heritage, though it is nothing to be ashamed of. Most of us in the heritage movement are idealists; we are interested in matters of the spirit, in striving for the ideal. In the following remarks I will restrict myself to a discussion of inner traits and all that derives from them. Our heritage comprises our national characteristics and all that comes from them, as well as our ancestral language.

This, then, is our heritage. Whatever is worth preserving of this heritage we should strive to save—first and foremost for our own selves, and next for our country, for America. We believe that our country needs our heritage. After all, what use does it have for us, if it cannot make use of our heritage? We are neither more nor less than what our heritage has made us.

We cannot reconcile ourselves to the idea that it is an advantage to our country for all its inhabitants to be alike. That is to say, identical, cast in the same mold, with all differences polished away. We believe this impoverishes us as a people. Let me illustrate this with a simple example:

Let us imagine a family with four children. The eldest is a boy, and our Lord has intended from the beginning of time that, if all goes well, he should be a pastor. The next child is also a boy; when you get right down to it, he ought to be a blacksmith. To take two white-hot pieces of iron and weld them together, or to take hard steel and make the cleverest things from it is life for this boy. Otherwise, life is hardly worth living. The third child is a girl. She has her ambition too. She wants to be a farmer's wife, to have a nice home out in the country with a large flock of children. Out there she will rule like a queen. If she can't do this, then life isn't much worth living. The fourth child is also a girl. She has no particular plan, no special ambition. She likes best to hang her head, act refined, sit at the piano, and plunk out simple melodies. There are girls like that.

Imagine now that the parents decide that all these four children should be treated exactly alike and should become the same thing. All four should be pastors. Or all four should be blacksmiths. Or all four should, if you please, become farmer's wives. Or all four should be forced into a life of idle uselessness. What would you think about such people? Most likely you would think that these people were too dangerous to let loose. You would perhaps consult with the neighbors to see if it wasn't safest to have this pair sent to the asylum for the feeble-minded. And in that you would be perfectly right.

But we cannot deny that in our striving for national unity in this country we carry on in exactly the same way as these parents. We attempt to attain unity by first attaining absolute uniformity, by polishing away all distinctive characteristics. Those of us in the heritage movement, however, believe that this is a completely erroneous view. In the first place, it is scarcely possible to nurture a feeling of unity in this way; and even if it were, that unity would be bought at too high a price. Such a country, if one can even be imagined, would count for nothing in the family of nations.

4

Several years ago I was fortunate enough to spend a summer vacation up in Nordland in northern Norway. I have so many beautiful memories from this vacation. One is large as life for me.

I was visiting some poor fisherfolk who had lived up by the Arctic Sea all their lives. They had no education beyond what the rather modest grammar school up there had to offer. In spite of this, they were particularly intelligent and enlightened people.

My stay there lasted until the end of August. Up there in the north it sometimes happens that you get remarkably beautiful nights in the late summer. The sun hides itself for three or four hours in the middle of the night, and even then it isn't quite completely dark. On a clear night, the play of colors on the sea and sky and mountains is perhaps the richest of the whole year. It is like being transported to the wondrous magical world of the fairy tale.

On just such a night I happened to be walking along a path with a couple of fisherfolk who were going to their little cottage down by the sea. Both the man and his wife were well known to me from my childhood. They were inquisitive people, eager to learn. I came from the outside world, had roamed about a good deal, and there were many things they wanted to find out from me—while I was trying to get as much information as possible from them about people and conditions in Nordland.

In any case, as the dusk of night grew deeper and the play of colors richer and more magical, conversation between us died away. America the great was forgotten, conditions in Nordland too. If someone spoke, no answer was made, and so silence fell. Our hearts were full, we were completely lost in the richness of color.

The wife was a middle-aged lovely and sensible woman. Suddenly, I noticed that she was weeping as she walked along. I could not understand what was the matter with her; just a bit ago she had been conversing quite cheerfully. Greatly alarmed I asked her:

"What is the matter with you? Are you ill?"

Then she looked at me with joy in her glance, and said quietly:

"Don't you think this is beautiful?"

This woman's question illustrates the point I want to make: *An*

idealistic view of nature has always characterized the Norwegian people.
This is a part of our heritage. Old tales tell of people in Norway all
the way back to heathen times climbing up to the high mountain
peaks in midwinter to see if the sun would not soon return. When
they caught their first glimpse of it, they came back down and held
a celebration—a celebration of light, a celebration of thanksgiving,
a celebration of joy because the light once more had been victorious over the darkness.

Norwegian literature down through the ages is extremely rich in
nature poetry, especially the more recent. Many poems have been
dedicated to the sea, to the mountains, and to the valleys. Every
beloved flower also has its song. Even the animals have become a
part of the poets' worship of nature. It would be a terrible loss to
Norwegian literature if all nature poetry were removed. Just think
about some of Bjørnson's lyrics and prose pieces, of [Johan Sebas-
tian] Welhaven's nature poetry, of Jørgen Moe, Theo. Caspari,
[Arne] Garborg, [Herman] Wildenvey, and many others, but first
and foremost think of Henrik Wergeland. His enthusiasm for nature encompasses not only mountain and sea, forest and lake, farm
and flower, but all of creation. In his famous poem "To an Illustrious Poet" he sings:

> Forget not the stars! Forget not the flower!
> Forget not the worm in the dust![6]

Our poets have expressed what the people have felt. These
thoughts lay hidden in the soul of the people, and the great singers
of songs came along and released them. Musicians followed. What
the lyric poet endeavored to say in words, the composer strove to
make even more expressive by providing a suitable melody. This
kind of literature could never have become so beloved of the people
if the feelings did not already lie hidden in their souls.—The impoverished fisherwoman up by the Arctic Ocean is certainly not the only
one who has been moved to shed tears over the beauty of nature,
and at the same time felt deep joy and happiness at the sight of it.

What does this idealized view of nature mean for our people and
our country? First, it ennobles the mind. When you get right down

to it, the person who can be deeply moved by the beauty of nature is a good person. Much of the child remains in this person's soul. This feeling for nature enables people to develop genuinely human qualities.

The idealized enthusiasm for nature does something else, which in its way is just as important: it contributes strongly to the connection people feel to a given place; it causes people to love their homes. For even if that place is not the most beautiful one can imagine, this passionate disposition will foster a readiness to idealize and draw sustenance from the beauty that is there.

I will attempt to show in connection with another branch of our heritage that we need to foster this feeling for place. Here I will just remind you that in this country neither we nor other nationalities have acquired a sense for the abundance of beauty that surrounds us. It is something of a mystery that the great plains—both the cultivated areas and the wild prairies—do not yet have their great poet. The closest attempt has perhaps been made by a newcomer from Norway.[7] He went back across the Atlantic because we Norwegians over here did not bother to buy his vivid descriptions of the Wyoming wilderness. Therefore he could not make a living from his writing, and so he went back.

But the prairie is genuinely beautiful. And the forest country in northern Minnesota and northern Wisconsin with its almost countless forest lakes where the black bass has its home and the loon calls so magically in the evening. Isn't this beautiful? You can see a sunset there that you cannot find the likes of without going all the way to Nordland in northern Norway. One thing is certain: if we are to truly love the homes we have created in this new country we must open our eyes to the beauty surrounding us.

5

This matter of the idealistic view of nature leads directly to another branch of our inheritance, *Love of home*, for this is also a part of our Norwegian heritage.

Of course it is true that love for the place you live is universal. It is found in all peoples, but in different degrees and manifestations. Love of home is different, for example, in nomadic peoples than in people who live up in Setesdal, where the same farm may have been passed down in inheritance from father to son in the same family for several hundred years. In the latter case, there are deep roots that are not so easily cut off. With such people their love of place encompasses not only the farm itself and the house they live in, but also the local community and the valley where the farm lies.

It must be obvious that the idealized feeling for nature contributes strongly to fostering love for one's home. When a child's mind has absorbed the beauty that surrounds its childhood home, this "first love" is not easily forgotten later; it binds a person strongly to his home community. Then it becomes true as the poet sings

> You will miss the earth where your mother wept
> Where as a child you sang in the woods.

"Never have the hillsides seemed so beautiful," said Gunnar of Lidarende [in *The Saga of Burnt Njal*], when he mounted his horse and was about to ride away into exile. The hillsides of his home seemed so beautiful to him that he could not tear himself away. He stayed in his home and thereby lost his life.

One finds this love of home clearly reflected in literature. The most beautiful words in a language and the loveliest thoughts the mind has been capable of creating are woven around the home and the ideas we associate with it. The best and most beautiful in Norwegian literature is connected directly or indirectly to the home. Of all the twenty-nine works written by Jonas Lie, scarcely a one does not in some way or another touch on the home. He is called by this lovely name "the poet of the home." Yet Jonas Lie is no isolated case. The Norwegian people are a home-loving people; home plays a large role in their emotional and intellectual life. It is quite natural therefore that the home looms large in their literature.

This trait is clearly revealed in the history of our settlement in this country. Norwegian immigrants usually landed in New York. But it hardly occurred to any of them to settle there. They traveled westward, to the great plains and the wild forests, past the large towns, and the small ones too—past the farthest outpost. Why? Because it was in their nature to look for a place that was suitable for a home for themselves and their extended families. A home cannot be rented, you see. According to the Norwegian point of view, a home must be owned, otherwise one cannot call it a true home.

That is why the Norwegian immigrant did not stop in the cities he traveled through. He simply could not. Because of his heritage he could not remain in the large city living from hand to mouth as an industrial worker. America has not suffered because he was like this, for thereby great plains and wilderness areas have been fruitfully cultivated. There is also another trait that has played a role here, but more of that later.

Will it have any significance in the history of American culture if we make a point of preserving this part of our heritage? Or is this just more of that foreign trash which we would do best to throw on the scrap heap? I cannot recall our opponents ever recommending that we strive to preserve this part of our heritage. I have heard them speak nicely of father and mother; but that is done by every person with the least bit of good breeding. I have also heard them praise this or that place to the skies as the best under the sun, as a place worth so and so much, with the possibility of rising tremendously in value. I have heard glowing speeches on local pride, because the place is financially advantageous; but I have yet to hear speakers attempting to waken love of place because it will provide a good home for the same family generation after generation.———Here we *boost* our places. We are judged by our ability to boost. We work hard to find suitable slogans for a place, slogans that promote local pride, public relations, and advertising. Especially the latter. One never hears a word about *love*, which is after all the one necessary element in making people satisfied with a place.

How can we have an eye for that side of the matter, here where everything is for sale? Across the Northwest we don't have many true homes. That is a part of our spiritual poverty. We have money, well-being, riches, but very few real homes. We have lodgings, places to live. But there is an enormous difference between a lodging place and a home! Impoverished spirits don't even comprehend this.

It is hard to understand how one can buy a home, still more difficult to understand how one can sell it when one has first created it. One can buy a dwelling place but a home must be *built* or be inherited from one's father.

But we don't regularly do this any more out here in the Northwest. Here we build or buy with future sale in mind. If a place is salable, that is good; if not, we have acted foolishly. But in this way we do not create homes. For *memories* and *traditions* belong to a home. The spirit of the family makes its mark on the place generation after generation. That is the Norwegian view.

It is hard to believe how good people can make such foolish decisions. Here we have a decent farm couple, hardworking, honest, who have lived on the same quarter-section of land for 40 years. With care and thoughtfulness they have created a model farm. Forty of their best years lie there. Perhaps they grew up in the settlement, maybe one of them inherited the farm that their parents cleared. According to all the rules of nature the lives of these two people ought to lie in this quarter section of land. Here they have watched nature blossom and ripen, here they have harvested crops and brought grain into the bins year in and year out. Their lives ought to be there, and yet they are not.

For this has not become a home for them, neither the land nor the settlement. They are not attached to the place. For several years now these people have been on the lookout for a good opportunity to sell advantageously. They don't think they have quite as good a life as they should have. Now they want to sell and move into town—and just take it easy the rest of their lives. They are perhaps around sixty years old, and time goes so terribly fast. They can't wait too long if they are going to have any time to take it easy.

Finally the opportunity arises; they make the sale even more advantageously than they had expected. Without any emotional wrench they part with the place where they have lived all these years. They abandon their life, cut it off—that causes them no pain either—and move into the small town with their bits and pieces to find the happiness they believe has eluded them so far. All the swarming, sprouting life out there, all that is healthy and wholesome, they leave behind in order to take it easy.

They move into the small town in order to enjoy life and they settle down on a back street. It wouldn't do for folks without riches to live on Main Street or one of the finer residential areas; it is so unreasonably expensive there; the lot alone costs as much as a good forty acres just a few years ago. And the taxes are terribly high too.

Well, these two old people settle down someplace on the outskirts of town to take it easy in their old age.

How does it work out for them? Well, just as the laws of nature say it must: they dry up and wither away like two trees that have had their roots cut off. And it is the lord of life that has decreed it to be so.

This migration into town by a large portion of our older farming population in order to take it easy—we ought to note that this is the goal of the majority!—is the saddest aspect of our rootlessness. It shows so clearly that we have not yet succeeded in setting roots and building true homes. We have mere dwelling places, not homes. No, not homes. This is unspeakably sad.

It is almost as sad to realize that our leaders do not cry out to the people in speeches and writings to tell them that if a people shall endure they must settle and create homes. If we do not do this, the soul of our people will die.—There are a few spokesmen among other ethnic groups who see this and are not afraid to speak out. An editor of one of our largest newspapers recently wrote that "We are fast becoming a nation of movers and renters." People must see that everything higher and nobler in the life of a society, true culture, cannot blossom if people do not feel themselves to be at home. The famous Englishwoman, Lady Asquith, created a sensation in New York last winter by saying: "It seems to me you have a terrible lot of noise, but very little civilization."

But our own leaders are silent. Don't they see it? Or is this what they want? They speak loudly about patriotism! They ought to comprehend that true love of country is impossible without love of home. If the latter is absent the former becomes mere blather and hysteria.

This matter of the sanctity of the home and family is in essence a religious question; therefore our pastors ought to be the first to see it and explain it to our people. What a great source of support this would be for our youth in their uncertain chase after the joy of living. Perhaps then they could be made to understand that the innermost and truest source of joy is a good home, a home their forefathers built with their hands and their hearts. And yet, with a few exceptions, even the pastors are silent. In fact, they themselves may very well be on the lookout for a favorable opportunity to move!

One thing is absolutely certain: if we truly want what is best for this country, for the people who now live in it as well as for those who will come after us, then we ought to encourage this Nordic concept of the home.

Let me close this simple reflection with a few lines of poetry, which emphasize what has been said above:

We like to roam, but our home is best,
Home forever!
It has no equal in east or west,
Home forever!
Here round about things are good and right
And over all is a gracious light,
Home forever!

Upon this hillock I safely dwell,
Home forever!
This home my father did build so well,
Home forever!
Here I alone am the rightful lord,
'Tis mine to rule at this precious board,
Home forever!

Here I can work, so happy and free,
Home forever!
Our Lord Himself will stand by me,
Home forever!
Yes, here at home on my quiet isle,
Here I will live and here I die.
Home forever![8]

6

I remember from my childhood how much I loved one of the stories from the sagas. This story from the Saga of St. Olaf told about the farmers at the Mora Assembly and how they wanted to have peace between the kings of Sweden and Norway. But the Swedish king wanted the exact opposite and was very angry with the farmers.

One of the farmers stood up and spoke to the king. Remember, he was just an ordinary farmer and was speaking to the king himself. Nevertheless he spoke his mind. His words vibrated with righteous anger over the king's pride and foolishness.—"We farmers demand," said this farmer, "that you as king do what is right in the eyes of reasonable people and make peace with the king of Norway. If you do not, we farmers know how to solve this problem for ourselves. Our ancestors threw seven kings into the bog here at the Mora Council when they refused to listen to reasonable men, and we intend to do the same to you if you don't listen to our advice." And thus it was done as Torgny wished.[9]

The sagas tell of many similar incidents. Farmers were not afraid to speak to the king—with decorum and respect for the most part—but always as his equal *under the common law of the land.*

And here we see another trait in the Norwegian heritage: *the democratic-aristocratic feeling that permeates the best of Norway's rural populace.*

These great clans of farmers, in saga times and later, were aristocrats and democrats at one and the same time. Nothing like it is found anywhere else in all of world history. The Norwegian farmer felt equal to the leading man of the country. He submitted willingly to the law of the land—but that law had to be common to all. Conflict between farmers and government officials arose during the period of Danish domination because these officials were foreigners, not chosen by the people; and besides most of them tried to govern arbitrarily. They would not take into account the interests of the people. These officials came from a country where such things could be done to farmers; in Norway it was impossible because of our national character.

We might also note that the great farming families were always connected to a definite place. They felt a deep love of home. The farm and the family that lived on it became as one. This was true in Iceland as well as in Norway. In the Icelandic sagas, when the farm went out of the hands of a family, the family generally disappeared from the saga.

This is another reason why Norwegian immigrants traveled thousands of miles into America and settled in the wilderness. We might not have expected this of immigrants from Norway. After all, most Norwegians lived by the sea; the sea was theirs; they had traveled over the ocean in their journey to America; they landed on the coast. Nothing would seem more natural than that they would seek homes along the coast in this new land. If anyone decided to return to Norway, this would also have made the way back easier. But the Norwegians did not stop at the coast. They pushed far into the country in search of land. They seldom stopped in the cities, even though it would have been easier to earn a bit of money there. But the Norwegian immigrant wasn't out after mere cash.

The Norwegian immigrant had to have a *home*. To earn a few dollars and live from hand to mouth wasn't enough for him. The national instinct in him demanded more: it demanded soil to till; for with that it was possible to raise an independent home, a home where he himself could rule and be the ruler of his own kingdom. That is the way he felt and he acted accordingly. The Irishman is well suited to the town; he can always elbow himself forward in the crowd; the Englishman too—he has the practical business sense; the southern European is better suited for large industry; he can live from hand to mouth crowded into large tenements and be tolerably well satisfied with that. Those who come from northern Europe, and not least our people, are farmers. All people, including the Irish and the Italian, are the way they are on account of their national characteristics. To deny this is simply foolish.

Again I ask: would it not benefit our country if we would emphasize this part of our heritage? Doesn't America need it?

For some time now a split has been taking place within American society, with capitalists on the one side and industrial workers on the other. The conflict sharpens every year. Right now, as this is being written, the newspapers report over two million men out on strike, among them coal miners. At the large depots in Superior and Duluth, which at this time of the year are usually overflowing with coal, the bins stand completely empty. And winter is at the door! I just mention this to show the results of this conflict.

Both capital and labor are attempting to get as much political power at they can. Both wish to control our legislatures. Where will this conflict end?

Capital includes large industries and all of the country's natural resources—oil, coal, iron, timber, and so on—together with the large financial institutions. This is a powerful force,—and one with little thought or consideration for other classes in society.

Labor includes all those who perform physical work, with the exception of farmers. Until now, farmers have stayed outside this conflict. We can only hope that they manage to do so in the future as well. Lately we have seen several attempts by labor to get the farmers to side with them. This is quite natural; for if farmers were organized as many workers are now, they would be a powerful ally in the struggle.—Labor is quite strongly permeated by socialism; and this will only increase as the battle sharpens and the workers become enlightened. Socialism is growing in America. We ought to note that this socialism is of a much more radical type than is found for example in Norway. In Norway, and the same holds true throughout Scandinavia, socialism stands for approximately the same ideas and reforms as those supported by the progressive politicians within the two old parties here in this country. Socialism in America is much more extreme.

An important factor which only makes this unhealthy condition worse is the growth of large industry. This in turn causes the large cities to expand and increases slums and slum life.

If these conditions continue to develop as they are now, how will our country look in twenty years, in forty, in sixty? One thing is sure: We must slow this trend down, otherwise we will go right over the cliff. We cannot simply be content to comfort ourselves by pretending that "things will get better." Things haven't gotten better for the last twenty years. Nor will things be all right if we merely pray like the Pharisees, thanking God because we Americans are so much better than all other people. We must learn to tolerate well-meaning criticism no matter where it comes from.

One of the strongest brakes to this trend is a strong, enlightened population of farmers with the democratic-aristocratic view of *ownership*, *family*, and *home* that has characterized the best of the Norwegian farming population. In addition, we need an intense effort to improve all aspects of farming. This must go hand in hand with speeches and writings which extol the conditions of life in the country as opposed to city life. The state must find ways to make it possible for people of limited means to acquire homes and as much tillable soil as is necessary to live on. Just in the three states of Michigan, Minnesota, and Wisconsin there are millions of acres of farmland lying fallow, among them some of the best arable land one could wish for. Perhaps this land will never be cultivated if the state does not make it possible for poor folk to get ahead. Not only the price of such land must be taken into account, but also the time needed to clear it before it can produce.

Such help would be a powerful counterbalance to socialism. For, you see, a landowner doesn't readily become a socialist. In addition, if that landowner has a Nordic view of family and home, it would be highly unusual if he concerned himself with those kinds of ideas.

In this respect, Norway has led the way. There the state pays farmers, and pays them well, for bringing land they already own under cultivation. Norway has figured out that this pays off in the long run, and without a doubt this is correct.

We Norwegian Americans should also lead the way. How can we do that? Well, we have become farmers since we came to America, perhaps in greater proportions than any other group of people. But we are not as fond of the beautiful farms we have cleared as we ought to be. We have not developed a sense of connectedness. The restlessness and chasing after wealth and pleasure which we find in the general population is attracting us too. We stand at the verge of losing part of our heritage. We must return to it!—The place we live must become a *home*, for us and for our descendants.

If our leaders truly want the best for our country, they must proclaim this "gospel". Our pastors ought to preach it too. Let them read the law Moses proclaimed about the sanctity of the earth and the right of ownership and then preach on that topic. In a country parish such a sermon ought to be timely at least once a year. Such a sermon would do much good; it would bring joy and satisfaction to souls and minds.

I can't get away from the thought that what the Northwest—and the whole country—needs right now is a strong class of farmers with precisely that Norwegian view of home and family. We need a class of farmers who consider it an honor to be farmers and who think owning a home is their greatest earthly blessing. We need people who will improve their homes and rule there like kings. If we can get this view firmly entrenched within our people, then we will be spared such sad sights as seeing fine older farming couples selling their homes, moving into town, and settling on the outskirts to take it easy in their old age.

We are few against the many—that is true. But it doesn't take so many if they just have the right stuff in them. Raise the heritage! Let it light up and shine over the whole country!

> Against the millions, we are few,
> But for the Chieftain's clan, that's nothing new.
> Leif it was who discovered this land,
> Let the ones who win it with spirit be from our band.[10]

Along with this love of home and the democratic-aristocratic view go hospitality and good breeding. (For examples of hospitality and manners, read the sagas and Sigrid Undset's great historical novel *Kristin Lavransdatter*). Norwegian hospitality is known the world over. Tourism these last decades has disturbed it; in several places it has been quite destroyed, but it can still be found in Norway!

This too is part of our ancient heritage. In "Sayings of the High One"—the wisdom poem in the Elder Edda—we read:

> There must be a fire   for the frozen knees
> of all arriving guests,
> food and clothing   for those who come
> over the hills to the hall.[11]

In the old days there were laws about hospitality. If an enemy should seek shelter with you, it was considered a bad deed not to receive him well. He must be allowed to leave unmolested. The sagas tell of a woman in Iceland who built her house right across a path, with a hallway down the middle. In the center of the hallway she placed a table with chairs around it, and she saw to it that there was always food on the table.

Gunnlaug Ormstunge and Ravn were deadly enemies because they both loved Helga the Fair. They fought a duel in Iceland, but one of them was only slightly wounded and the matter between them was not settled because their friends and kinsmen were there to part them.

Then one morning Gunnlaug stayed in bed a little later than usual. He was alone at home. All the others in the house were working away from the farmyard. Suddenly Ravn came riding up to the farm, fully armed, with eleven men in his company. Gunlaug sprang up and grabbed his weapons. But Ravn would not do battle just then, even though his deadly enemy was now in his hands. He said to Gunnlaug: "The last time we met, we did not settle the matter between us because our kinsmen were nearby. Therefore I suggest to you that we go to Norway and hold our duel there, where no one can part us."—"Now you speak as a worthy man," answered Gunnlaug. "Stay here with your men and enjoy our hospitality."[12] These two were deadly enemies, take note of that!

When beloved and welcome guests came, they often stayed several days on the farm. Not only were they well treated while they were there, but when they left the most distinguished guests were given gifts. A cherished guest must not be sent away empty-handed. At all the big holidays there were great feasts. This was also true of celebrations such as weddings, christenings, and funerals.

A large, well-cared-for family farm must have been a picturesque sight on such occasions. It was filled with the joy of celebration; flowing with food and drink, games and merriment and athletic contests, happiness and pleasure. People sang folk songs, danced, held poetry contests, and told traditional legends and stories.

Of course it could sometimes get wild on such occasions. People drank heavily, there could be fights, and even killing. We must remember that the morals of the time were no better than they are today. What I want to draw attention to is the need for joy and celebration and hospitality in *our homes*, and the *generosity* accompanying it which has characterized us as a people from ancient times.

If we want to compare the violence of those times with our own, we would find that ours are not so much better that the old times can't stand the comparison. I will just remind you that one scarcely dares to show oneself on the streets of Minneapolis after dark without fearing for both life and property. And yet we live in a country that boasts of being the best in the world, and this is the twentieth century!

Furthermore, I wish to emphasize that the desire for celebration, joy, and pleasure is disappearing in us as we gradually become Americanized. We notice it in all areas, not least in family life and in the life of the church. Nowadays it is becoming the fashion, especially in town, to have baptisms at home. The pastor is invited to come over on a weekday or a Sunday afternoon and baptize the child. After the ceremony there may be a little bit of refreshments. The solemnity of it is gone. The joy and festivity too. Weddings too have become out of date. Now it is considered good form for the bride and groom and couple of witnesses to get in a car and drive off to a strange pastor—seldom their own—and get married there, in his living room or in a small office. This takes care of the whole business. Now one would think that if there were any pastoral acts that belonged in God's house, it should be these two, weddings and baptisms. If there are any things that ought to be solemnized in our lives, it is these. But such is not the case.

Why don't our pastors write about this? Why don't we hear about it in their sermons? They ought to educate the people on these matters. Who is closer to these questions than they are?

7

Another characteristic feature closely connected with the love for home and kin which I described in the previous section is *obedience to the law, respect for the law of the land.*

"With law shall the land be built."

That is an ancient saying from the Old Norse sagas. We can find it on the lips of our people long before the coming of Christianity. Far back in our history we find living evidence of that belief. The law assembly was an established institution long before the time of Harald the Fairhaired; the job of law-speaker is considerably older than the coming of Christianity. The assembly grounds were sacred once the assembly had begun. Woe to the man who broke the peace after the assembly had been proclaimed! Anyone who did so became an outlaw.

Other people who came into close contact with our Viking ancestors were astonished by this characteristic. Wherever the Norsemen settled and formed colonies, these brutal Viking warriors showed that they had a remarkable ability to rule themselves, to organize a society, and to keep law and order. An amusing story is going around here in the Northwest about a lawyer who didn't want any "damned Norwegian or Scotchman" on the jury. With that kind of people sitting in judgment he was afraid it wouldn't be possible to win a shady case. How far this tale may be true I don't know, but a people could scarcely have a more beautiful testimonial.

"But for heaven's sake! Don't people steal in Norway! Don't people cheat there! Don't people swear false oaths!" I can hear this around me on all sides. And I answer, "Yes, unfortunately they do." People in Norway steal and rob and commit all kinds of sins. Paradise does not exist there either. Nevertheless it is true that obedience to the law has characterized our people like hardly any other nation. People broke the law—and break it now—but not with an easy mind. I discount the mentally and morally stunted criminal. Of course people steal, but they do it with a bad conscience, with the knowledge that it is wrong. The question is not just: Can I get by with it? No, you are always conscious of breaking the law, committing a wrong.[13]

I remember so well from my teen-age years, when we boys began to try to take on the mannerisms of the grown-ups. We believed that to be grown men we had to put in some curses every now and then. How deathly afraid we were that we would swear to something false! Swearing went with being grown up, but swearing to something untrue would be the same as perjury. And that was not only a bad deed, it was a *mortal sin*. We were not especially good boys; nevertheless, this point of view was part of our nature and we couldn't get away from it.

Do we need to preserve this characteristic? Does America need this aspect of our Norwegian heritage? Well, just look around and answer for yourself. The record of criminality in our country is terrible. In this domain we stand indisputably higher than any other civilized country; here we can say quite truthfully that we have attained a world record. Those who do not care about preserving our national heritage better take note of this and consider their choice of words more carefully when they speak out against the usefulness of the Norwegian heritage for America.

Along with respect for the law of the land follows something else which is a great advantage for society: obedience to father and mother and respect for older people. We were brought up to raise our hats to the elderly—even if they looked strange to us. It was simply proper manners to be polite to older people.

Let's look at obedience to father and mother. They were the closest authorities, they personified the law for us when we were young. We were to show them not only obedience but also *respect*. I have not investigated the situation for other areas of Norway, but up in Nordland we used the formal pronoun when we spoke to mother and father after they had grown older. We did this for all elderly people, for that matter. "Only a custom," you may say. Yes, that is true enough, it is only a custom, but it is a very beautiful custom to show respect for your father and mother. And what are customs if not a reflection of values?

When we became adults ourselves, we understood why our parents should be respected. Perhaps they lived on the place where their family had lived for generations. Through mother and father we ourselves became a part of the great company that had gone before. Through them we were made a part of the spirit of a Norwegian home. Through them we became one with our people; the history of our country became our spiritual heritage and property. We could go all the way back to the great deeds of the saga age and recognize that they belonged to us.

It is much more difficult to foster this feeling of respect here, in the conditions we live under, and in the way we have ordered our lives. There are so many difficulties here, and we have refused to face them.

Here mother and father are mere *foreigners*, or such close descendants of them that the odor still clings. Our young people do not feel that their fathers' history ties them closer to the history of this country and its people. During a certain time in their lives, young people may even feel the exact opposite. They fear that the closer they stick to their mothers and fathers the more they themselves become *foreigners*. It is just this closeness, this togetherness, that people need in order to develop fully, yet our young people avoid it because of the common opinion around them. I myself know a little boy who didn't like to go with his parents to the Norwegian church services because he was afraid his friends would find out. I mention this to show how strong an influence we are fighting against.

Mother and father seem so terribly backward! In the first place they are just *foreigners*, and in addition they can't even talk properly! Children don't have to work their way through many grades in school before they understand that much, before they realize that they can speak *better* and *more correctly* and *more elegantly* than mother and father. And they are most likely right; the children can do this.

This situation becomes even more difficult because we entrust so much of the upbringing of our children to the schools. After children reach the age of six, school takes on the most important role in raising them rather than the home. At home we don't have time. If our school system had the slightest bit of understanding of psychology, it would do everything it could to encourage ethnic pride in the children, instead of trying to break it down. In this way, young people would come to feel their worth as human beings. This feeling is an essential provision for the road ahead.

It is not only the public schools that fall short. Our own are scarcely any better. And that is harder to forgive. For we ought to see the situation. At every one of our schools there ought to be a good course in pioneer history, that is, the *history of Norwegian immigration*. It doesn't matter whether English or Norwegian is used for instruction; I teach such a course myself and I use English. As a matter of fact, I think English is best, for it makes the course accessible to everyone. Such a course pays for itself, for it opens the eyes of our own youth to the fact that we really do have a part in the history of America—even the immigrant who has just arrived, so long as he had some human worth when he set foot in this land.

8

The three inherited characteristics I have already discussed are like compartments in a large drawer in the same dresser. They are so closely related that they hang together. Now we will look in another drawer, at another pair of compartments close to each other. In this drawer I can find several more treasures that have been part of our family heritage since time immemorial. These beautiful treasures are *desire for knowledge and appreciation of art*. Let us take them out and examine them one at a time.

> The men who live   the fairest lives
>   know just a number of things.[14]

So it says in the "Sayings of the High One," the wisdom poem in *The Elder Edda*. Other old proverbs touch on the same theme. "Things are bad when wisdom is lacking." "There is nothing worse than to know little." "Ignorance is no man's friend."

This view, that learning improves life and makes it fuller and richer was widespread among our people in heathen times. They also understood that a life lived in ignorance is impoverished.

This view has characterized our people ever since. There is scarcely another country where the level of education is higher than in Norway. It was widespread even in the saga age. At that time young men from leading families went on raiding and trading expeditions to foreign countries—not only to rob and pillage or to buy and sell, but also to learn foreign customs and ways, courtly manners at the palaces of kings and earls, and languages and all sorts of useful knowledge. These expeditions were part and parcel of a young man's education. People who sat at home all their days were frowned upon. All the knowledge gained by those who went out was brought back to other people in their homes and local communities. In this way a blending of cultures took place. One spread one's own culture and reaped from other cultures to sow in the soil at home.

After the saga period with all its great deeds had ended and the ranks of the great families had thinned out came the time of folk songs, tales, and legends. Traditions survived in the mouths of the ordinary people. In the fisherman's hut, around the lumberjack's campfire, up in the high mountain meadow, in the long fall and winter evenings in the homes of ordinary people, stories were told and songs rang out. Words and melodies fell with remarkable lightness from the lips of the storytellers and singers. If a stranger happened by who could tell tales of people and conditions in foreign lands, he was a welcome guest.

In more recent times, the Scandinavian countries—and not least our own ancestral people—have become models of public education.

In elementary school we learned this verse by heart.

Reading and growing
help us get big!
Those who will be grown up
on this earth
must be healthy and strong
and wise too
so all will praise
their work in life.[15]

The great Danish poet N.F.S. Grundtvig expressed this thought more simply, and gave it a classical form.

"True enlightenment is to man as sunshine is to the soil."[16]

The school system in Norway has made great progress recently. A hundred years ago it was nothing to brag about. The same was true in other countries; it is only in the nineteenth century that popular education has taken off. But the *desire* for enlightenment was in our people all along. People valued education. Books were cherished guests in the home. Children were required to learn to read. A person who didn't know anything was really backward.

Thirty years ago up in Nordland it was considered the worst sort of disgrace if someone took two years to learn enough to be confirmed. Such a person was marked for life. People figured there was something wrong, and had a hard time forgetting about it. This was true in spite of the fact that we scarcely had a model elementary school. When I first started going to school we didn't have more than nine weeks of school per year. But we learned something anyway, and we learned even more at home than at school. People took it for granted that children had to study at home; it was the parents' duty to see that they studied. I remember well my mother sitting at her loom with a child on either side of her, each reading a book. Or father mending fishing nets, one of us standing beside him with a book. Sometimes the switch lay close by. They were strict, those old folks. It even happened that one of us children had to go without eating because we hadn't learned our lesson by the appointed time.

This desire for knowledge is the aspect of our heritage that we as a people have taken best care of since we became Americans. The struggle to maintain schools has characterized all of our work in the church, and we have done reasonably well. Though we are one of the most recently arrived of all ethnic groups in the United States, we do more for higher education in proportion to our numbers than any other group in the country. We have reason to be pleased about this. Yet no one should be complacent and think that we have done enough. We have the resources to do much much more! If we did everything in our power, everything our heritage demands of us, we would set a fine example for the whole country in the field of higher education.

Just suppose we did! The Lutheran Church has been in America a long time now; still it has not managed to create a seat of learning that is first-rate either in size or influence. Historically the Lutheran Church ought to be the church of enlightenment *par excellence*. Suppose we Norwegian Lutherans really exerted ourselves and led the way, perhaps taking a slightly different path than the one others have trodden before us? We have the power to do it both financially and intellectually.

But I was talking about national characteristics. It is overwhelmingly just ordinary people who emigrated from Norway—farmers, fishermen, working people. Yet they had vision. There had to be schools; talented youth had to be given the opportunity to get ahead. These Norwegian immigrants were individualistic enough that they had to build their own schools. Blessings on them for this!

Here in the Northwest it may not be so important to emphasize this part of our heritage, because here the rest of the population is mostly northern European, and popular education has always had a high value among them. On the other hand, if we look at the country as a whole, this aspect of our heritage takes on a whole new meaning. During the last war [World War I] the military draft revealed the sad fact that as a nation we are among the least educated people in the world. Of the 3,750,000 draftees who were tested, there were 75,000 who could not read or write. And it is interesting to note that most of the 'illiterates' came from states where there are the fewest 'foreigners,' where Americans of old stock have done just as they please with no foreign-born to spoil things.

Earlier I said that, as far as the Northwest is concerned, it mattered little whether we emphasize this aspect of our heritage or not. Let's take a closer look.

Ostensibly we have built up an excellent school system. In theory we have nearly approached the ideal. Our schools take children at the age of six, and have them for seven, eight, or even nine months of the year until they reach the age of fourteen. In towns a large percentage stay on through the four years of high school, attending school until they are eighteen. In many places, school buildings and other equipment are as good and as modern as money can buy. We have not spared on the schools! We have no reason to find fault with the curriculum either. So we should expect the best results.

And yet, throughout the country we hear voices asking serious questions and raising doubts about whether we really are reaping benefits in proportion to expenses. Doubts are becoming stronger. Fears are growing. We are finding that our young people do not have the solid foundation of knowledge that they should have after so many years of schooling. Even more serious, their moral character is far from what it should be. Instead of leaving school with solid knowledge, maturity, seriousness, and a deeper view of life, our young people are leaving as painfully superficial human beings who know little of serious matters and have no desire to obtain such knowledge. They seem to have gained an insatiable appetite for 'amusements,' but little or no ambition. They just float along with the crowd. In addition our criminal records show us disturbing news. Criminals are as a rule young people—the great majority are under 35 years of age and a substantial percentage have attended high school. In spite of this they are able to do evil deeds.[17]

We must take such information seriously if we want to be true patriots. These matters will not improve by themselves, and certainly not just because we brag about being the most enlightened and advanced people in the world. It will take more than that.

Here our Norwegian heritage could be a big help, if we only bothered to nourish and promote it to a greater degree. According to the Norwegian point of view, we don't go to school just to be there, just because others are doing it, or because it is part of growing up. We go to school because life demands the greatest possible store of knowledge and maturity. Life simply demands it. "Things are bad when wisdom is lacking." "There is nothing worse than little knowledge." "Ignorance is no man's friend."

This is one side of the matter. Another is that, according to the Norwegian view, it is impossible for school to be the only place where children and youth are reared—no matter how good the school. We see this more clearly all the time. Norwegians believe that the home *must* and *shall* do its part, not least when it comes to

morals. It is the home that must sow and plant; the school will cultivate. The home has the greatest responsibility.

This is a part of our Norwegian heritage. God help us plant it in
America's soil so that it will always grow vigorously and provide
shelter and shade for the coming generations!

9

Since becoming Americans we have tried to nourish our desire for
knowledge and have valued this part of our heritage highly. Unfortunately, we have disdained that part of our heritage that concerns
a love of art. We have simply had no use for it. Some of us have even
wondered if it was not evil. As a group we have neglected it shamefully. This is true for all areas of art with the exception of music.

Art dimly reveals the mysterious in our existence. In this it re-
sembles religion. A human being is so moved by all the beauty
around him that he feels compelled to interpret this feeling for others—in melody, in words, in color, in line. His own deep emotional
response is thereby transmitted to others.

There are hearts that see beauty everywhere and in everything.
Most of us don't find it strange that people see beauty in high
mountains, blue skies, broad seas, and running rivers. We probably
have noticed it ourselves. We may have observed the beauty of sunrise and sunset too. Many a love song has been written when hearts
are touched by the beauty of flowers.

It is more remarkable that some people have the gift of seeing
beauty in pain and sorrow, in joy and laughter, yes, even in death.
Some have found life itself, in its ceaseless race towards eternity,
more beautiful than anything else.

All this may seem strange, and yet maybe it's not so strange
either. Our Lord is all powerful; He can accomplish all things. And
in His all powerful wisdom He has equipped some people with this
ability to find beauty everywhere.

Yes, it is He who has done this.

Out of all the many peoples in the world, the Lord chose one to
be his own people. He gave this people great and wonderful ances-

tors. He let them grow in numbers in slavery among a foreign people. And then He led his people for forty years of wandering in the wilderness. His people had to become mature before they were worthy to take possession of the Promised Land.

On their long wandering, this people had a place of worship where they could assemble for prayer at the times the Lord Himself had decreed as holy days. They needed a place to bring their offerings of atonement, their thank offerings, and their sacrifices. They needed a house where the Lord could meet his people. Therefore the tabernacle was built. After all, there had to be a tabernacle if there was later to be a temple!

But the house over which the glory of the Lord was to shine had to be beautiful. And not only that, those who were to serve the Lord as priests and high priests, who were to go into the holy of holies, had to have garments that were seemly. These servants needed beautiful clothing.

Listen now to the story from the book of Exodus that tells how all these things became beautiful.[18]

"And the Lord spoke to Moses, saying: 'And you shall make holy garments for Aaron your brother, for glory and for beauty.. And you shall speak to all *who have ability, whom I have endowed with wisdom, that they make Aaron's garments to consecrate him for my priesthood.'*

"The Lord said to Moses, 'See, I have *called* by name Bezalel the son of Uri, son of Hur, of the tribe of Judah: and I have *filled* him with the *Spirit of God*, with *wisdom* and *intelligence*, with *knowledge* and all *craftsmanship*, to devise artistic designs, to work in gold, silver, and bronze, in cutting stones for setting, and in carving wood, for work in every craft. And behold, I have appointed with him Oholiab, the son of Ahisamach, of the tribe of Dan; and *I have given to all able men skill,* that they may make all that I have commanded you.'

"And then Moses spoke to the people: 'And let every able man among you come and make all that the Lord has commanded: the tabernacle, its tent and its covering, its hooks and its frames, its bars, its pillars, and its bases; the ark with its poles, the mercy seat, and the veil of the screen; the table with its poles and all its utensils, and the bread of the Presence; the lampstand also for the light, with its utensils and its lamps, and the oil for the light; and the altar of incense, with its poles, and the anointing oil and the fragrant incense, and the screen for the door, at the door of the tabernacle; the altar of burnt offering, with its grating of bronze, its poles, and all its utensils, the laver and its base; the hangings of the court, its pillars and its bases, and the screen for the gate of the court; the pegs of the tabernacle and the pegs of the court, and their cords; the finely wrought garments for ministering in the holy place, the holy garments for Aaron the priest, and the garments of his sons, for their service as priests.' Then all the congregation of the people of Israel departed from the presence of Moses.

"All the women whose hearts were moved spun with their hands, and brought what they had spun in blue and purple and scarlet stuff and fine linen; all the women whose hearts were moved with ability spun the goats' hair.

"And Moses said to the people of Israel: 'See, the Lord has *called* by name Bezalel the son of Uri, son of Hur, of the tribe of Judah; and he has filled him with the Spirit of God, with wisdom, with intelligence, with knowledge, and with all craftsmanship, to devise artistic designs, to work in gold and silver and bronze, in cutting stones for setting, and in carving wood, for work in every skilled craft. And he has inspired him to teach, both him and Oholiab the son of Ahisamach of the tribe of Dan. He has filled them with ability to do every sort of work done by craftsmen or by a designer or by an embroiderer in blue and purple and scarlet stuff and fine linen, or by a weaver—by any sort of workman or skilled designer.'

"Bezalel and Oholiab and every man in whom the Lord had put ability and intelligence to know how to do any work in the construction of the sanctuary shall work in accordance with all that the Lord has commanded. And Moses called Bezalel and Oholiab and every able man in whose mind the Lord had put ability, every one whose heart stirred him to come to do the work."

And then follows a careful description of how all the work was done. The story ends like this:

"And Moses saw all the work, and behold they had done it; as the Lord had commanded, so had they done it. And *Moses blessed them.*"

I have cited this at such length for two reasons:—I wanted to show that God is the source of *all* love of art in human beings. And in addition, that He has given special abilities to *some* in order to encourage love of beauty in *all* people, so that his name may thereby be glorified. It really ought to be unnecessary to call attention to this!

There are scarcely any people who love art as much as our own people, not even the Jews or the Greeks. My opinion about this is based on what our people, in proportion to their numbers, have produced in the realm of the arts.

This love of art is as old as our people; it must have been there from time immemorial. It can be clearly seen in the proud lines and grandeur of the Viking ship, in the carved dragon heads and row of shields decorating the sides. Truly, these ancient shipbuilders had an appreciation of beauty, as well as the practical skill to translate it into reality. We find art in the form of the stave church, in its beautifully artistic carvings. Where can one find anything like that! We see it revealed in the rose paintings in the homes of Norwegian farmers. But this love of beauty comes out most strongly and clearly in literature; here we encounter the greatest and purest art.

The art of poetry was widespread in Viking times. High-minded young people competed to learn to create poetry. One of the greatest compliments you could pay a man was to say that he was a good poet.

Everyone with the least bit of culture valued this poetry highly. The poet was an honored guest wherever he went, and especially at the courts of the earl and the king. He was paid lavishly for the poems he created—if they were any good. He might receive a lot of money, rare weapons, magnificent clothing, ships, and often a place of honor among the king's retainers.

It is no wonder that this early poetry has such a high reputation—several degrees higher than the literature produced in other countries at that time. Today this poetry is read and studied and admired throughout the literary world, in spite of the fact that it was created in one of the world's smallest countries!

We see the same if we look at the prose literature of the time. No other people have a comparable treasure to show. Two things especially stand out in Old Norse literature: style and form and the depiction of character. The form is so simple and natural, the style so pure, so powerfully epic. And the depiction of character is incredibly profound. The authors of the sagas knew their characters. In addition, these stories reveal an epic view of existence. Life is ultimately tragic; and yet it requires each human being to meet it with joy—not like a fool, but like a hero. One might be tempted to think that the creators and tellers of the sagas had been raised on Old Testament literature all their lives.

And as I have noted earlier, after the saga period was over the age of folk literature arose. The other two Scandinavian countries excel when it comes to ballads and folk songs, but Norway more than evens things up when it comes to the folktale. In this art form, Norway has gone far beyond any other country. The Norwegian folktale has provided a playground for the imagination of the people. And play they did! People used this medium to translate their dreams and longings, their ideals and moral views into easy, playful words and lively tales that were told and listened to generation after generation, creating in this way the highest art of its kind anywhere.

Let us also take a look at more recent literature. I will just point out the fact that Norway in a short span of time has had two Nobel prize winners; and experts maintain that a third is not far away.[19] That's the record of poor, tiny Norway. Our huge, rich country with a population of over 100 million people has not produced a single writer who could even be considered in all the years since the Nobel prizes were founded. No other nation in proportion to its population has made such an impact on world culture in the area of the arts as the small country of Norway has done in the last hundred years.

If we heritage people were the only ones who talked like this, it would be easy to accuse us of egotistical blindness and of stubbornly promoting ourselves. Fortunately, however, we have said little about this part of our heritage. People who understand such things, people to whom "The Lord has given the gift of love of art," say the same the world over. I will demonstrate this with a few brief examples.

"*Peer Gynt* is the greatest poem of the nineteenth century," wrote a German critic at the beginning of this century. Last year a St. Olaf graduate was studying at Princeton University, where he met a student from Japan.[20] "Oh, so you are from Ibsen's homeland!" exclaimed the Japanese man, as happily as though he were meeting an old acquaintance, when he heard that the other had been born in Norway. "And from Bjørnson's," he added quickly. The Japanese man had read *Synnøve Solbakken* [*Synnøve of Sunny Hill*] in his own language. Last year an editorial in one of this country's leading daily newspapers stated that "Since Ibsen's day, drama can never be what it was before; Ibsen has brought it to a higher level." And here is what the well-known English writer Bernard Shaw said about Ibsen's influence on England: "The influence which Ibsen had on England is almost equivalent to the influence which three revolutions, six crusades, a couple of foreign invasions, and an earthquake would produce. The Norman Conquest was a mere nothing compared to the Norwegian Conquest."

This will have to be enough, though I could continue for many more pages. Ibsen has been translated into all modern languages; and one could fill a large bookshelf with critical works on his writings. More are coming out all the time. Last year a bibliography of works on Ibsen was published; it came to seventy-five pages and was still incomplete. In addition to Ibsen, Bjørnson may be read in many languages, as may Knut Hamsun and Johan Bojer.

Though our people have reached the highest level in literature we have also made great contributions in other art forms. Let us look quickly at music and the visual arts. Ole Bull, Edvard Grieg, [Johan] Svendsen, [Halfdan] Kjerulf, [Christian] Sinding are well known names.[21] Likewise [Hans] Gude, [Adolph] Tidemand, [Gerhard] Munthe, [Gustav] Vigeland, [Stephan] Sinding, [Christian] Skredsvig, and many others.[22]

I began this reflection by saying that love of art is the part of our heritage that we have cared the least about. In order to document this, I will repeat here a part of what I wrote several years ago.[23]

It seemed impossible that our people over here would be able to produce any literature, any poetry in the Norwegian language. All historical indicators gave a clear and decisive "no". No immigrant ethnic group in this country except the English had managed to create a body of literature in their own language. Not the Swedes. Not the Germans. Nor any others. That made it seem impossible for us Americans of Norwegian ancestry.

It did seem as if this was right. Most of our writers who have touched on this matter and those cultural leaders who have spoken about it have assured us over and over again that a literature in the Norwegian language in America is and will remain an impossibility. When we finally get far enough along to produce a body of literature, it will be in English. Popular opinion agrees with this. (I am tempted to ask parenthetically: How long will it be before we produce it in English? Most of our people have left pioneer conditions far behind them. If the second and third generation have not yet learned English well enough to produce literature, we have little hope that this will ever happen. As a group we have become materially wealthy. Some of our talented young people are getting the best education the country has to offer. We have time, we have money, we have the language. Where is our literature? Strangely enough, almost all who have attempted to write in English were born in Norway. I think there is scarcely a single exception. I repeat my question: When will the time come?)

Those who have discussed this matter have seemingly documented their assertions with great thoroughness. The difficulties are insurmountable. For example, we have no language any more. There are so few who read. Genuine literature makes such great demands; it requires so much of its servant. First and foremost it demands people's entire will, their complete devotion, their undivided heart, their undivided mind, their entire personality, their total commitment. No one will make such sacrifices, they cannot be made. Such devotion will mean death to the one who ventures out on this path. "Do this, and starve to death!" This is the judgment—short, cold, and inexorable. Our cleverest minds and our cultural leaders have analyzed the matter and judged it to be so.

What do ordinary people think? I again draw your attention to the fact that the majority of Norwegian immigrants are just ordinary people—farmers, craftsmen, fishermen. They came here because they wanted to explore the world; they wanted to better their economic condition; they wanted to save a few thousand crowns and then go back home. Most of those who came after the 1880s probably intended to return to Norway to live permanently. Unfortunately, this mindset led to restlessness and hindered the feeling of being at home. Newspapers in Norwegian have been and still are read. People have to follow along with the times and see what is going on in the world. But books? Works of literature?—Who has time and money for that? And especially literature created here in this country—in Norwegian?—Hm!—The newspapers say that sort of thing is impossible. Our poets and authors after all are back in Norway. And in addition to all this, much of our best preaching has cast doubt on secular literature. In several cities here in the Northwest one can find small groups of people with a genuine interest in literature, but whose entire literary lives are lived in Norway. They will not touch a Norwegian-American book. They think they know beforehand that it cannot be worth anything for the simple reason that it is written by a Norwegian in America.

These attitudes have turned into apathetic indifference. Among Norwegian Americans we can scarcely find any interest at all in books written in either Norwegian or English. People look at book reviews in the newspapers, and if it is not immediately apparent that the book has a religious content, no one even reads the review, much less the book. Just ask our publishers!—

That is the way ordinary people feel and that is why we have not been on the lookout for talented writers. We as a people don't see the usefulness, the blessing, and the uplifting influence that comes from true poetry. We feel no longing for poetry. In many a soul there may lie a vague dream of a beautiful world of words and a mild longing to slip into that wonderful land. But it never goes beyond that. We have been convinced that literature in Norwegian in America is impossible. Our preachers either ignore it or call it questionable. And we ourselves have neither time nor money. We simply don't care.

This is the situation. Such are the attitudes. But in spite of all this, something miraculous has happened. A Norwegian-American literature in Norwegian has appeared. It is a strange, fantastic creature to be sure, and yet so alive and with such power in its lungs that it is not possible to shut our eyes and swear that it doesn't exist. For the creature does exist. We can easily count seventy, eighty, yes even a hundred Norwegian-American books—books which are so unmistakably good that you have to call them literature whether you like it or not. And in addition to fiction there are thousands and thousands of lyric poems buried in dusty heaps of newspapers.

We may not like either the books or the poems. We may not be bothered to look at them. But they exist, in spite of all the disdain and the prophesying that they could not come into being.

If we call these books and poems provincial literature or emigrant literature, we give the child a wrong name. For they are neither of those things. They are American literature in the Norwegian language. And yet they are unlike all other American literature in that they look more deeply at life and tell more truthfully about it.

Well, now. Seventy or eighty or even a hundred volumes, that isn't such a large shelf of books. But take a peek at that of any other national group—with the exception of the English—and you will look in vain for anything comparable. Our literature is that large and that rich in spite of all our indifference, our contempt, and our lack of faith. Is this not proof that the love of art is deeply incorporated into our family heritage!

As a group we have had little use for those who interpret in living words the desire for beauty. As a result, we have not rewarded our writers but rather have neglected them. How then could it be expected that we would be any more generous with our painters, who attempt to express the same thing in line and color. Indeed, we have neglected even more those among us who have used canvas as a medium of art. There are several eminent Norwegian-American artists, but with the exception of a few portraits of famous persons we have scarcely a single example of Norwegian-American visual art.

Our own artists have had to leave us even though we have needed them. A people needs those on whom the Lord has bestowed special gifts!—We needed our artists, but we didn't have enough wit to see it, and therefore we did not procure the means to hold on to them. In this we were the losers, but the artists gained by it. That is, gained financially, but lost spiritually. They were able to receive compensation for what their spirits created, but they suffered by losing contact with their own people. Some of these artists have won a reputation which resounded across our land and reached all the way to Europe, where their works are very favorably received.

This ought to be a source of pride and joy for us, but the tragedy is that so few of us know anything about either these artists or their works. I venture to claim that the great majority of our educated people do not even know the names of these artists. Even if they ever heard or saw them, the names have escaped their minds as something completely irrelevant. We Norwegian Americans don't need any tabernacle, therefore Bezalel and Oholiab cannot remain among us and we will be forced to wander in the wilderness for many years before we get a temple!

Contempt for this aspect of our heritage and the consequences of it meet us everywhere we turn. The Norwegian Society has tried for ten years to scrape together a few nickels for a statue of one of our most distinguished men, the patriot and hero Colonel Hans Heg. We have still raised only a third of what is needed.

In 1915 a group of men got together and decided to spearhead a movement to put up a statue of Saint Olaf on the campus of St. Olaf College. At that time such a statue would cost about $3,000. The committee included men who had the confidence of the community. They willingly put their names on the challenge that was sent out to people. Remember now, they only needed $3,000. Surely you would have expected it to come in at once? Well, it did not come in. To date the fund has raised only $800. Either 800 people had enough interest in art and sense of history that they donated one dollar each or there were 100 who gave 8 dollars each. It doesn't matter how we figure it, what we get is proof of spiritual poverty.

I'll just leave you with one more example to prove my point.

Shortly after President Hoyme's death, someone made the lovely suggestion that we ought to build a Memorial Chapel at St. Olaf College in honor of this beloved pastor and president.[24] This was a beautiful thought and, besides, such a chapel was needed at the school. A collection was started.

We rightly expected a positive outcome. In the first place, Hoyme was one of the most beloved people of his time. In the second place, St. Olaf was then and is now the largest seat of learning our people have. A great number of our best youth would enter this chapel daily to learn of all that is highest and most beautiful in life. The impression made here would carry into their entire lives. And the result? Well, a building was built, that is true. It is still standing there, so anyone who wants to see it can do so. But everyone who sees it says the same thing. "This really looks more like a barn than a chapel." Besides that, the "barn" is much too small![25]

This will have to be enough about this aspect of our heritage.

I must add just one more thing. America can make good use of this inherited treasure if we care for it and share it. We who have inherited this characteristic have the duty to lead the way in using it for our own benefit and for that of the whole nation. If we could only shake off our apathy and our materialism, which, like rust on the wheat, threatens to ruin our lives. What a blessing we could be for the whole people!

10

Those of us in the heritage movement have been accused of many absurd things. Among them, that the only thing we talk about and the only aspect of our heritage we promote is the language. Our critics say that the Norwegian language is all we care about and wish to preserve.

This interest in the Norwegian language, they say, precludes all others. Children must learn the language, even at the expense of religion. And to the degree that we acquire Norwegian our ability to learn other things, especially English, declines. Our children and young people and adults will go around in the towns and on the prairies speaking nothing but Norwegian all their days. In this way we intend to secure an earthly paradise for them and for ourselves.

This surely must be counted as one of the deadly sins. But now for something even worse!

Some years ago there was a clever fellow among the promoters of English monolingualism who, in a moment of sheer inspiration, deciphered the real plan behind what we are doing. He described our plot in words that came to him from above.

"These people are attempting to build a little Norway in America!"

Now we were in a fine spot! All our secret plans and wicked schemes were at once revealed to an innocent and unsuspecting people. At last it was possible to point a finger at us, and in writing and in public speeches we were told to pack up and get ourselves back over the Atlantic Ocean. We did not belong on this side!

A terrible storm broke loose over us. We shivered and froze, and didn't know where to seek shelter. We dared not speak. If we used Norwegian, that was wrong; if we attempted English, that was even worse. Even for those of us whose words fell lightly from our lips, when we spoke English the language was what we could in the best of cases call *'speckled.'*[26] People stood up in meetings and complained of the misfortune they had suffered because they had learned enough Norwegian as children to be confirmed in that language.

An obvious lie, a lie that everyone can see is a lie, cannot be taken for truth in the long run. That is the case with this particular lie too. The assertion about a "little Norway" has begun to wither; by now it has become quite pale and thin in the mouths of our accusers.

This was inevitable. Sensible people looked around and did not discover a trace of such a structure. No one has been able to spot a carpenter busily building!——There are neighborhoods in which Norwegian is used quite frequently at home and in public, but even in such places you cannot find a person making plans to get King Haakon or the crown prince to come and rule over the settlement. No one has ever even dreamt of getting the mountains and fjords moved over to the prairie.—Quite the opposite, one finds that such neighborhoods are generally more intensely American in spirit than others.

By now, this statement has become something of an embarrassment to those who made it. Not even among the most avid spokespersons for our ancestral heritage can we find a single individual who has attempted to prevent our children from becoming just as fluent as other children in the language of our country.

These revelations have caused some concern, for our opponents did not expect them. Indeed, if one bothers to investigate the mat-

ter and not just repeat idle talk, one can find many cases of bilingual children whose English is better than that of monolingual
children. Examples are easy to find. Just go through the records at
our schools, and you can find all the proof you need. The children
of our heritage people have not avoided English as a subject nor
have they done more poorly in it than other people's children; the
opposite is rather the rule. It is only natural that it should be so.
For "to him who has will more be given."[27] These facts are indeed a
disappointment to certain people!

The accusation that the only part of the heritage we wish to preserve is the language has been thrown at us thousands of times in
writing and in speeches as well as in private conversations. When
our opponents run out of arguments or become so angry that they
have to find real insults, then they resort to this matter of the language. It is high time for them to stop it. It is usually considered
poor sportsmanship to lie about your opponents. And this nonsense about a little Norway that some people are trying to build in
America is really too stupid even to be mentioned by anyone with
the least claim to education and enlightenment.

Here I must take the opportunity to pose a question to our opponents. What part of our ancestral heritage do *they* want to preserve? Yes, what is it? For sometimes they too can utter fine words
about the heritage of our fathers. If they could elucidate this clearly
and tell us the method they would use to preserve it, there could be
some hope of reconciliation and cooperation. And both of these are
needed! I have heard some of them mention the Lutheran faith, but
that is just nonsense; Lutheranism is not Norwegian heritage. That
much we all know. We must have another answer!

No, we are not interested only in the language. But luckily we are
not so blind that we can't see that language is also part of our heritage. It is one of the most precious treasures in our culture. We see
that. Our heirs must have the right to inherit the language of their
kin! We think this is crystal clear. Sometimes it is hard for us to forgive our opponents for the scorn with which they occasionally
speak of the ancestral language, and for their callous indifference
to the necessity for their children to learn it. It is certainly human

to get angry at a fellow human being who throws away a precious possession!

Languages are the greatest and richest storehouse belonging to the family of man. In languages we find preserved that which a nation has thought and dreamt and felt in its long journey forward through time. All this is contained in the language, in its idioms and vocabulary, in its sound and rhythm, in its poetry and wisdom, in the works of authors, philosophers, and scientists. All this is stored and preserved in language like golden grain in the farmer's bins. Whoever wants to can go in and help himself.

Therefore it is self-evident that the study of languages and literature has great value for the person who seeks knowledge and wisdom. It is interesting to note that such study has been carried on with great diligence during historical periods of advancement, while the opposite is the case whenever materialistic tendencies get the upper hand. Just investigate, and you will see that this is true.

If the study of languages in general is so important, shouldn't it be even more important to acquire the language of your own kin? This language ought to possess even greater value precisely because it does belong to your kin. It is much more important for Americans of Norwegian descent to learn Norwegian than, for example, to learn Spanish or German, and in any case they don't learn much of these languages with only two or three years of study. (The purely economic side of the matter I will touch on in another connection). And yet we find thousands of our own youth laboring under the misconception that it is much more fashionable to know a little French or German than to be able to speak and read Norwegian fluently.

This view comes partly from the home, perhaps even more from the elementary and high school, and not least from the leaders among our own people—from our politicians, teachers, and pastors. They have not taught our people about their kin and their heritage, and the usefulness and blessings that flow from understanding the language of our people.

Only a very few of us who are fathers and mothers comprehend how invaluable it is for children to learn the language of their own people, and therefore we just don't do as much about it as we should. It is most unusual to find teachers in the elementary or high schools who understand the educational value in these languages; and so young people get no encouragement from that direction either. Our own leaders as a rule keep totally quiet about it. When they do speak, it is in such vague generalities that it is hard to tell exactly what they mean; or else it sounds like a half-grudging admission. It is seldom that one hears an urgent appeal. Am I saying anything untrue?

You have often heard harsh words from the supporters of our heritage about the lack of interest among the youth and their great indifference to the language of their ancestors. This kind of talk is as unjust as it could be, and we ought to be quiet. The way things have gone for the last ten years, we could not have expected our young people to have any great desire to study the Norwegian language. But we cannot place the blame at their feet, for they are children of their times to a much greater degree than we are. Again and again, they have been given the impression that everything that has grown in the soil of America is good, while everything that can best be described as *foreign* is at best of doubtful value. Many of our own people have followed along in the path of the jingoists. "Norwegian church services! Why should we have Norwegian church services in America? No, preach in English; then the whole country will lie open to us. By our preaching let us persuade all of America to join the Norwegian Lutheran Church in America. This ought to be our goal, therefore let us take away the foreign emblem in our flag. No full-blooded American could be expected to join a *Norwegian* church!"—It is words like these we have heard and are still hearing.

Young people are particularly sensitive creatures when it comes to their honor and especially their patriotism! It has been—and partly still is—a matter of honor to be able to document that nothing *foreign* sticks to oneself. Under such circumstances how can we possibly expect our young people to show any special warmth or enthusiasm for their ancestral language. That would be to expect the impossible.

Yet if a renaissance of interest in our ancestral heritage should take place then a deep interest in the language of our forefathers would quite naturally follow. And if this does happen, it will be led by our young people. Consciously or unconsciously, the most intelligent among them are beginning to feel that something is terribly wrong, that the bough supporting them, which before was merely bent, is now broken.

Some things that we have regarded as essential truths are not. They are just a noisy stream of words—mere hot air. Really intelligent young people revolt against this mirage we have been following. And quite naturally. For if all that is of foreign origin is trash, and our youth are close descendants of foreigners, and the laws of heredity were not repealed yesterday, then they must themselves, with the merciless inevitability of logic, also be trash. For only bad comes from bad. It's that simple.

The most intelligent of our young people have slowly begun to seek the fundamental sources of their own nature, and to search there for values. In my work these last years I have clearly noticed this uncertain groping and searching.

I fully and firmly believe in a renaissance. I do not know how and when it will come, but it will most likely be led by our young people. When this renaissance finally comes, the study of the language of our forefathers will naturally take its rightful place. Yes, this renaissance will come. History has never shown a single national group or a single individual who has been able to defy the laws of life. It is not possible to turn your back on your heritage and continue to exist as a people. The person who does this must perish.

The relationship between a people and their language is so intimate that mere words are too coarse and rough to make it clear. It is like all the vital parts of the body; they cannot be separated from each other without extinguishing life. This connection cannot be fully clarified either.

Language preserves an unbelievable richness for a people, and this of course applies to ourselves and our own ancestral language too. The Norwegian language seems so commonplace, so ordinary to us. It has also suffered some injuries by being transplanted to a foreign land. It has acquired a terrible accent and often sounds unnatural. Our language is a bit like Kari Woodenskirt in the Norwegian folktale. She was really a princess who disguised herself as a poor servant girl by hiding her golden dress under a skirt made of wood.

We can scarcely think of a better tool for transmitting our culture and education. After all, Norwegian is the language of the great poets and philosophers of our people—Wergeland and Welhaven, [Magnus Brostrup] Landstad, [Jørgen] Moe, and [Peter Christen] Asbjørnsen. In this language Bjørnson spoke and sang to his people—showed them the "brighter hillsides" that led the people back to their true selves. In this language Ibsen carved out the fates of his characters and wrote down all his knowledge of human beings. It is the language of Garborg, of Jonas and Bernt Lie, and of [Alexander] Kielland. In their hands the Norwegian language sparkles as brightly as the sunlight playing on the meadow. Great authors following in their footsteps have not disdained our language either, but have lifted it to even higher glory and honor and influence. For the Norwegian language is also the language of [Knut] Hamsun, [Johan] Bojer, [Hans] Aanrud, and Sigrid Undset, as well as all the others, great and small, who have used it to tell their dreams and visions. All of them have worked in and with it. Each time a great artist uses it, the language becomes more supple and refined, more melodious and clear. Should not the Norwegian language be important to all of us who are "members of the family"?

There is yet another consideration. The person who learns Norwegian thereby also opens the door to the world of Danish thought and intellectual life. This person can easily make friends with [Adam] Øhlenschlæger and Grundtvig, [Bernhard Severin] Ingemann and [Søren] Kierkegaard, as well as [Holger] Drachmann, [Johannes] Jørgensen, [Harald] Kidde, and [Martin Andersen] Nexø.

Furthermore, from Norwegian to Swedish is but a tiny step. Whoever knows Norwegian, and wants to, can take this step. With it, the door to another beautiful storehouse is thrown open and access granted to yet another group of great minds. Anyone with Nordic blood who seeks a true education ought to be able to read in the original language the works of [Esaias] Tegnér, [Johan Ludvig] Runeberg, [Carl] Snoilsky, [Gustav] Fröding, [August] Strindberg, and Selma Lagerlöf, as well as all the other great Swedish poets and thinkers!

For the person who wants to go even beyond this, the Norwegian language opens wide the door to another beautiful hall, to the gallery of our ancestors itself. Norwegian "Landsmaal" as it lives today in Norway's country districts is essentially Old Norse.[28] And from Norwegian "Landsmaal" to Old Norse—the classical language of the saga age—is a step that any person with normal talents can take with some study. And that step is well worth taking. By combining the study of language with that of history we are carried straight into the marrow of our own people. Therefore it seems to me that the study of Norwegian for people of Norwegian descent will pay better than the study of any other foreign language.

We ancestral heritage people see this. Is it any wonder that we get angry at the stupid preaching of the opportunists? We might not be quite so angry about the indifference and neglect of language-teaching among our people if this were the only reason to study the language, but we believe there are other advantages as well. We believe in the challenge set forth by the wise man: "Know thyself!" Knowledge of ourselves, our kin, our people, all our national characteristics, positive as well as negative, is of inestimable value to the individual, precisely because it makes it easier to become a true person. We must learn to know ourselves. We know that no course of study gives greater and more intimate knowledge of our kin—of our own history—than precisely the study of the language and literature of our people. We value these things because they are *ours*, they belong to us. When we who support the ancestral heritage carry on with such seeming stubbornness about the value of our language for our children, it is not with the intention of sneakily creating a "little Norway" either here in America or in Africa. We simply wish to make ourselves and our children into better and more capable people. If we succeed, we are naive enough to believe that this will benefit our country as well.

I willingly admit that it is not so easy to persuade American children—even if they are of Norwegian descent—to learn the Norwegian language. I will even agree that there are some cases in which it will be impossible. For example, when both mother and father go to work during the day and the children are left to the streets, the matter is worse than difficult; for neither school nor friends will give the least bit of encouragement, rather the opposite. But luckily only the smallest percentage of our population is in this position; most of them live in better circumstances. But even under the best of conditions it can be difficult enough.

Everything depends on the mother. The Norwegian language in America will live as long as she wants it to and no longer. If she sees the necessity for children to learn Norwegian, then they will. And if she does not, then it will no longer happen. Mother is still the best teacher.

We Norwegian Americans have been foolish when it comes to language teaching, even those of us who really want to do it. We teach our children to speak a little Norwegian, then we place a hopelessly inadequate first reader in their hands. When they are a little older, we give them Luther's Catechism and Pontoppidan's Explanation to read. We take them to Norwegian church services and send them to four weeks of parochial school with a teacher who may well know only a little Norwegian, and we think that is all that is necessary. This is what happens in most cases.

It is astonishing how much Norwegian some of the smartest children have acquired in this way. But one thing is missing: love of the language. In many cases the result is neither fish nor fowl, neither Norwegian language nor religion. Some children even acquire an aversion to both. The long, difficult words and, even more, the abstract concepts in the Catechism and the Explanation choke their interest in the language. We haven't even bothered to give our textbooks a modern, natural language form. Both the spelling and the usage are *Danish*, such as was used in Norway around the middle of the last century. And this is the kind of *Norwegian* we most often hear in our Norwegian sermons too!

We are in a bad position with these two texts in dogmatics being used as Norwegian-language textbooks for Norwegian-American children. We haven't done much better with our first books for children. We don't have anything suitable for Norwegian-American children. What we have is simply not good enough. We have to consider what our children encounter in our public elementary school. At the age of six or seven, the child gets a primer, that both in illustrations and in content is quite a bit more appealing than the Norwegian equivalent. In addition, the two books are based on different methods of instruction; the Norwegian text is based on the spelling method; the American primer begins with whole words—pure reading. The illustrations in the latter are beautiful and appealing, the content for the most part folktales, which engage the child's imagination. Take any one of our Norwegian first readers and compare it to one of the best American primers. Then ask yourself how we can expect our children to like the Norwegian book. It is unbelievable that our publication committees have been meeting all these years, knowing these conditions, and yet have not tried to do anything about it. The first book a child encounters is incredibly important because it has to capture the child's interest and fix it for the future.

One would expect an old Norwegian teacher discussing this theme to give some specific advice regarding teaching Norwegian to children. Yet I cannot do this, because both situations and individuals—mother and children, father and children—are different in almost every case. But I will venture to offer a few hints, some from my own experience, others just theories and therefore of unproven worth.

First and foremost, tell stories to your children! Take a few minutes every evening and tell your children stories. These times will later be some of the brightest moments in your family life.—Stories from the Bible are excellent, but only if you are able to retell them in your own and the children's language; you must try to do this. Fables are also good. Folktales are best of all because they come closest to the child's own imagination. A child's fantasy can build bridges over the deepest abysses and leap them with the greatest of ease.

If you have memories of Norway, tell your children about the country. Tell them what happened when you emigrated, how you took leave of your home and your dear ones. Tell about your family, about customs and ways of life, about nature and people. Tell about your childhood, about your grandmother and grandfather, and even farther back in time. This is good, for it shows the children that they come from an ancient people. Tell about the sagas if you know them, about the Vikings and their hardy lives. There you have room to use your imagination too. You can tell stories in English sometimes too. But don't use that language if you sound strained and fumble for words in order to make the story childish and natural. Use your dialect instead, for then the words will fall easily from your lips.

And don't forget to tell about pioneer days, about our own lives in this country in the first years! Let the children hear about the hard work and privation of our people, about their innumerable struggles and victories. You must know something about the pioneer period. Such tales will make the children conscious that we too have helped to build America.

I put great weight on stories, interesting, lively stories that bear the mark of one's personality. They are of inestimable value.——And when you say you don't have time, that is just nonsense. You must know that "man does not live by bread alone"!

This is one tip.

And here is another. You should sing *to* the children and *with* them. Sing Norwegian words and melodies into their minds—and, above all, Norwegian emotional life! Sing simple hymns and children's songs. There are plenty to choose from. Sing Norwegian folk songs. The collection *Norges Melodier* [Songs of Norway] ought to be found in every home where there are children and young people of Norwegian descent. You can scarcely imagine how much Norwegian—both spirit and language—you can *sing* into your children. You ought to try it!

Those of you who can afford it, whether you live in town or in the country, ought to get two, three, or four families together and conduct Norwegian school for your children for a month or more every year. There are hundreds of thousands of you who can manage it. This will be a much cheaper language school than at a college or university later in life. And the rewards are greater in relation to the costs. But be sure to get a teacher who *knows* Norwegian and who *loves* Norwegian. Preferably a woman. If she is of the right kind, she will be closer to the children than a man.

There is even more that you must do.

Acquire some Norwegian children's books and easy books for

young people. No other nation has produced so much excellent literature of this type as Norway has in recent times. And you surely understand that if children are to learn to love to read Norwegian, they must have something to read!—Get some good books about Norway in English too.[29]

Those of you who are so fortunate that you can afford a trip to Norway ought to take some of your children along—all of them if you can. Show them the country and your family's old homestead. This will strengthen their family feeling. They will of necessity learn a little language on such a trip too. As a rule it is more important that your children visit your homeland than that you see it again yourself.

And above all: Speak Norwegian with your children! Let Norwegian be the main language within your home circle. It is so much better for them and for you that you speak good Norwegian with them rather than bad English. It is better for their Norwegian; better for their English; better for the relationship between you. In this way you are linguistically superior to your children, rather than the opposite. Your children ought to look *up* to you, not *down* at you—and this applies in the area of language too.

Let your children understand that it is wonderful to *know* something, not least languages. Knowledge is power. And of all the foreign languages under the sun, the one belonging to the child's ancestors ought to be the one closest to the child. This is just as obvious as that 2 plus 2 equals 4. Hold fast to this thought.

We could add many more hints to these. But that would just be a waste of time. For each and every mother will have to find her own means and methods. And yet what has been mentioned above has been tried, for the most part. Therefore it will be of value to others.

But let us not hear anyone say that it is impossible to teach our children Norwegian. It is true that it takes quite a bit of thought and sacrifice on the part of the parents, but it is still possible,—even in town, where the children have to use English as soon as they stick their heads out the door. Even there it can succeed, if only the mother wants it. Both the credit for so many American children having learned Norwegian and the blame for the large percentage who know so little fall on her. Father may help her bear both credit and blame; for he naturally has a part in this too. But as I said, it really depends on the mother.

This is all I have to say about the children, but now I will add a few words about the young people who enter our secondary schools and colleges. I am vitally interested in them. In the first place, for almost seventeen years I have made my living by trying to get some of them interested in Norwegian; in the second place, we all know that most of our future leaders will come from our own schools. Therefore the impressions, values, and education our young people acquire there is vitally important. If young people get the impression in school that Norwegian culture has left no monuments, this impression will remain later in life. On the other hand, if they are convinced of the greatness and richness to be found in the cultural treasure of our ancestral nation, they will take away a completely different impression. And these impressions will affect their actions.

The neglect of Norwegian in our schools is nothing to be proud of. It is appalling how we who support the ancestral heritage have neglected our duty. What have we really done to advance this work? We have often complained that our schools have failed us with regard to Norwegian, but that is all we have done. Only a handful of us have bothered to consider the difficulties facing our schools. We have taken for granted that Norwegian should be taught; and we have a right to expect that, but not many of us have investigated to what extent the schools are really capable of giving such instruction.

Remarkable things can happen in our times. This summer I was told that one of our schools sold some of the few Norwegian books that were in the school library! This is supposed to be true! There really was a school so richly supplied with Norwegian books that it could afford to sell them!

On the other hand, in most of our schools there is such a dearth of Norwegian books that it is worse than slim pickings, it is utter destitution. And we who support the ancestral heritage deserve a reprimand for this; for we have certainly not done what we could and should do. We have let our concern for our heritage be expressed in words rather than in deeds. Some years ago I visited one of our schools; the first thing I asked to do was to see the library. As soon as I came in, I looked around for the collection of Norwegian books. But I didn't find any. There were only a few worn-out copies of Bjørnson's peasant tales, and a few—also worn-out—of Ibsen's plays. That was all. No historical works. No translations. No books for children and young people. The only dictionary to be found was my little glossary to one volume of Rolfsen's reader. Yet one of the warmest supporters of our ancestral heritage had sat for many years on the board of this school!

This situation is enough to make a grown man weep. The case I have mentioned is by no means isolated. A few years ago I wrote several newspaper articles about the necessity of getting more Norwegian books for our schools. At that time many of those who were warmly interested in the fatherland were sitting on school boards. Some of them are even well-to-do men of considerable influence. But nothing was done, absolutely nothing. The few books to be found in the schools have been acquired by the Norwegian teachers. Three years ago our two Norwegian societies at St. Olaf College started a campaign to raise funds for a scholarship to study Norwegian at our school. We set a goal as high as $4,000. The committee wrote a fine request appealing to all persons in America who were interested in Norwegian. All the newspapers published it; *Decorah-Posten* even wrote a fine editorial about the matter and recommended it warmly. What was the result of this appeal in the newspapers? Well, we collected *one dollar*. Yes, *one dollar*. And that came from a man with a German-sounding name. By looking at his name, no one would guess that the man was Norwegian. This was three years ago, when times were still quite good. Still, the young people didn't give up; when they saw that they couldn't raise any money this way, they began to write personal letters to people they thought might be interested and who had the means to help them. During their vacations they worked to raise money for the cause wherever they were. In this way, they have now raised $1,000. (In parentheses, I will note that two young people's organizations have given something over $100; and one individual gave $500. It's hard to describe the joy in the ranks when these three large gifts came in!)

I tell you all this to demonstrate the painful lack of interest we heritage people have shown. It is indifference and thoughtlessness more than anything else. Our opponents are justified in disdainfully asking us what we have done other than talk about this cause that we so vigorously defend.

Providing collections of Norwegian books for our schools is one focus of our work among the young. We treat our young people badly when we talk about Norwegian literature, Norwegian art, and Norwegian culture without anything to show them. Pupils come into the library; here they encounter the world of books and begin to look around in it. Here they find large, beautiful works of American and English literature, perhaps German and French too, and a quantity of translations from other languages. But of Norwegian there is little or nothing. The impression they already have that we Norwegians don't amount to much is strengthened; and so they go back to their Norwegian class and wonders if what the teacher is saying isn't mostly empty bragging.

As this is being written, we have 425 students in the Norwegian department at St. Olaf College. We hope to reach 450 this year. This is a commendable number. Here we have a golden opportunity. But in our library we don't have nearly the books we need—not by any means. I could easily have used $25,000 this year to buy books for the Norwegian department at the school—books in English and in Norwegian—without wasting any money. I have lying here beside me a list of over 4,000 volumes that I would like to buy for the library, but which I cannot touch because of poverty. And this list of books is not nearly as complete as I would like. Only someone who has attempted to teach Norwegian can understand how this kind of poverty makes our work difficult. We ancestral heritage people could easily remove this hindrance if we only saw the need and its consequences.

In this connection I might add that in order to make good use of the opportunities afforded by our schools, we must have *people* and *means*. It is unjust to lay all the blame on our schools. They are completely American institutions, and they must be. That is self-evident. If they are to survive, they must keep up with the competition in both equipment and quality and even more so in the quality of the human beings they send out into the world.

If we ancestral heritage people are going to get new leaders from
our schools, leaders who can take up our cause when we can't manage the work any longer, then we must set our sights on educating
such leaders. Our homes must first of all do their part for those
youngsters who show desire and talent for learning. And if the
schools are to continue the work, they must be put into condition
to do it.

And how can this be done?

First and foremost every school has to have a comprehensive collection of books! What else are the pupils to learn from? What else
will kindle their enthusiasm? What else will strengthen and nourish and carry their interest further once the teacher has awakened
it? Of course there must be books, books of science, of art, of literature. And woe to the teacher who doesn't understand how to use
what is there! He is an unfaithful servant. He has buried his talent
in the ground.[30]

Next, those talented young people with desire and ability must
have the opportunity for further study after they have graduated
from our colleges. They must have the opportunity to travel to Norway to study. For many years we have had two or three students in
the senior class who really wanted to go to Norway and further
their education—young people who had never seen Norway—but
who couldn't do so because of lack of money. Most often it is the
poorer boys and girls who have such interest. And this is to be expected. For wealth as a rule chokes intellectual interests. It is like
the rust which consumes the wheat.

I see it as a necessity for our future work that gifted students be
given the opportunity to travel to Norway and further their studies
there. I have made that trip myself and know from my own experience how important it can be. I can find many American examples
that show the same. For instance, the recently deceased Professor
[William Henry] Schofield and Dr. H.G. Leech have made invaluable contributions toward furthering the interest in Scandinavian
culture in America. Both are descended from old New England
families. How did these two men receive their intellectual baptism?
Well, they did it first through study at American universities, where
they came in touch with Nordic culture and intellectual life through

books. And next and most important through long periods of study in the Scandinavian countries. And there are other "old Americans" who have been "converted" in the same way. The men who awakened my interest were my two beloved teachers, professors J.S. Nordgaard and P.J. Eikeland. Both of them had sat at the feet of Thrond Bothne and listened to his inspiring words. He motivated them to such a degree that they simply had to study in Norway. Then they returned and became teachers among our people. Professor J.A. Holvik, who wrote the two textbooks most frequently used to teach Norwegian in our high schools, also received his intellectual baptism over there. He had never seen Norway before he went there as a student. It would be easy to multiply these examples with many more from both our own and the other two Scandinavian groups.

However, it is not only to provide Norwegian teachers at our own schools that we must get our talented youth to Norway. That is needed. But we also need people with the right values in other positions in life. We need many people who have visited our ancestral home and have drunk from the original source of our culture, people who have come into living contact with the Norwegian spirit.

One thing is certain. If our heritage movement shall survive, we who now are working for it and who believe in the necessity of our cause must call young people to the work and must help them to get the education they need. The resources for this must come from those who believe deeply in this cause. Unfortunately, we are still marked more by words than by deeds in this work to keep our heritage intact.

And now I ask all of you older folk who believe in the necessity of our cause for our people and for our country—come and help us with the Norwegian work at our schools! I am not thinking first and foremost of St. Olaf. I am asking for *all* our schools! If the good Lord has blessed you with earthly goods, then leave a legacy to help promote the study of Norwegian at one school or another. This is a beautiful way to perpetuate your name. And in addition such a legacy will be of greater value to the cause you want to promote than you can know. If only we could see that every great cause demands sacrifice! Sacrifice of wealth, sacrifice of devotion. Anyway, we really shouldn't call it a sacrifice to give to a cause we are devoted to! Such gifts ought to come of themselves!

11

I remember one time when I was sitting in a smoking car on a train here in the Northwest. We were stopped at a well-known small town. People streamed past; some got off, others got on.—I sat there as I usually do on such occasions, studying the appearance of those coming and going, and trying to guess which ones had Scandinavian blood.

But this time I was torn out of my reverie by the resounding Sogning dialect being spoken behind me. The seat there had just been vacated, and now two new passengers occupied it. It was impossible not to notice that one of them was from the district of Sogn in Norway. After I had arranged my face into an expression of the greatest indifference I turned so that I could get the two newcomers into my sights.

It was a hot summer day. One of them, the Sogning, looked rather agitated and angry. This impression was heightened by seeing his round, fiery red face, the color of which became deeper and deeper as the man continually mopped away the perspiration.

The first words I could grasp of their conversation came from the Sogning.

———"No siree, I'm damned if we'll do that!——If the pastor starts the collection without first calling a congregational meeting, then I will leave the congregation.——Either he does it or I go!—It's about time he learned that he can't carry on like this!"

This sounded as if it could be interesting. In order to avoid disturbing the two behind me with any untimely attention, I sat there as though I didn't understand a word of what they said, lit my pipe indifferently, and bent over my newspaper. But my ears were wide open!

The other man must have been somewhat phlegmatic; at any

rate, the Sogning's anger and revolutionary plotting didn't seem to disturb him in the least. I desperately wanted to study his face, but the situation would not allow it.—I could not tell from his speech what district in Norway he or his forefathers had sailed from; the peculiarities of his dialect were nearly obliterated, but most likely he was from Telemark.

It was clear that he was not at all sure the attitude of his companion was justified. He answered rather reluctantly, as though he was searching carefully for the right words. His voice was mild and gentle.

"Yes, yes, you may be right.———We can, of course, consider this later.———I think maybe you are being just a bit hasty.——After all, you were a delegate to the annual meeting; and you told me yourself that you voted in favor of this fund drive."

This conciliatory spirit did not affect the Sogning in the least. When he answered, he sounded even more agitated than before.

"I don't give a damn how the annual meeting voted!——This is up to the local congregation. Now it's their turn to decide. No annual meeting can tell us what we should do or not do. We decide that for ourselves.—And our pastor better not try to do it for us either."

"But you aren't actually opposed to the fund drive, are you, John—?"—I thought I detected a tinge of laughter in the man's voice as he said this; it could be that he was teasing the Sogning.

"Against it!——I don't know which way I will go. But until the congregation has voted, I am against it—that much I know.—This time the pastor is going to bite the dust!"—

I sat there, all ears.—From the conversation that followed, I gathered that the issue at hand was the special jubilee fund drive that the United Church had just decided on at its annual meeting. Further I discovered that the Sogning had attended the convention as the delegate from his congregation and had voted for the general drive for the entire synod.—In spite of this, he was determined to create a hullabaloo in the congregation, because the pastor had announced the previous day that he expected a visit from Dr. Kildahl[31] and he wanted to start the fund drive in connection with this upcoming visit. The Sogning remained firmly convinced that the pastor had overstepped the bounds of his authority and had violated the rights of the sovereign congregation. Only the congregation it-self could make such a decision.——The annual meeting had only voted on the principle of the matter; it had no authority to decide how this would be handled within each individual congregation.

———"We will soon be like sheep if this continues!" was the last thing I heard the Sogning say, as I got up and left the train at the next station. By then, the discussion had been going on for a long time. The Sogning had not been budged in the least by his com-panion's thoughtfulness or his logical arguments.

I relate this little incident because it demonstrates so clearly one of the essential qualities of our people: *the passion for liberty, the in-sistence on self-determination and the rights of the individual under the com-mon law of the land, and with this right of democratic self-government has also come the capacity for self-government.* This is one of our people's strongest traits; and therefore also the one in which it is easiest to take the wrong course. History confirms this.[32]

From Norwegian history we learn that the noble idea of unity first began to dawn on the Norwegian people over a thousand years ago. At that time Harald Halfdanssøn came forward and "saved" the country. In using the term "saved" the poet indicates that though the country, that is to say the people, had existed for a long time, now Harald brought the country safely into the new day that was dawning.

What did he "save" the country from? What darkness ruled over the people? At that time rampant individualism was destroying both the land and the people. There was a separate king in every province; in each country district there were one or more chieftains. Both the kings and the chieftains wanted to do just as they liked and live their lives exactly as they pleased. They didn't want any in-terference from anyone else. No one could come and tell them what to do. It had been this way from time immemorial and it was un-thinkable that it would not continue forever. *The greatest possible free-dom for the individual* was the compass people steered by.

Then along came Harald. He had a greater vision, perceived greater possibilities for the whole country. With him dawned the idea of unity. He felt that it must be possible to preserve individual freedom under a greater unity. He didn't see clearly how this could be done, but he did perceive it dimly.

The battle was a long and bitter one, as it always has been whenever the Norwegian people have felt that their freedom, their God-given right to follow their own judgment without the interference of any stranger, is in danger. According to the sagas it took ten whole years before Harald could realize his vision. But Harald was a talented fellow, and eventually he succeeded by means of two great traits, cunning and might. By using a combination of generosity and guile Harald persuaded one small king and chieftain after another to join with him and accept his idea for the future. Where these means did not work he used force. By the year 872 he was the sole king over the whole country.[33] Unity had been achieved.

But, if only one man was to rule over the whole country where many had ruled before, the others would have to learn to obey. They had to be silent when the king spoke.

In order to strengthen his position, this one person had to have great power. He needed an army and a navy too, for the position he had created needed to be defended both internally and externally. He also had to live in a manner suitable for the greatest person in the country.

All this was expensive. Harald needed money. And there was no other way to get it than to tax the people. And here we see what we have seen ever since—in North Dakota, for example, and not least among our churches here in this country. It is difficult to tax Norwegians against their will.

This was the case back then too. Rather than pay taxes to a man they had not chosen, Norwegians preferred to emigrate. They wanted freedom at any price. Norwegian colonies had existed previously, but now they got a fresh impetus and flourished as never before, leading to the greatest period of Norwegian colonization.

History repeated itself when St. Olaf came to the throne and attempted to complete Harald's work. Harald had raised the foundation. Olaf wanted to build upon it, fill it with life and spirit and consecrate it. It was wrong for Olaf to force people to believe and think in one way and to prescribe the way they should worship. But even though it was wrong, this could still be tolerated. There could be no barriers to thought, for no one could know what you thought or believed. The king could not see everywhere; those who preferred to serve Odin and Thor rather than Christ could safely do so.

However, the king did something much worse; he insisted that the laws must be obeyed, not just by the weak and lowly in society, but even by the most powerful men in the country. *Everyone was equal under the common law of the land.* Punishments were the same for all. From the day that Olaf proclaimed this principle it was impossible to have him as king anymore. He was taking freedom away from people!

With this unquenchable desire for freedom in our people goes the capacity for self-rule—rule by the people. Norwegians have shown this trait the world over. They showed it in Iceland and on the islands of the Atlantic, in Normandy as well as on the American prairie. And of course in Norway. In heathen times the people chose both their religious leaders and their local chieftains. When the new era dawned and the light of Christianity streamed across the land, this old system was admirably suited to many of the new ideas. Just as the independent farmers previously had chosen both religious leaders and chieftains, they now chose their priests. It was not until well into the thirteenth century that the bishop had anything to say about the appointment of priests. Some of our free church organization over here is based on old Norwegian tradition!

The desire for freedom and self-rule—yes, take a peek at the Norwegian people in any place and time, and you will find these characteristics. Even in the darkest days of the Danish period you will find them. As long as the Danish officials were friendly and allowed the Norwegian farmers to organize things more or less as they pleased, things went smoothly. On the other hand, if they acted arbitrarily, there was strife and conflict. The farmers wished to be left to their own devices. As long as they were, they didn't pay any attention to the weakness of their country.

The tide turned early in the nineteenth century. When it became known that the Danish king had surrendered the country to Sweden, the Norwegian people declared that they wanted to decide their own fate. "That is every person's God-given right," they said.

With that they began to hammer out the constitution under whose shelter they and their children would live in the future. Typically, the constitution they wrote placed most of the power in the hands of the farmers even though few farmers sat in the constitutional assembly at Eidsvoll. That was no accident. The men of the constitutional assembly acted as they did on the basis of ancient tradition, on the views they had inherited from their forefathers. The new ideas that came from the outside—from America and France— assured them that their views were correct.

We have often heard that the Norwegian immigrant, in comparison with other immigrant groups, makes a good American. Everyone seems astonished at how easily and quickly the process of transformation takes place. What people say and write in this regard is correct. However, it would be even more true if they changed the tense of the verb. The Norwegian immigrant doesn't *become* a good American. He *is* one already before he emigrates. He was one already in the saga age!

.   After all, what is the core of the *American Ideal*? Is it not precisely this: *the greatest possible individual freedom under the common law of the land*? I don't know of any other. Nor do you. And if we shine our light far back into the history of the Norwegian people, we will see that this has been their great political goal too. It is even possible that this ideal and many of America's free institutions *are actually inherited from ancient Norwegian traditions*, that they have their origin in Norway.

Many writers, some of them renowned British and American scholars, have held this view. Historical research on this topic has not yet progressed to the point where we can map the way clearly. This matter is still at the stage of belief, without satisfactory proof.

I will offer just one quotation on this matter. I have chosen it tactlessly because it will irritate and annoy our opponents. It is taken from an essay published by Price Collier, an old-stock American, in *Scribner's Magazine* in the fall of 1914. He says: "The Statue of Liberty properly belongs on one of the small, bleak islands off the coast of Norway."[34]

The man begins to rave like this when he starts writing about the

Norwegian sense of freedom. And he is not even a socialist or a Bolshevik; on the contrary, he is an American millionaire!

Does it matter to America that we Americans of Norwegian heritage work to preserve this part of our ancestral heritage? Does it belong on American soil? Or has this country already reached the ideal? Have we won "the greatest personal freedom within the law of the land?"

There are several ways to answer this question. Naturally, the apathetic masses and all those jingoists whose greatest sport is speaking to these masses will answer *yes*. "Yes, of course we have reached this goal! Is this not the land of freedom par excellence, the only one in the world on which God's sun shines? Woe to the one who dares to disagree!"

Every country has people like this. Even Norway. They existed under the old patriarchal system. They can be found among the nomads, in the ancient states, in Nero's time, during the worst period of absolute monarchy, during the rule of Caesar as well as under the Republic. They are probably not unknown in the Russia of today; one will also find them in the most capitalistic state in the world. The law of inertia has its strongest support from them.

Luckily, there is an opposition party. I am not thinking of the revolutionaries here—those who want blood and destruction. But I am thinking of "the quiet ones in the land," of those who go and pray "in secret" that the kingdom of God in all its beauty will soon be found on earth in our political-social life as well. And in addition, we have that small brave flock who lead the way and "dare to build with their sword at their side."

Both of these groups look to the fulfillment of this ideal—"the greatest possible personal freedom under the common law of the land"—look to it and work for it in America too. And isn't this a beautiful ideal to work toward! Is it unreachable? Perhaps. Henrik Wergeland didn't think so. In a moment of inspiration he saw it come true in a place where every man would be "King on earth and priest before God."[35]

Even in this land of freedom, we are still far from the goal. We have to admit that there are other countries that come closer than we do.

In another reflection I have drawn attention to the fact that one of our largest and most important industries is at a standstill because of a strike. The employers will not agree to the demands of the workers. The workers will not give in to the employers. The whole rest of the country is left powerless and helpless. Right now, I could not buy coal for the winter even if I had money in hand and was willing to pay any price. A railroad strike is also threatened. The radical newspapers are recommending it warmly.

What then becomes of your freedom and mine? If the coal strike doesn't end soon, we will be free to freeze this winter whether we want to or not. And if there is a railroad strike, we will be free to sit at home whether we want to or not. That is as far as our freedom in these two areas goes at present, and it isn't very far.

Two years ago we were about to have a presidential election. Three candidates ran within the strongest political party. If we belonged to that party, we had to vote for one of those three. That was as far as our freedom went. So then we went and voted for one of these three, you and I and our neighbor. But we didn't exactly agree on which of these three ought to be president. Therefore we each voted for a different one!

Did you get your choice? Did the neighbor get his? Or did I get mine? No, the strange thing is, none of us got our choice. When the convention opened in Chicago, it was informed by big business here in this country that none of these candidates was acceptable. And that was that. Neither you nor I nor our neighbor was able to vote in the general election for the candidate we voted for in the primary. The situation was pretty much the same in the country's second largest party too. Here we cannot speak of great freedom!

Farmers have experienced hard times the last two years. Compared to the prices on things they needed to buy, the prices on the goods they produced were almost nothing. For example, when the farmer took wool and hides to town to sell, the prices were laughably low. When this raw material had been converted into clothing or shoes the poor farmer had to pay fantastic prices in relation to what he himself had received. He had to sell his raw goods if he was to have anything to keep himself alive; he had to buy things for the same reason. Did he have anything to say about it in either case? No, he did not. How great is his economic freedom?

Just look at the schools in your own town or in your own neighborhood. How much freedom do you have for your children? Can you make choices for them? Your children have to learn exactly the same things as other people's children. Your children and Russian, Black, and Indian children all learn the same things. A child with a single talent will go through exactly the same curriculum and at exactly the same pace as a child with five talents. The same subjects and the same pace for all, the same games, the same lessons, the same morals, the same views.

I have just pointed to a few examples. It will have to be enough. If you haven't seen the disparity between ideal and reality, it wouldn't help you to read many more pages; you wouldn't see it anyway.

We are still a long way from our goal! But we are duty-bound to try to come closer. Upward and onward. It doesn't matter how many hills lie between us and the ideal, we are duty-bound to "steel ourselves," as Espen Ash Lad said in the fairy tale.

Through countless battles and endless sacrifice we have made progress. And our ancestors have always been among the leaders. The greatest possible freedom under the common law of the land is the social-political ideal they have striven for ever since the dawn of history broke over our people. This passion and drive and will is one of our main character traits. God grant that it will continue to be! Then we will be a blessing for our new country in the days to come. Those who promote our Norwegian heritage and give it to our country in the greatest measure will become the greatest Americans in the future. It will be to our everlasting honor if we can lead in the great march of progress and not hang back with the masses and stragglers.

Here we stand before a seeming paradox: The best Norwegian is the greatest American!

12

"The church holds a high place in the estimation of the peasant; he sees it standing apart, lonely and hallowed," says Bjørnson in *Synnøve Solbakken* (*Synnøve of Sunny Hill*).[36] Bjørnson expresses this truth in pithy, beautiful words.

The Norwegian people have always lived a deep and strong emotional life. Such strong feelings have even caused some to become visionaries. People *felt* until they could *see*. In this way fairy-tale creatures such as underground folk and household spirits, water sprites and ghosts came into being. A peasant boy might wander dreaming and longing through forest and meadow, might feel the distinctive beauty of nature and at the same time feel unspeakable fear as dusk turned into the blackness of night. That's when the *hulder*, the alluring siren, appeared. The fisherman might feel the awful terror of the sea and the storm until at last he saw the terrible headless ghost portending imminent death. When the mighty waves came chasing toward the land, roaring and booming in the growing darkness, then the fisherman heard the ghosts and the moans of the dead. He knew they foretold death. Out in the farmyard mysterious forces quivered in the dark evening. Of course the home fields were fenced in, but the houses stood close to the wild, dark mountains. Entering a well-filled hay barn, or going into the stall where the horse whinnied and the cow mooed gave an element of security on a dark night. Yet even the bravest soul felt his nerves quiver just as he slipped into the barn. This is how the household spirit came into being. We will probably never know how much these creatures of the folk imagination are reflections of ancient heathen spirits, and how much they are the personification of impressions from nature.

A people whose emotional life is so strong must necessarily be *religiously* inclined. And the Norwegian people are. Religiosity is another characteristic feature of our people.—Go back to the time of the ancient gods, and you will find this characteristic. The ancient Norwegians were faithful worshippers of the old gods. They took their faith seriously and did not give it up easily. Christianity had to fight a long and hard battle before it got a firm foothold.

But the Norwegian people are not just religiously inclined; there is also great stability and faithfulness in their religious lives. They don't change beliefs easily. Just as the introduction of Christianity was slow and difficult, the change from Catholicism to Lutheranism was no easier or swifter. It also caused a long and bitter struggle.

To Bjørnson's words, "The church holds a high place in the estimation of the peasant," we can add that it forms a central point around which his whole life revolves. This is the first place he is carried to in baptism. He goes there as a confirmand in order to renew his pact with God—an act whose great solemnity is seldom forgotten. There bride and bridegroom are consecrated. There he also makes his final journey on earth.

Not only does the church speak to him in all the important moments of his life, but, whenever the *state* has anything important to say to him, this is also done from the gates of the churchyard.

And because the church is nearly always located in the center of the rural community, people come there for worldly reasons too, to meet friends, to exchange news, to transact business. And people come there—as a lay preacher is once supposed to have said—

to speak of weather and wind
and admire the roses in the ladies' cheeks.

The church is integral to the lives of the farmers and the rural community. Everyone participates in its life, rich and poor, young and old.

Nothing could be more natural than that the Norwegian emigrant took his church with him when he left for the New World. Before his church was built, he somehow didn't feel quite safe. There was something missing.

We don't need to look very far around us to be assured that the church has been an important part of our life here too. Our history in this country is in many ways the history of the Norwegian-American church. And yet we must painfully acknowledge that the church has not always been able to hold people and gather them under the shadow of its wings.

Attempting to idealize, one runs the risk of saying more than one really means. This may be because ordinary everyday words acquire a stronger fire and color than we are used to giving them.

That's true for these reflections too. For I certainly don't mean to say that the Norwegian people are angels, that they detest sin, that over there everyone goes to church and knows the Bible by heart. I don't mean that and I haven't said it either.

What I have said and what I stand by is this: that we *as a people are strongly inclined toward religion*.

I want to draw attention to the notion that our people have a relationship to God that is different, for example, from that of the English or the German, the American or the southern European. Norwegians have a *distinctly personal* relationship to God. It is God and the individual, not God and the group or God and the masses. A person is saved or lost *individually*, not as part of a *community*. And here our distinctive Norwegian personality plays a role. Strangers as a rule find Norwegians to be rather serious people, and often characterize us as melancholy or morose. This may very well have some justification. A person who is conscious of guilt, who knows that he alone carries the responsibility for eternal life, will quite naturally look at life seriously. At a meeting of educators held in Minneapolis several years ago, an Irishman spoke to us. He said that he didn't dare to try to be funny in a meeting where there were so many Scandinavians. They never laughed; or if they did, it was only inwardly. They had no sense of humor, he said. He had *heard* that we were like that. He believed he had *seen* that we were like that. And it is true that with respect to *religion* we are serious.

The Norwegian is a religious being. He is seldom able to tear himself loose from God. He can deny Him in words. He can even loudly proclaim that he doesn't believe in a higher power. And yet he feels the presence of God. Something in his consciousness witnesses to a secret power within him and outside of him, a power that he cannot escape. For him, God *is*. The doubter senses Him. The unbeliever battles Him. The anxious soul fears Him. The believing heart beats in childlike awe and joy over belonging to Him.

That's the way it is among the intellectuals. The characteristic is clearer in ordinary people. For them God is even more personal.

God is there in the storm, in the lightning, in the thunder. He is there in the depths of the sea and in the wild majesty of the mountain. God is there in joy and in sorrow, in good years and lean years. God is the power that surrounds life and cannot be escaped. And God is often—too often—incomprehensible and stern. He punishes severely. The person upon whom God has laid His hand bears the marks of it all the days of his life.

But God is always personal. There is always a relationship between Him and the individual. For example, when Ibsen has Terje Vigen say, after the great reckoning of his life is finished:

Perhaps it was all for the best, in some wise,—
so the thanks, God, are rightly yours![37]

It is no mere accident that Ibsen has Terje Vigen express himself in these words. This great judge of character has gotten his man exactly right. It is just the way an old salt like that would talk to God. That is how *personal* the relationship is. What else *could* an old Norwegian sailor say to his God!

There must be some explanation, some reason that the Norwegian people are more religious than other people, that they have this view of their relationship to God that I have outlined above. And sure enough, there is—not just one reason, but several acting together. Let us look at them.

I have already mentioned our deep temperament and serious nature. These are inborn characteristics. "Øivind was his name, *and he cried when he was born.*"[38] How quintessentially Norwegian Bjørnson was here! That children cry when they come into the world is characteristic of the Norwegian view of life. That's what we expect them to do. An American would say that they *laughed.* One's disposition is inborn. Conditions of nature and the values of the people develop it further. Norwegian nature reminds us strongly of God. There we find majesty and power, authority and mystery, purity and divinity. A person from northern or western Norway, or from a narrow valley where the forest whispers the same eternal song, finds nothing particularly strange, in reading Hamsun's novel *Growth of the Soil,* about Isak Sellanraa meeting both God and Satan. Hardly anyone would stop to question whether there are still fellows like that to be found out in the hills. Quite the opposite, one feels that this could happen to anyone. We also readily accept the clairvoyant, the sick mind, the person whose imagination easily slips over into mental illness. Jonas Lie gave us a masterful portrait of just this kind of person in his earliest work. Not even the most critical reader of Norwegian descent would ask if there really are people who can look into the concealed world and clearly see what is about to happen. His sixth sense tells him that such could easily happen to him too. Isn't it natural for the Norwegian people to think like this? Haven't people been humming "The Dream Ballad" for all of 700 years?[39]—And, of course, Norwegian nature and the values of the people have done their work too.

Of course we must also take into account the way children are brought up. It is impossible for Norwegian children not to know God. They meet Him everywhere. If the home is silent, then the school speaks. Religion, which is a required subject, occupies a large part of the curriculum in Norwegian schools. Not as much as it did thirty or forty years ago, but if you take into account the increase in required attendance and improved teaching methods and textbooks, then the results should be better rather than worse.

Even children who are excused from religious instruction at school and who hear nothing about God at home still can not avoid Him. Perhaps it will be through lay preachers. Scarcely a rural district, remote valley, or fjord is not visited at least every other year by a traveling lay preacher. I don't know anything about the situation in towns. But I have seen that the Calmeyer Street Mission in Kristiania is packed evening after evening. No doubt it might be better if some of these lay preachers were set to work clearing land and grinding grain rather than preaching. But after all, the same could be said about pastors and people in all walks of life. I remember well how as a child I listened to the fire-and-brimstone preacher until I couldn't sleep at night for fear of "the beast with many horns and the lake of fire where the serpent never dies and the fire never goes out."[40] Today the activities of the lay preachers are on a higher plane, and to deny their great value to Christian life in city and country would reveal both little understanding of Chris-

tianity and also great stupidity. Through these lay preachers many
Norwegian children and young people have met God so intensely
that they will never forget Him.

I might also mention sermons in church and confirmation instruction. However, I will not take time to do this. Their influence
should be clear to all.

Have you ever considered the place of God in the classic children's songs which play such a rich role, both in text and in melody,
in Norwegian literature?

Let me remind you of several of them:

"Lord! Oh hold in Thy hand my child,
Guard by the river its playing!
Send Thou Thy Spirit as comrade mild,
Lest it be lost in its straying!"[41]

Or take this one:

"Asleep the child fell
When night cast its spell;
The angels came near
With laughter and cheer.
Her watch at its waking
the mother was keeping:
'How sweet, my dear child,
Was your smile now while sleeping!'"[42]

Or yet another:

"Now rises roof and rafter
To starry vaults of blue;
Now flies my little Haakon
On wings of dreaming too."[43]

Oh, no, there are so many it is impossible to continue! I must
stop! When I think about it, I realize that it is impossible to include
them all. I will even leave out the Norwegian-American ones.

But I will just remind you of one cradle song, whose melody is perfectly classical. Search the whole world through; listen well, listen long, and then tell me if you have ever heard the like:

> "Hush, hush little child,
> The porridge pot hangs over the fire
> full of creamy porridge for our little babe.
> Father sits and sorts the grain.
> Mother plays the lovely horn.
> Sister spins the cloth of gold.
> Brother goes into the woods
> hunting all the game.
> If it's white, bring it home.
> If it's gray, let it go.
> If it's brown, let it free in the woods."[44]

Stop at the first picture presented in this song, and see how genuinely homey it is. There you see the whole family circle—father, mother, sister, and brother, and then the little child. They are busy with domestic tasks. Father is the breadwinner; he is sorting the grain to make the porridge. Big brother is out in the forest taking care of the livestock. The song warns him to watch out for wild animals. Mother and sister are busy doing handwork.

But "man does not live by bread alone." Not even in a simple farmer's home. "Mother plays the lovely horn." We do not know whether it is father himself or big brother who has the God-given artistic creativity to make this horn for mother. But mother has it and she uses it! And sister "spins the cloth of gold." What can we make of this? In Norwegian farm homes linen and wool are spun, but hardly gold. Is this pure romanticism? No, it's not. Don't you remember that sister sang while she spun? It is the beautiful melody that the little child turns into threads of gold. Her song is so beautiful that sister's spinning turns into gold—beautiful shining gold. And you can be sure that God is in that song!

We have analyzed a bit of the text. Let's look at the melody. It's Mother's melancholy that moves it. Who has composed this melody? No one person is responsible; all the people, all the moth-

ers have had a hand in composing it. It has grown out of the pain
and care of all of the mothers. Now and again, hope and joy break
out, soon to dip down into seriousness again. The little child "cried
when it was born." How genuinely Norwegian both text and
melody are!—The melancholy and the seriousness of the people are
heard even in the rocking of the cradle!

Listen to all the wonderful songs for young people, the kind you
hear wherever young Norwegians gather together. You will have to
look far and wide among other people before you can find such a
treasure. I cannot start to name one, for fear that another better one
will be left out. There are simply too many. In addition to all the
songs for young people, one would also have to include large portions of Landstad's hymnbook—that pearl among all songbooks.

I must mention Ingemann's great hymn to life, "Deilig er jorden"
["Beautiful Savior"]. Of course, it is not of Norwegian origin, but it
has a place in Landstad and in nearly all songbooks for Norwegian
youth. It even appears in many of the older elementary-school readers. There is scarcely any hymn that has been sung so often by Norwegian young people; it is the queen of all their songs. It praises the
beauty of creation in the simplest and clearest of words. The basic
theme is so genuinely Nordic, almost remarkably Norwegian. Life
is tragic, our journey on earth is a "pilgrim's way"; nevertheless it is
happy and beautiful.[45]

Just as I said, a Norwegian child cannot avoid meeting God. Nor
can a young person who bothers to read or to open his mouth in
song. I started this reflection with a quotation from a book which
is found in every library in Norway. I doubt if a single young Norwegian can be found who isn't familiar with it. The basic motif of
Synnøve of Sunny Hill is strongly Christian. This is true of all of
Bjørnson's peasant tales. God is present, as is to be expected in a
realistic story, since God is such an important part of the spiritual
life of our people.

Christianity plays a fundamental role in most of Norwegian literature. Start with the works of the brother and sister Henrik
Wergeland and Camilla Collett. Remove God and all references to
Christian ethics, and see what is left. Next try to carry out the same
procedure on the works of the trio of Welhaven, Jørgen Moe, and

Landstad. When you are through with them, you can try it on Bjørnson, Ibsen, and Jonas Lie.

I have already mentioned Bjørnson's peasant tales. I must also mention the work in which he reaches his highest poetic greatness and intensity—*Arnljot Gelline*. This poem glorifies the victory of Christianity over heathendom. The heathen hero seeks the ultimate throughout his life, and finally finds it in Christ. At once the mystery of life is solved, and he thereupon goes gladly to his death. Just listen:

> "While now the host of the foeman
> Ranged itself in the distance,
> Pious the King held discourse
> Life and death concerning.
> Wondrous things met Arnljot's vision.

> "*There*[46] for him were answered
> All of the thousand questions;
> *There* his life transfigured,
> Raised to the sunlit uplands,
> Dawned then the day of his longings."[47]

After you have finished *Arnljot Gelline,* read Ibsen's three classic works: *The Pretenders, Brand,* and *Peer Gynt.* Then ask yourself: Where in all of secular literature can one find such intensely Christian works which at the same time contain such rich poetry and beauty as these? Answer the question for yourself. Some foreign critics have found fault with Ibsen for preaching religion in these three works. They maintain that he has exchanged the poet in himself for a puritanical pastor. Jonas Lie's literary works never touch directly on Christianity; and yet in every one of them the moral tone is crystal clear. No other author is so popular with pastors and with ordinary people. And what would be left of Garborg's work if the religious content were cut out?

You can hear the same strong theme in the works of many younger authors too, for example Nini Roll Anker and Kari Gløersen, Bojer (*The Great Hunger* and *The Last Viking*), J.A. Vinsness,

Gabriel Scott, and J.B. Bull, yes, even a devil-may-care genius like Herman Wildenvey can write such a lovely religious-lyrical poem as "Eventyr til Ellen."

I must beg again not to be misunderstood! By religious literature I do not mean sermons and hymns and pious devotions. I mean literature which strives seriously to clarify the great questions of life; literature in which characters are true to life; literature in which new thoughts illuminate the depths of the human heart; literature in which morals are based on Christian ethics.

This describes the best of Norwegian literature. God has a large place in it. We meet the thought of God everywhere in it. Young people with any kind of sincerity must feel solemnly religious when they sing songs like "A Singer's Prayer,"[48] "Hymn to Norway,"[49] "The Sailor's Last Journey,"[50] or "I saw Him as a Child"[51] (which has become Norwegian by adoption). Any intelligent person will of necessity be gripped by the *dead seriousness* of Christianity for the individual when reading such works of literature as *The Lost Father*, *Brand, The Golden Gospel,* and *The Church*.[52]

The idea of the personal relationship between God and the individual, along with the responsibility to strive for the best, appears again and again in Norwegian literature. As far as I can see, this idea characterizes Norwegian Christianity, and by that I mean *Norwegian Lutheranism*!

This is closely related to our national character, with its focus on individualism and personal freedom. Norwegian Lutheranism suits our national character and our national character suits it.

From my discussion one might get the impression that the beautiful time of the millennium was approaching in Norway. However, to anyone who has been reading our Norwegian-American church publications the last ten or twelve years, this would seem ludicrous. There we have often read that people coming from Norway nowadays are a bunch of godless rascals who are simply immune to religion. If nothing I have said would suggest the millennium, neither is there any evidence to support the assertions in our church publications. I have not touched on the present situation of the church in Norway, or on Christian life there. The traveler who visits Norway today will get two widely different impressions of the power of Christianity over the minds of the people, depending on which social class he associates with. In elegant circles in grand restaurants in the capital, it may seem that there is little or no Christianity in the country. On the other hand, if he spends a few weeks at a Christian school, he may come away with quite the opposite impression.

I know very little about the situation of the church in Norway. But if the reports of serious people are to be believed, people I am convinced know what they are talking about, then there has never been so much Christian activity in the country as there is now. According to what they say, there have never been so many young people flocking under the banner of Christ. In Norway, serious Christians, not fanatics and visionaries, believe that the time will soon come when Norway will be the standard-bearer of the Gospel to all people. They believe this and they pray that it will happen.

Well, now. That was something of a digression from our main subject.

I had been talking about the religious consciousness among the Norwegian people, their relationship to the church and to God, their religious seriousness, and the reasons for these things. The question that then occurs to me is this: Does not America have use for this part of our national heritage? Does our country not need us to live in such a way that our children cannot avoid meeting God? Does our nation not need the seriousness which arises from such a meeting? In other words: Does not America need *Norwegian Lutheranism*? And will not this part of our heritage provide a counterbalance to the endless desire for *amusement* that characterizes our people over here?

Most will answer "yes" to these questions. It will benefit America if we bring our Norwegian Lutheranism with us. Probably most who are interested in Christianity will agree.

But look, friends, if we believe this, it is not enough that we talk nicely about Lutheranism in general, we must stress that it is *Norwegian* Lutheranism. The term Norwegian Lutheranism is perhaps somewhat clumsy and unfortunate. I would have preferred something else instead, something like "the Norwegian view of Christianity," or "the Norwegian understanding of Christianity."

But it doesn't much matter what we call it, if we only agree on what it is. If we do, then we must act on it. For it is not possible to follow the advice of some of our church leaders who tell us we must try to preserve the religious part of our heritage! They think it is possible to preserve that part of our heritage without preserving the rest. And in this they are completely wrong. If we are to have any hope of preserving the religious part of our heritage, we have to start farther back, with our national characteristics and our heritage! It is folly to deny that Christianity is colored by national characteristics. If there is any religious heritage that we can call ours—and I have never heard any doubt about that—then this heritage has grown out of our national characteristics. So we must go in the exact opposite direction to what is now being recommended. Instead of starting with the end, we must start with the conditions which have brought about that end. Either that or we must create the conditions necessary to bring about the same result!

But here we are approaching the *sancta sanctorum*: our emotional attachment to the country we have become citizens of, and where our children will live and build after us. The anxious heart will ask with serious and deep concern: How can a person with a distinctly Norwegian view of life—with a "Norwegian soul"—be a good American citizen?

Well, what makes a good citizen? What is a bad citizen? If the anxious person would look for clarity on this issue instead of climbing up on the rooftop to see which way the wind is blowing, his worry would soon disappear. For me the answer is quite simple. Let us promote the Norwegian ancestral heritage, and our emotional attachment to America will be just fine. For it is *human* beings this country needs, not just *beings*. First and foremost, let us promote our own feelings for home. Let us have true homes, and not just the dwelling places we now inhabit. A home for every family. Every head of a family an owner. A home for every single individual. If we could truly be so thoroughly Norwegian, so radically Norwegian on this point, then we would also be as intensely American in our emotions as anyone in the whole country. You can be sure of this! But homes first and foremost. Homes for the body.

Homes for the spirit. Tramps are no benefit to the country. The tramp is mere human wreckage floating around in society.

Here I return again to the simple parable I used in the third section of these reflections—the parable of the four children. In which case would they love their father, mother, and home the most—if the home and parents helped each child to develop its inborn gifts and aptitudes, or if the home and parents did everything they could to obliterate their aptitudes and take away their gifts?

There are still more precious heirlooms to take out of our chest of drawers and admire. Much of what I have shown you deserves a more well-rounded and complete treatment than I have time or space for here. That is as it must be. Others will take up the work and improve upon it.

I have left untouched all the rubbish that is down in the bottom of the chest. There is much of that too. And it needs to be looked at as well. But there will always be those who can manage to dig *that* out!

SIMPLE REFLECTIONS ON

Our Literature

1

In January of 1922, Professor D.G. Ristad wrote an article about Norwegian-American literature. It was called "In Which Language?" I am going to quote it in its entirety.

"In which language have all those things been written that represent the cultural contributions we have made to date in this country? In Norwegian or in English? Which language is used by those who most completely and competently interpret our lives in this country at present? How many of those who speak most intimately and truthfully for us today have found and still find that they can communicate best in Norwegian? In English? If Hjalmar Rued Holand publishes another book about the Norwegian immigrants, will he write it in Norwegian or in English? Strømme, Ager, Wist, Prestgard, Norstog, Baumann, Rølvaag, Kildahl, Buslett, Foss—to name just a few of the men who have managed to write original interpretations of the lives of Norwegians in America— could they, and can those who are still living, reach so far down, so far in, and so high up in their task of placing us face to face with ourselves and our own fate and our own duty that we acknowledge the situation and shoulder our responsibility—could they and can they do it in Norwegian? Does the language mean anything to them and to us? Could they have done it as well in English as in Norwegian? Does language have any cultural value for us Norwegians in America?

"For whom is it most important that our people—with all they are and all they have, their temperament and their needs—become conscious in their minds, their wills, and their emotions of all that is characteristic of Norwegians as a people? For us ourselves, or for the others we share this land with? What is most important: *that a people grow in self-acceptance or that they grow in acceptance by others*?

"Just because the younger generations are steadily speaking more English, is that any reason to hurry the process so that the transition goes even faster?—So the distance between them and the older generation of Norwegians increases as quickly as possible? Among the American-born Norwegians, who are most likely to honor and respect, love and cherish their own people, those who retain some knowledge of the Norwegian language, or those who do not retain it?

"Perhaps someone would like to take up some of these questions for discussion."

This is Professor Ristad's article.

While he was going around over in Wisconsin thinking about these matters and formulating his questions in this way, Mr. N.N. Rønning was sitting up in Minneapolis contemplating "our poverty." In the Christmas issue of his journal *Familiens Magasin* [The Family Magazine] he included an article with the title "This Is Our Poverty." I will quote the entire piece here.

"A man wrote recently about the impossibility of having a Norwegian-American literature. 'If we ever get to be that literary' he wrote 'then we will have ceased to be Norwegian. Our literary future is to be American, not Norwegian.' This is undoubtedly true. It is difficult to sound the right linguistic tone, because we have no literary language that people use in daily life. (Cited from a book review in *Minneapolis Tidende*).

"It is true that we don't have a literary language which we speak in daily life, but that is not completely necessary either.

"The peasants in Bjørnson's peasant tales speak the same language that Bjørnson himself used in daily life. But that was not the same language they themselves spoke in daily life. Aase in *Peer Gynt* doesn't speak her dialect. Neither does Peer. The sailors and the slaves in Shakespeare as a rule speak an elegant language. Only now and then do they use their own speech. In Garborg's stories the city people speak *Landsmaal*, a language which at that time was not considered to be literary.

"Of course it would be best if the characters in a story, novel, or drama spoke the language that they use in daily life, but if it is not the literary language, authors let them speak the literary language. Why can Norwegian-American authors not let their characters do the same?

"But do our authors themselves use a literary language? Oh, yes, some of them do. They use about the same language as is used in *Minneapolis Tidende*, and in that language one can express just about anything one has to say, and in a quite literary manner. Just read the book reviews and music columns in *Tidende*.

"No, the lack of a literary language is not our greatest lack. It is not our greatest source of poverty. This is our poverty.

Our authors don't have anything much to say.

They don't dare say it.

They can't say it forcefully enough.

They don't get anything for saying it."

I took up both Ristad's and Rønning's pieces in my column "For Fædrearven" on January 12, 1922, and added the following comments:

"These statements invite discussion. On the whole, I am in agreement with the thoughts which underlie Professor Ristad's questions. I will only add that I believe the time will come when literature written in English will blossom among us, and will be so beautiful and truthful that it will be a joy and a benefit to mankind. However, this will happen only if our national characteristics are not erased too soon."

But it will scarcely be the generation now coming to maturity that will create this literature, and hardly the next one either. The youth of our time are not particularly enthusiastic about either beauty or truth. Their interests lie in the practical realm, in struggle and in pleasure. Especially in pleasure.

It is depressing to think that within the second, third, and fourth generations among us there is so little interest in higher intellectual and cultural matters. But it is true. Gustav Mellby was born and confirmed in Norway. Belle Hagen Winslow was also born there. The same is true of Hjalmar Hjort Boyesen and Henry Olaf Oyen. As far as I know they are the only ones who have tried in any appreciable degree to create literature in the English language.[53]

I join Professor Ristad in asking: "What is most important: that a people grow in self-acceptance or that they grow in acceptance by others?"

Here he touches on the heart of the matter. We don't want self-acceptance; what we are looking for is acceptance by others. What do we care about our own authors and thinkers? Not the least little bit. We wave their names around on festive occasions. We are even rather good at doing that. And every time we hear someone of another nationality praise one of our great men, then we get excited, then we think this is "awfully great"!

In the course of the last year people have often said to me, "It is too bad you don't write your books in English; then something could come of them."

And the underlying thought is not what this could mean for me personally. No, the thinking is, your books don't matter very much to us, we can manage just fine without them; but it would be nice if genuine Americans and others around here could see that we too have fellows who can put together a readable book. What matters, then, is to get others to see what damn clever folk we are, and thereby earn their praise. But we are totally indifferent to what other Norwegians think.

What else could lead them to speak such nonsense! The younger generation as a rule doesn't care in the slightest about what is written by our people, no matter what the language. Gustav Mellby has published—isn't it four?—collections of poetry in English. Ask young people if they recognize his name! Last year Dorthea Dahl published a remarkable collection of tales in English. Did the young buy the book? And ask some young people if they know Simon Johnson's excellent novel *From Fjord to Prairie*? Of course they have never heard of Henry Olaf Oyen. Boyesen is too old, too far back in time, so we can't expect them to be familiar with him. Belle Hagen Winslow's work was heavily publicized. Augsburg Publishing House advertised *The White Dawn* better than they have any other book, but our younger generation didn't buy it, nor did pastors or lay people.

It is hopelessly stupid of us to sit here and wait for the golden age which will come after the transition to English is complete. We won't become better human beings just by changing languages.

Wilson had fourteen points. N.N. Rønning manages with only four. But they are bold assertions.

There is much we all can agree with in his introduction to the four points. I agree completely with Rønning that language doesn't have much to do with the matter. Language issues are the least important. If we don't know standard Norwegian *Riksmål*, we certainly can manage a Norwegian dialect. If we don't know either of those, then we know Iowa-Norwegian, or English. It is possible to create a literature in any of these languages.

Language doesn't have much to do with the matter. The most intensely American patriotic work was not written in English, but in Yiddish. It is the play *The Melting Pot*, by the Jew Israel Zangwill.[54] The other day we received a poem written in Telemark dialect by a boy who was born and raised in the far northern Canadian prairies, far from civilization. And it is a really beautiful poem!

It is not until we get to Rønning's four points that we disagree with him. I will take up these points one at a time and examine them.

Point One. Our authors have nothing much to say.

Perhaps. But they have said, and continue to say, quite a lot of things. No doubt Rønning means that there is no heartfelt urge in them. They are not deeply moved, and therefore they do not "prophesy" either.

Does he think they are carrying on just for the fun of it? Is it just for fun that Norstog has stayed out there in the wilderness and written one Biblical drama after the other? That Ager has stolen hours from the night, hours that he couldn't afford to lose, in order to write his tales and stories? Well, if it is not for fun, then it must be due to inordinate ambition. Or should we believe that our authors are such aesthetes that they write just for the love of beauty? But that can't be, for Rønning doesn't think we have any such needs.

And Rønning himself declares that they don't get anything for what they write, so it can't be for the sake of income, since they don't write for money. So would Rønning kindly explain *why on earth they write*!

I disagree completely with Rønning. Let's look at the Christmas issue of his own magazine. When I read the story "The Old Pastor's Surprise" it seems clear as sunshine to me that here Rønning has something important to say. I even have the feeling Rønning himself must have thought so as he sat writing the piece.

Point Two: They don't dare say it.

See, now he's got you, all of you! Take that and chew on it for a while! You are a bunch of cowards, all of you. You, Ager and Baumann and Buslett, Norstog and Simon Johnson, and Ristad and Wist, or whatever your names are. You too, Dorthea! Yes, even you Rønning yourself, for you have dabbled in the trade too. You don't dare to come forward with what you have on your minds. Curl your tails between your legs now and run on home and lie down!

But to speak seriously, fear is scarcely the reason that our literature is not richer than it is, or that our authors are not more widely read than they are. Rønning doesn't really believe that either. One can hardly accuse our two Wisconsin boys, Ager and Buslett, of being afraid, nor any of the others either. I don't dare to speculate on how far Rønning himself may have felt the paralysis of fear as he sat there on his stool trying to write something extra good, but I find it hard to believe that is what is wrong with Rønning.

So I suggest that Rønning drop these first two points.

Point Three: They don't say it forcefully enough.

Here we take things very seriously, we writers. Here Rønning hits us where it hurts. And here he scores a point.

Not quite a knockout, though. There is some life left even after the fatal blow has been struck. Ager's tale "He looked small and insignificant" could scarcely have been better told. "John McEstee's Cradle Song" could hardly hit the mark more squarely than it does. Within the genre of the sketch, it would be difficult to find anything livelier than this little tale. That is also true for much of Simon Johnson's writing.

As I page through Baumann's poems, I find much beauty in them. This is genuine poetry, not just rhyming verses with a so-so rhythm. This is true poetry, and it hits home. One day a man from Solør confessed to me (and this is a man who has never met Baumann) that "Baumann is a really great poet!" This man from Solør had been affected by his poetry! That's the way it is with many of our authors and their products.

So this argument about not being forceful enough is not as convincing as it seems at first glance. When Henrik Ibsen's *The Warriors of Helgeland* first came out it was almost unnoticed. It didn't go much better with *The Pretenders* either, though that work is now considered one of the masterworks of world literature. And both *The Warriors of Helgeland* and *The Pretenders* are surely "striking" enough.[55] It would be easy to find such examples from other countries too.

Even so, I admit that there is some truth in Point Three. Too much, unfortunately. Much of what we writers have put out into the world has not been as substantial as it should have been. It is too green—not yet ripe fruit. But on the other hand, no matter how ripe it might have been, it would not have made any impression on readers who couldn't be bothered.

Point Four: They don't get anything for saying it.

In this we are in complete agreement with Rønning! No one will try to contradict him here.

But I would have preferred to have Rønning formulate this point a little differently. I would say: There is very little appreciation among the general public, and among the educated, almost none. *This is our poverty*. And it is such naked poverty. The lack of interest from the general public is oppressive enough, but even worse is the lack of *vision* among most of those who are supposed to be the leaders among our people. And this poverty will be difficult to climb out of.

Here I must add something that was not said in the newspaper article, as an explanation of where this poverty comes from.

Rough seas do not come up in calm weather. Flat lands do not give an echo, for on the plains there is nothing sticking up to reflect the sound. And spring does not come if the sunshine and warm south winds stay away. That's the way it is in the world of nature.

And in the world of the intellect it is much the same. There can be no true intellectual life where self-satisfied indifference abounds, where intellectual arrogance rules, where ardor is lacking. Only the hungry appreciate nourishment. It is those who "hunger and thirst after righteousness" who "shall be satisfied."

I find this same thought expressed by Professor Gerhard Gran[56] in his work on Henrik Ibsen.

"It is a tragic fate to be born an artistic genius in a small nation, in petty and narrow-minded circumstances. The great author has not only a mighty passion to produce, but a nearly equally strong need for response. Where these two factors do not meet, the soul of the poet suffers unspeakable torment, which we ordinary people can only vaguely apprehend. Even Henrik Wergeland, with his bright spirit and eyes always focused on the sunrise, had moments when he was nearly tortured to death by the murderous indifference of his cramped surroundings. There were times when he felt himself

> ". . . like a bell, men hush,
> muffled close in clammy folds;
> like the rose's radiant bush
> which a covering basket holds."[57]

The "tragic" with us is not that we are "a small nation." We are large enough. But we are "small" and the conditions we have created are "narrow-minded." In these conditions, we can find no "response." It doesn't make the slightest difference to us whether or not we have someone to tell tales or create poems. We don't care in the least. We are fine just as we are, we are satisfied and happy with our condition. Above all we want to be left in peace. People who write books are often rather bothersome. It is best to beware of them. We see and understand our times perfectly well, and we don't need them to explain things to us.

That is the way we reason, consciously or unconsciously. But such a point of view can only be found in a people who are completely weighed down, oppressed by cultural poverty. When I say this, am I either untruthful or unloving? Well, look around! It is true that our literature is nothing to brag about. Yet much of it has traces of springtime in it. Do we see these traces? And do we try to protect them? No. Just look at the reception our books have had.

Will this reception encourage even more writing? A friend of the author or the publisher might write half a column in a newspaper, or a whole column (or maybe just a short paragraph) praising the author. The reviewer pats the reader on the shoulder and says now we must be kind and buy the book, for it is a good book and the author is a good man. And after that there is silence, dead silence.[58] Have there been any discussions of literature in our newspapers that might waken interest in books and writing? No. Do our pastors try to guide people? Do they recommend books when they are talking to people? That is, novels and poetry? No. Is anything done in our various organizations to waken interest in literature? Not that I know of. Both Baumann and Ager are warm friends of the Sons of Norway. One of them is perhaps the most faithful worker the organization has at the moment. It would not be too much to expect that the Sons of Norway could give him, or both of them, an author's stipend so they could carry out their work with their whole heart. But the Sons of Norway has not done this. There are many organizations which could sell reliable fraternal insurance, but only the Sons of Norway could take care of these men and help them write a proper book. That they have not done so is just a further example of the oppressive cultural poverty amongst us.

Let me give more examples.

Professor [J. A.] Holvik down at Waldorf College published textbooks in Norwegian and school editions of Norwegian classics for our high schools and colleges. It could be expected that we would thank him for this. We did not. We starved him out of this occupation. "We have enough Norwegian teachers!" said a highly-placed official within the church when the debate over the name change raged at its worst. This man meant exactly what he said, and the sad part of it is, he expressed the prevailing opinion of our educated leaders.

There sits Dr. [Knut] Gjerset down in Decorah. He has written a monumental work about the history of Norway. And he has written it in an understandable and popular language. The work is written in English. Anyone can read it. We might expect that Dr. Gjerset would be excused from teaching beginning classes in Norwegian. Others could do that, and he could devote all his energies to writing the history of Norway in English. But we haven't done that. We have not lifted a finger to help him continue his work.

And even if the church didn't show any interest in this matter, one would think there might be individuals who would do so. There are so many who *could* do so. And Dr. Gjerset wrote his book in English, so we can't blame the language here. But so far not one of our rich men has offered to help. Perhaps this is too much to expect, since spiritual riches and material riches seldom go hand in hand. It is unusual to see them on the same path.

As far as I know, there is only one Dr. [O.M.] Norlie among us. It will probably be a long time before we find another man with his ability to do research. One would think that we would make use of his talents. But have we done so? No. Now we have finally buried him in a poor teacher's position down in Decorah.

But why not take Rønning himself as an example; after all, he has worked faithfully for us and among us. We let his English language publication, *The Northland Weekly*, starve to death, and if the signs are not altogether wrong, he will have a hard battle to keep *The North Star* going. He wouldn't need to do this if our educated people would show the interest in his journal which it deserves.

I have mentioned these examples to show how low our so-called higher spiritual and intellectual life lies. What if for once we were honest enough to admit that no such higher spiritual life exists among us Americans of Norwegian descent. This is our poverty. And in this poverty such a tender and fine flower as literature cannot blossom. In this we find the entire explanation.

2

The above article was printed in the *Duluth Skandinav* and, together with Rønning's four points, it immediately created a great uproar. For three months now the battle has been raging, and it still continues. And the controversy is spreading to some of our other smaller newspapers.

I find it significant that all our larger newspapers have maintained strict neutrality. They have stood back as silent observers, cool, composed, calm. It seems as though this strife does not interest them.

But in *Duluth Skandinav* the controversy has been as hot as it could be. A man said to me this winter, "I haven't seen anything so refreshingly lively in any of our Norwegian-American newspapers as the battle which is now taking place in the *Duluth Skandinav*." And this is true. But then, some of our sharpest observers have taken part, some with several contributions.

I myself have written five articles. These consist mostly of remarks on literature and life. I will repeat them below, in a slightly altered form.

What prompted me to write the series, and also enticed others to join in, was the article titled "What kind of literature," which was signed "S."[59] It is not a long article. And so that you will understand my remarks, I will quote it here. Anyway, it deserves to be preserved. I will print it exactly as it appeared in *Duluth Skandinav*:

"I see that several people have taken up the question of literature in this paper. Even though I am not terribly interested in the question as it is posed, I feel it is my duty to shed light on the subject from a side that up until now has not been mentioned, namely the Christian side or, if you will, the side of the church.

"Professor Rølvaag, Julius Baumann, and others complain about our cultural and spiritual poverty. What do they really mean by spiritual poverty? Well, they mean that the Norwegian people in America are spiritually impoverished because they don't read the books that these gentlemen have written.

"But what right have these men to call the Norwegian people in America spiritually impoverished, and can we look at the question from just this one side?

"Let us look more closely at the issue.

"Have Professor Rølvaag, Julius Baumann, Waldemar Ager, Buslett, or any other of these authors given us a book that a responsible pastor in good conscience could recommend from the pulpit? One that he felt would help him in his work for God's cause?

"I think not, and I would add that a book that a pastor cannot recommend wholeheartedly in church is meaningless. From a spiritual point of view.

"There are two kinds of spiritual poverty. I don't care one whit about the kind of spiritual poverty these authors complain about. What matters is to be rich in the spirit which belongs to the coming kingdom, to the kingdom of God.

"These gentlemen will no doubt call me narrow-minded and limited. I will just permit myself to pose one question. Has the world become a better place lately with all this modern literature? Has it not rather become worse?

"How many books could be found among our forefathers who settled out on the prairie? Well, one found the Bible and the hymn-book and some kind of devotional book, and not much else. And what did these people do? They were the ones who cleared the land, broke the soil, made the way for the generations who now live because of their work. And no one can say that spiritually they were any worse off than the current generation, in spite of the fact that they held themselves to Christian literature. They didn't need any *Boat of Longing*, or any *Two Fools* [*Pure Gold*], any *From the Prairies,* or whatever these books are called. They didn't need a Waldemar Ager, a Buslett, a Simon Johnson, or any other of these writers. They were satisfied with their Bible, and I believe the same is true of every man and woman today, even though of course everyone will admit that a pure literature has some justification within our society.

"President [Gjermund] Hoyme[60] said in an ordination sermon in Minneapolis in 1900: 'Therefore, Brothers, it is important to preach the gospel without the *admixture of human wisdom*.' I believe it would be well for the Norwegian people in America to hold more to the gospel and less to the 'human wisdom' which these our authors want to force upon us as a spiritual necessity.

"Can we perhaps find a single one of these authors who has any particular interest in the church? Or have any of them attempted to give us Christian literature—make us spiritually richer? If we look hard, we may even find that some of them deny the faith of their childhood!

"When the day comes that one of these authors gives us a book each and every pastor can gladly recommend from the pulpit, that day they will be read, whether they write in English or in Norwegian. But as long as these authors write the kinds of books they have written, books filled with sensual and worldly matters, then I for one am glad that there is so much spiritual poverty among us that they are not read.

"These authors of ours ought to take the St. Olaf Choir as an example. This choir has reached the pinnacle with church music. The best critics in the country have declared the choir to be the best in the country—and they sing only church music.

"Christian literature will in the long run pay off just as well as Christian music—for God is for it."

That is the way "S" writes.

And I feel compelled to answer him, since so much of what he says concerns me personally. I would have appreciated having him sign his name, for then we could have spoken more easily together. If the thoughts presented in this piece were just those of one individual, I wouldn't have bothered to answer, but they represent a school of thought, they give expression to a rather common view; therefore I am compelled to answer.

"S." says: "Rølvaag and Julius Baumann complain about our cultural and spiritual poverty. What do they really mean by spiritual poverty? Well, they mean that the Norwegian people in America are so spiritually impoverished that they don't read the books these gentlemen have written."

I can't answer for Baumann in this matter, he will have to take care of that himself. I don't know what his opinion is either, but it has never occurred to me that people are spiritually impoverished because they don't buy *our* books. No, I don't think that. I hope this statement is quite clear. I don't think that people are spiritually impoverished because they don't buy our books, I do think the fact that they don't buy any books at all of the type we are talking about here is an unmistakable sign of poverty. For books, works of literature, carry the message of life, they emanate from burning souls, from suffering and compassionate hearts, from minds angry over injustice, from happy minds that celebrate with joy, from minds filled with beauty. Books give birth to thoughts, and all this has the effect of setting minds on fire.

But our people don't care about such books. Just go into their homes and see what you find. Well, maybe there is a bookcase, for that belongs to a well-furnished place. Maybe there are even some books in it, for it looks best that way. Look at the books! Talk to the people in the house about the books you have found, then you will find out how many of the adults living in house are familiar with them.

Go into the parsonages, and you will be met with the same poverty when it comes to literary works. The great majority of our pastors have no interest in fine literature. If you try talking to them about a famous piece by a great author, you might be embarrassed to find that they have not heard of the work and perhaps not of the author either. All of you have heard the strong condemnation these last few years of recent Norwegian literature. This negative view has been passed from person to person, and has become something of a slogan, just about as well known as the dogma about the Norwegian immigrants' indifference to Christianity. One often hears pastors expatiate upon the theme of "filthy literature from Norway." But ask them if they are familiar with Gabriel Scott, and they will just stare at you in astonishment. "Gabriel Scott? Is he Norwegian? What books has he written?" This has happened to me not just once, but many times.

Right now no country in the world has such an extensive and healthy children's literature as Norway. This would provide nourishing fare for us Norwegians over here, especially out in the countryside where Norwegian is still alive and kicking in so many homes. But the majority of our pastors—the only class of educated people who come in close contact with our people—don't know anything about these books, and so we can't very well expect that the people will know about them either.

I have met only three of our pastors who knew anything about Selma Lagerlöf. And she is perhaps the world's greatest living author. I have never seen in her work the slightest thing that could cause the most piously holy mind to blush in shame. The basis of her literature is deeply religious. Read *Jerusalem (I–II)*, *The Wonderful Adventures of Nils Holgerson*, *The Teamster*, *The Tales of a Manor and Other Sketches*, *Thy Soul Shall Bear Witness*, *The Emperor from Portugallia*, *The Girl from the Marshcroft*, *Christ Legends and Other Stories*, or *The Outcast*, and you will see that this is true. Here we have one of the greatest interpreters of the human soul of our time. An author with astonishing insight into the secrets of life. In addition, she is deeply religious. One would imagine, therefore, that our pastors would be familiar with her work (several of her books have been translated into Norwegian, Danish, German, French, and English), but just ask them!

No, it is not because our people don't read *us*, that we complain, it is because *they don't read*. And if they read literature, if they were interested in literary works, then they would also be interested in our works, even if our works are not yet mature.

Has "S" never noticed this spiritual poverty? Has he not felt how it has oppressed him, boxed him in? Has he not noticed how sometimes it is difficult to breathe? Well, then "S" is a lucky person!

But doesn't "S" visit people's homes? Through his whole piece we detect a tone that suggests he is a pastor. He would scarcely have written as he did if he were not a pastor. So he must be familiar with our homes. What kind of conversation does he hear there? What do people talk about when they get together? Is it about art, literature, poetry, music? Or is it about science and aesthetics, questions of morality? Or are there discussions about the great problems of life? Or schools of thought, great and inspiring ideas? No. It is about business and more business; or it is about entertainment and politics; or it is gossip, vile gossip; or in the best case, a theological discussion; or, or,—they play *Rook*!

Let "S" take a close look at these amusements, and see if he can find culture in them. There can be culture and ideals in such things too. Compare modern dance to traditional folk dance, for example. Or think about our movies, there can be ideals there. And athletics certainly needs to be ennobled by ideals. Let "S" take notice of political discussions within our circle. In politics there surely ought to be much idealism and spirituality, but does he find it there?

Or "S" can take a look at our Norwegian-American press and, with a few exceptions, see what he finds of culture there. What do they write about? About what people want, of course. And what do people want, judged by the content of the newspapers? He will find notices of deaths, pieces about crops, about good years and bad years, about rich black soil, about elections and politics, and more about politics. Or about banquets. We are very good at writing about banquets, and giving banquets, and giving speeches at banquets. But does "S" find much culture at these banquets of ours? And in the flood of speeches, has "S" noticed any sparks of spirituality that have burst into flame and led to action? I ask, now let him answer!

"S" continues in this way:

"Have Professor Rølvaag, Julius Baumann, Waldemar Ager, Buslett, or any other of these authors given us a book that a responsible pastor in good conscience could recommend from the pulpit? One that he felt would help him in his work for God's cause? I think not, and I would add that a book that a pastor cannot recommend wholeheartedly in church is meaningless. From a spiritual point of view."

Now that was a real bolt of lightning! First I must ask "S" a few questions. What does he really mean by "a responsible pastor in good conscience?" Or did I read it wrong? Should it be read as "could responsibly recommend with a good conscience"? Well now, it doesn't really matter how you interpret it, either way it is equally meaningless. If "S" had just mentioned when he wrote this what kind of books "would help the pastor in his work for God's cause," we could have discussed it more intelligently. But he didn't do that. And I would like to know when a pastor—in what circumstances, that is—"recommends wholeheartedly in church" and when he recommends *half*-heartedly? And does "S" know of any congregation where the pulpit is used to advertise literature?

I am not at all sure that I understand "S" in the above quotation. It seems to me that he is preaching with great "admixture" to use one of his own expressions. I will answer him according to my understanding of his words.

And so I say to him. I have written four novels, as well as some stories and sketches, and right offhand I cannot think of one of them which "S" could not recommend from his pulpit, that is to say, assuming his pulpit was to be used for that purpose. I am even stubborn enough to think that my books would have helped "S" in his work for God's cause if he just had sense enough to use them.

I have written a novel in which I attempt to depict the change in mentality that takes place in all who trade one homeland for another. Presumably "S" has some people like that in his congregation; therefore, he needs to study the psychology of transition in order to be able to reach into the hearts of his parishioners. And you don't find that kind of psychology in works of dogma or collections of sermons, or in devotional books or Bible stories. If he is ever going to understand this psychology—and he must if his sermons are to be more than just empty floods of words as far as this class of people is concerned—he will need to search in the books that deal with psychology. Does "S" not understand this?

It is very immodest—I understand that!—to refer "S" to my own works, but I really believe that he will have to preach many sermons about "the daily crucifixion" before he will make the impression I have made in one of my novels on the same theme. "S" ought to read it! But now I will be even more bold: I am certain that "S"—"S" himself—will never manage to preach as well about the sin described in *Pure Gold* [Two Fools] as I have done. It is not because I am so much better a preacher than "S," but rather because the topic is so much better suited to literary portrayal than to a sermon. And since "S" mentions my last novel several times in his short piece— he clearly thinks it a godless book—I will merely say that if "S" shouted himself hoarse from the pulpit about the inscrutable longing of the human soul for the good and the beautiful, for the source of love, he would never get as far as I did in *The Boat of Longing*. "S" would be wise therefore to refer to this book whenever his sermons touch on these topics.

Now I won't say any more about myself! If "S" had not so boldly condemned books that he had not even read, I would not have said so many foolish things.

But "S" and I must continue.

He paints quite a moving picture of the pioneers and the pioneer period. The only thing wrong with it is that it is both stupid and false. Let us look at it again.

"They [the pioneers] were the ones who cleared the land, broke the soil, made the way for the generations who now live because of their work. And no one can say that spiritually they were any worse off [and what does he mean by worse off?] than the current generation, in spite of the fact that they held themselves to Christian literature. They didn't need any *Boat of Longing* or any *Two Fools* [*Pure Gold*], any *From the Prairies,* or whatever these books are called. They didn't need a Waldemar Ager, a Buslett, a Simon Johnson, or any other of these writers. They were satisfied with their Bible, and I believe the same is true of every man and woman today."

Here "S" speaks falsely about life. And he should not do that, for such things usually come back to haunt one. If "S" doesn't know any better than what he says in the above quotation, then his own spiritual poverty is so great as to demand our genuine compassion. But if he knows better, and says it anyway, then it is really a bad deed for one who should be a teacher in Israel. And it is not so easy to lie about life either, for truth will out. But I will take his statement at face value and write it off to ignorance.

Yes, the pioneers read books! As a class they were inordinately fond of reading, even the reading of novels. That is the truth. They were so fond of reading that they got together and formed small reading groups, and they bought books which circulated in the settlement until sometimes there was not much more than tatters left of them. These collections contained many different kinds of works. For instance, there were Bjørnson's peasant tales, Jonas Lie's tales of the sea, [B. S.] Ingemann's novels, several by [Carit] Etlar, Walter Scott, and Dickens (in Norwegian), [Frederick] Marryat's tales of the sea (also in Norwegian), some by Dumas, James's *Daughters of the Forest* and *The Pearl of Abyssinia* and even *Rocambole,* and many other strange things. One can still find remnants of these circulating collections out in the settlements and meet people whose voices become warm when they remember those times and those conditions.

And when "S" speaks about the pioneer time as though he knew something about it, he ought to remember what happened to *The Cotter's Son*[61] among the Norwegian immigrants. Hasn't he heard about all the people who left their work in the middle of the busiest harvest and ran to the post office to get the next installment? The truth is, for the most part the pioneers were eager for knowledge, intelligent, and interested in everything. That is why they founded Norwegian newspapers, first in one town and then in the next. And these newspapers always had at least one serial going. It is an example of his own cultural and spiritual poverty that "S" doesn't know these things which are so widely known.

And then "S" quotes a sentence from an ordination sermon preached by Hoyme. I repeat the quotation:

"Therefore, Brothers, it is important to preach the gospel without the *admixture of human wisdom*." "S" has even italicized the quotation to give it more power.

Well, if this sermon was preached at "S"'s own ordination, he has not complied with Hoyme's words. "S" "admixes" quite shamefully.

In any case, Hoyme is the worst example he could have found, for the man was a great lover of literature and poetry; he even wrote poetry himself. Hoyme must have been very familiar with the literature of the time; it shows clearly in the language of his sermons. There has been scarcely another Norwegian pastor in America who used the Norwegian language so poetically and with such picturesque power as Hoyme. I would ask "S" to read some of Hoyme's speeches! There he will find poetry, and thoughtfulness, and imagination! Truly, this man must have made use of literature as far as his time and strength allowed. And it served him well. And it would serve "S" well also if he would just try it.[62]

I will once again quote from "S"'s article:

"Can we perhaps find a single one of these authors who has any particular interest in the church? Or have any of them attempted to give us Christian literature—make us spiritually richer? If we look hard, we may find that some of them even deny the faith of their childhood!"

I have quoted word for word; even the exclamation point has been included.

The above is not only an example of spiritual poverty, it is nasty. Here "S" is trying to get the public to believe that the authors he has mentioned, at least some of them, are the kind of people that Christians ought to avoid having anything to do with. It takes quite a lot of "talent" to write something like that. And it is a nasty person who puts a cowardly "S" up in front of himself as a screen. The man really has a duty to read what we have written and document such assertions with facts. Don't you agree, "S," when you think the matter over?

Then I finally come to the climax of this article. It is so peculiar that I will cite it too:

"But as long as these authors write the kinds of books they have written, books filled with sensual and worldly matters, then I for one am glad that there is so much spiritual poverty among us that they are not read."

This is quite a powerful statement. It reminds me of a Norwegian folk tale. In this tale there is a really nasty and ugly old woman. She walks right into a strange house, where there is some freshly cooked porridge on the table. She picks up a spoon and digs right into the bowl of porridge and puts it right into her mouth. But she burns herself on the porridge, and "then the old woman said something very very nasty." Then she throws herself down in a chair, but the chair goes to pieces. And then the old woman says something "very very nasty" again. Finally, she lies down on a bed, but the pillow on the bed is too hard and, again, she says something "very very nasty." That is just what "S" does in his article.

I cannot help believing that in the little bit of our literature that he has read there must have been something he burned himself on, something that has caused the ground under him to fall apart, and something that was terribly uncomfortable for him to sleep on. Oh well, if this is the case, then our literature, poor as it is, has deeply affected at least one soul. And for that we ought to be happy.

In any case, I am prepared to believe that "S" doesn't really understand what he has said. So great is his spiritual poverty. Does he really know what lies in the expression "books filled with sensual matters" in the connection in which he uses it?

But I shall assume he understands what he says, that he really believes our books are lewd. And yet this is just another indication of his spiritual poverty. Our literature suffers from many failings, I will readily admit that. But there is one failing it does not have, it is not smutty. In spite of this he has pointed his finger and said with great authority, "books filled with sensual matters." He condemns our literature for the one thing that it contains not a single trace of. No wonder "S" has failed to notice the spiritual poverty among us. That man wouldn't notice that a fire was burning until his beard was alight.

If "S" has the slightest interest in truth, and we have the right to expect that of him, then he is duty-bound to name the collection of poems or the novel within our literature which is "filled with sensual matters." Come now, "S," be a man! When you have done that, then go to the pulpit and warn about that book. That is your duty!

No, our literature is not smutty. It is pure. That is just what is great and good about it. Our authors are driven by idealism. Therefore they have tried to make the beautiful so attractive that we who read would strive to reach it. The good is for them so positive that they are willing to sacrifice their whole lives for it. When our authors depict sin, it is always hideous. It is "very very nasty." As best they could, our authors have shown how sin ruins, how it destroys the lives of those who allow it to rule over them.

This is what our authors are seeking and have sought to do. But in spite of that "S" can piously fold his hands and thank God that so few people read them! It takes quite some "talent" to bring forth such thanks!

3

I didn't really have time to write about these matters just now, but the article by "S" cast such a garish light over this aspect of our cultural poverty that all its wretchedness became clear. This made it difficult to keep silent. The same church organization that "S" serves—if I am right in my assumption that he is a pastor—has hired me to teach literature to its youth. And "S" and his kindred souls hinder me in my work. Therefore I feel it is my duty to speak out.

It is not just what "S" says that reveals his ignorance, though that is revealing enough, but even more it is revealed in the way he says it. It is revealed in his self-satisfied indifference, in his casual certainty, his sleepily cocksure attitude which judges and condemns in smug carelessness without the slightest idea that he is doing anything wrong. No, indeed, he believes he is right to preach sermons instructing and warning ordinary people about our literature! With great confidence he outspokenly condemns people he doesn't know, and works he has never read. The principle that guides him is this: I can get along quite well without literature, "these worldly books," therefore it is wrong of others to feel any need for them. With that he folds his hands piously and recites the prayer of the Pharisees. He is happy that there are so few who buy our books. Happy the poor person who does not see his own nakedness!

"S," and unfortunately many other pastors with him, condemns our secular literature. We should be astonished at how little knowledge these people have of the history of our church and of our people. Is the saga of our kin a *terra incognita* to them? And they preach to the descendants of these very people—the children of our kin!

Some of the most brilliant figures in the history of Norwegian-Danish literature are pastors or people who were trained to be pastors. Have "S" and his kindred spirits never heard of Petter Dass or Ludvig Holberg? They ought at least to know the name of Erik Pontoppidan; and even he is listed in the literary histories as an author of secular literature. That is to say, he wrote books which "S" could scarcely "with a good conscience" recommend from his pulpit. Men such as Ambrosius Stub, Hans Jacob Willes, Hans Strøm, Thomas Stockfleth, we can't very well ask about these when they don't recognize the names of the better known ones. But they ought to recognize names such as Johan Nordahl Brun, Claus Friman, Edvard Storm, Jens Zetlitz, Jonas Rein, Steen Steensen Blicher. Note that it is only the *names* I am talking about here! But as spiritual leaders for *us*, as bearers of culture among us, we justifiably demand of our pastors that they should know a *little* bit about men such as Søren Kierkegaard, N.F.S. Grundtvig, [Vilhelm] Birkedal, [Wilhelm Andreas] Wexels, Henrik Wergeland, Johan Sebastian Welhaven, Elias Blix, M.B. Landstad, Jørgen Moe, Anders Hovden, and many more such shining lights from our Norwegian-Danish church and cultural history. I believe we have the right to demand of pastors who preach in Norwegian for people of Norwegian descent—and especially of pastors who condemn literature—that they have at least a passing acquaintance with the history of our people.

But here too I will judge them mildly. I know that many of our pastors have struggled to get ahead under very difficult conditions; they could not acquire any education beyond the strictly theological without great sacrifice and hard work. I will therefore excuse them for not knowing much about that part of our national history which took place in the old fatherland. But though I excuse them from this, I neither can nor will excuse them from knowing—at least somewhat—our Norwegian-American church history. For if they are not familiar with this, then what do they know? Don't "S" and his kindred spirits agree that I have the right to ask this? And when we look out over the history of the Norwegian-American church, we again find this phenomenon, inexplicable for "S," that some of the greatest names, some of the splendid leaders, many of the men whose names will live on in our history, not only loved books which "S" could not recommend from his pulpit, they even wrote such books themselves.

I have already mentioned President Hoyme and shown his interest in literature. Let me now remind you of another great leader from that time, Dr. Vilhelm Koren. (I could just as well mention Mrs. Koren too; her memoirs are some of the most beautiful and interesting that have seen the light of day in Norwegian America.) Dr. Koren had quite a considerable poetic talent. "S" can just take a look at his "Collected Works" and he will see that this is true.

I could name many others now dead around whose names some of us see a halo, and with good reason. Professor Th. Bothne, Pastor Johan Olsen, Pastor [L. M.] Biørn, Dr. Kildahl, and Pastor [Henrik] Voldal. Is it possible that "S" is a pastor within our church and doesn't know anything about the lives and the writings of these men? But let me just name a few others, for example: O[lav] A. Bu, Johs. Bothne, Sigurd Folkestad, [Andreas] Bersagel, [George A. T.] Rygh, O. Shefveland, Karl Xavier, Th. Eggen, Gustav Mellby (he doesn't belong to our church), professors Ristad, Wilh. Pettersen, E. Kr. Johnsen. No, let me stop naming names! The list will get too long, and I might leave someone out. But doesn't it seem strange to "S" himself that he does not know anything about what these men have accomplished in the literary arena, and does he really want to condemn them for what they have written?

He knows nothing about these men. And here he reveals again his spiritual poverty. For if he had known them, and then had read the poetry collection *From the Prairies,* which he so blithely con-

demns, then he would also have known that this poetry collection
of Baumann's contains some of the finest lyric poetry we Americans of Norwegian descent have brought forth to this date, along
with some of the poems of Folkestad and Ristad. And if he knew
about the pastors and teachers I have mentioned here from our history, and then looked to Waldemar Ager, for example, then he
would have known that no one among us has so far surpassed Ager
in the sketch and the short story. But now I must have permission
to repeat my statement from some time ago: We have the right to
demand of "S," as one who is a leader of our people, that he know
enough about our people to comprehend such things.

Doesn't it seem strange to "S" that some of the pastors and
teachers throughout our history both in this country and in our
fatherland—those who will never be forgotten as long as the nation
lives—loved books and even wrote some themselves. Doesn't it seem
strange to "S" that they wrote books of the type that he, according
to his own statement, cannot recommend from his pulpit? I just in-
quire in all innocence!

Yet when one reflects on this a bit, it is not in the least bit
strange. In fact, it is inevitable that such men would love literature
and write books.

Let's talk about this now, simply and clearly. Please don't get
angry if the discussion drags on a bit long.

This is inevitable because all literature that amounts to anything
at all *reflects life*, and in doing that it *explains life*. We see the picture
the author has drawn for us, we begin to follow its lines, and little
by little we see the whole drawing, we understand the picture of life
which has been produced for us.

These pictures can take many different shapes. They may depict
a soul in distress, battling itself or the world around it. They may
depict a grieving heart, a longing mind, a drowning faith. They may
show us joy and faith giving strength to life. Or the picture
may show us love, courage, power; or weakness, illness, diseased
souls, sin that rages and ruins lives. All these descriptions enable us
to see a picture of the human soul. We can see the effect one soul
can have on another, how mind reacts against mind. This interplay
in turn creates a picture of the protagonists—heroes and heroines.

The picture might show us some parts of society or a whole so-ciety. It might show us a particular time period. The author might paint a picture of trends—good as well as bad—and show how they can become a blessing or a hindrance. But whatever the picture is concerned with, there will be descriptions of humanity in it. In our time, description of the human condition has become the great as-pect of all true art. Life, human life in all its teeming multiplicity, provides the material in which the author and poet finds his sub-ject matter.

That takes care of the subject matter.

And now some words about the person who works with this matter, the poet. What is he like? And how does he work?

Henrik Ibsen once gave this definition: "To write is to see." To see what? we might ask. Life, of course. For there is nothing else to see here in this world. Even the person who sits down and conjures up a utopia does it out of the experiences he has had of life. Yes, even when Baumann writes his beautiful hymn in praise of morning, he presents a picture of life. (Is it possible that "S" has not read it? And if he has, could he possibly have us believe that he was not moved by it?) This poem shows us how a man feels at a high point in his re-lation to nature, nature created and equipped so richly and beauti-fully by Our Lord. In doing this, the poet has described the feelings of a mind moved by beauty as a flood of sunlight washes over him in the early morning. This is what all nature poetry does. It shows the effect of nature on a mind that is in tune with it, and in this way we readers have our eyes opened to the beauty surrounding us. Did I say we readers? Well, excuse me! Not *Spiritus Sanctus & Co*. They just sanctimoniously fold their hands and pray like the Pharisees.

"To write is to see." What a striking definition! To see life, to see everything growing and developing around us and in us—good as well as evil. See it in all its swarming multiplicity—see it and be moved by it. "S" and his compatriots ought to go down on their knees and beg Our Lord to give them eyes that can see life. And if He truly heard their prayer, then their sermons would grip us in a completely different manner than they do nowadays.

In this famous definition of his, Ibsen includes much more than the words reveal at first sight. For by these words he also means to

see with understanding. The one who writes about life, must *understand* life,—that part of life he wishes to portray.

Therefore a person who wishes to write cannot be indifferent to
life nor have an attitude of self-righteous saintliness toward the
phenomena that surround him. He must do like the Ash Lad in the
fairy tales, he must *marvel* at even the most seemingly ordinary,
everyday thing. "All knowledge begins with great wonderment,"
said one of the old Greek wise men. That is to say, with *sympathetic
wonderment.* By this we do not mean that the writer must run out
into the streets and byways and stare about him. We certainly do
not mean that. But when life comes knocking at his door, he cannot deny that he is at home. He must receive life with an open
mind, with a spirit that hungers after understanding. Therefore it
is also necessary for the writer to become completely absorbed in
the material and the people he wishes to tell about. The more intimately he understands them, the better. (It is said about Alfred Ten-
nyson that he smoked eleven pipes for each line in his poem *In
Memoriam.* I tell this for two reasons: one, to show how deeply the
man was absorbed by his literature, the other, to annoy "S," for I bet
he doesn't smoke!)

The greatest failing with so much of what we Norwegian Americans have written is just this, that we have lacked vision. We have
not managed to tear ourselves loose from all the noise and distrac-
tion around us. As a result, the pictures we drew have been unclear.
We have not been strongly enough nor intimately enough moved by
what we are portraying. That is why we do not say it "strikingly
enough." And in that connection, Rønning may be right in one of
his points.

But the writer, the visionary, must have one more ability. His
tongue must be formed in such a way that when he begins to speak
we see exactly what he has seen, we feel with him, and understand
life exactly as he has comprehended and understood it. He must be
able to express "the inexpressible." In other words, he must have
power over language, he must have the beautiful gift of words. I
would like to quote from *Diapsalmata.* (I won't bother to give the
name of the author, "S" wouldn't recognize it anyway.)

"What is a poet? An unhappy person who conceals profound anguish in his heart but whose lips are so formed that as sighs and cries pass over them they sound like beautiful music. . . . And people crowd around the poet and say to him, 'Sing again soon'—in other words, may new suffering torture your soul, and may your lips continue to be formed as before, because your screams would only alarm us, but the music is charming."[63]

When we happen (and this is rare) to find someone of the kind described above, then we have found a great poet. For a person who truly *sees* life, understands *sympathetically* what is seen, and has the gift of beautiful words is a true poet. It is these true poets who have brought into being the great literature of the world. We should not be surprised by this. For a person like this has looked long and carefully, has looked in wonderment, has stared till his eyes watered. And then has placed his keen ear close up to the beating heart of mankind, has listened with great excitement, and has heard inexpressible things.

And then the poet recited, he told the story of what he had heard and seen, giving the world great works of art that will never be destroyed by the ravages of time.

There are books by which the family of man has warmed itself on its journey through time as though seated around a common campfire. Books which perhaps "S" and his spiritual kin cannot recommend from the pulpit, but which they certainly cannot afford to ignore. "Many of these books" says the Norwegian literary researcher Professor [Christen] Collin (I am citing from memory) "were created in the summer of human life. They can be compared to the peat and the coal we burn. Both peat and coal store up the sunlight from long past summers."

When you folks up in Duluth warm yourselves next to a hard coal heater on a crackling cold winter day, it is really the energy of the sun from long past times that you are letting loose and warming yourself by. That is also the way it is with certain great works of secular literature. Even if "S" cannot recommend them from his pulpit, humanity cannot afford to be without them. If these works were suddenly lost, it would be a deeper loss to the household of humanity than would the loss of all the ore in northern Minnesota, and in the whole rest of the world too.

Now I hope "S" does not misunderstand and think that I am comparing what we Norwegian-American writers have managed to create with the works I mentioned above. I am not that depraved. But I will just remind "S" that when the history of Norwegians in America is studied in the future, then our poor products will be one of the most important sources for these researchers. And they probably won't even look at "S"'s sermons.

4

Literature reflects life, reproduces it in condensed form, concentrated, so to speak. We can sit down with a work of literature and in a few hours we have lived an entire lifetime, perhaps even more than one. Without literature we would know very little of life. But with literature we can experience in two hours what would otherwise take an entire lifetime. This phenomenon may explain why a quiet, reserved person can have greater insight into people than an extrovert who is always surrounded by others. Just as the still water of the fjord reflects the mountains around it, so literature reflects life. *Literature is the mirror of humanity.*

No other form of education can take the place of literature. Not sociology, or economics, not any of the social sciences, no, not even the study of history can teach us so much about life, give us such great insight into it.

Of course it is true that all knowledge is useful—for some people. For an American, for example, it is both useful and interesting to understand the racial composition of our society, or the principles on which our taxation system is based, or the economic law of supply and demand, and many similar topics. But all of these subjects treat only external things. Of course it is interesting for us to know that forty different nationalities (or is it more?) now live in the city of New York. But it is ten times more imperative for us to understand what these nationalities treasure in their hearts. For if we understand what these people think, *how* they think, if we know their hopes and dreams, their ideals, their characteristics, in other words, if we understand their psychology, then we will also understand what kind of influence these groups are having on this society which is now in the making. But only authors and poets can reveal these things to us with any clarity. Does "S" not understand this?

But "S" and his like don't care about literature. And it is not only the neglected homeless waif we call Norwegian-American literature that they despise. They are not interested in literature at all. For if they were, they would care enough about Norwegian-American literature at least to read it before condemning it. Unfortunately, their spiritual poverty is spreading to others. Their job is to be beacons of light, but they have no light. They cannot awaken interest in their fellow men for something they themselves are not interested in. And they care nothing about literature. In that, they suffer an incalculable loss, the loss of connection to life itself. They become narrow-minded and materialistic, and often rather pompous. Even worse, they lose intimate friendship with humanity itself. They don't hear the speech of time, or the song of their kin. For them the only reality is the present moment and "the coming day." That's why their preaching is so shallow, so lacking in sincere humanity, so often filled with mere pretentious nonsense or sentimental emotionalism.

Let me explain a little more closely what I mean—the winter nights are long, and you aren't as busy as you think you are.

As we read the three great Russians, Tolstoy, Turgenev, and Dostoyevsky, and after a while as we plunge ever deeper into their writing, we inevitably feel that the Slavic people are our brothers. Perhaps they are a bit more slow-moving than we are, they suffer from more consuming passions, feel stronger doubts, have a melancholy that is more musical than ours, and yet the more we learn to understand them the more strongly we feel our brotherhood with them.

The same is true for authors from other nationalities and from other times. For example, if we read *Ecclesiastes* and follow it with the work of the Persian poet Omar Khayyám, we find the views of life astonishingly similar. This is so in spite of the fact that the authors of these two works are descendants of completely different peoples and lived separated in time by perhaps 1,400 years or more.

This shows how intimately the study of literature leads us into humanity itself. On the other hand, if we neglect this study our lives become like small, isolated puddles of water, cut off from the endless, ceaseless stream of life. Without inflow or outflow our lives soon dry up. We lose contact with life and then there isn't much left to be interested in. Yes, what is there except for life?——Just to tease "S" I will quote some verses about this endless continuity of life—they were even written by a Norwegian American.

> I sat one day, by the Stream of Life
> and watched it flowing by;
> it quietly ran or thundered along,
> but carried me not away.
>
> There was a sight which caught my soul:
> All the ships so tall and proud!
> They skimmed along before the wind,
> here and there away they sailed.
>
> And some boats came and some boats went—
> more than language has words.
> They tacked 'round the headlands and out the fjords,
> sailed over the great wide world.
>
> I stared up at them till my eyes grew tired,
> but no end of them came into sight;
> even after the day sank into dark night
> the stream ran on and on.
>
> I've been rocked in the cradle of the deep;
> had to find out how far it went!
> And now I have traveled so far on land
> that I know the Stream has no end![64]

Does anyone think I am putting too great an emphasis on literature and the study of literature? I don't think so. Is there an educated man who has not felt the creative power hidden in great works of literature? As he sits reading, his pulse begins to beat faster, a hidden power stirs within him, a strength that he didn't know he had is set in motion. "Poets are the unacknowledged legislators of the world," says the great poet Shelley. This is true, but a great author is even more than that. He also the singer and the seer of humankind, its truth-sayer, priest, and prophet. What we ordinary mortals sense only dimly, only unconsciously—that is what the poet sees in the strongest light. Whether it is ugliness or beauty, joy or sorrow, or righteous fervor, the sublime soul of the poet trumpets it for us with painful clarity. He proclaims to us those things which we truth-seekers only dimly perceive. "Good company gives much pleasure" according to an old saying. We are richly blessed when we associate with the best minds through literature.

Truly great literature does two things. It reflects life, and it brings forth and enriches life in the mind of the person who associates with it. Let me now use simple language and a few examples to prove this.

It is possible for a botanist to examine what is growing in a field and from this ascertain the composition of the soil below. And that is not all he can discover, for the plants also tell him about climatic conditions. The botanist does not need to visit a country in order to find information on its soil and climate, all he needs is to know what grows there. It is the same for an intelligent person with literary interests. By studying the literature of a country, he can come to understand quite fully the cultural life of that country, its political, social, ethical, and religious life. By looking at literature, we can see life.

Let me illustrate this thought with a few examples.

Some years after the beginning of the period we call the Renaissance, educated people over there in Europe enjoyed reliving the life of ancient Greece and Rome. They acted like a bunch of children let loose in a big room filled with wonderful toys. Within this room they looked around and played and had a good time, until they matured to the point where they could create history. All this happened in spite of the fact that the time period they were reliving, parts of it anyway, was several thousand years earlier! We children of the twentieth century can read *The Iliad* and *The Odyssey* (and there are good English and Norwegian translations of both these works; Garborg's translation of *The Odyssey* is one of the greatest works of poetry I have read) and literally relive the time of Homer.

The fact that we are 3000 years distant from that time doesn't make a speck of difference. The Old Norse eddas and sagas do the same thing for us in regard to the Viking period. That is how *fully* the study of literature can lead us into humanity itself!

Let us take other examples.

We can sit down with Jane Austen's novel *Pride and Prejudice* and get a clear picture of society in England 140 years ago. Bjørnson's peasant tales paint living pictures of Norwegian country life around 1860. In spite of all the uproarious wit in Holberg's comedies, and the outrageous exaggeration of flaws and shortcomings, they still give a clear picture of the spiritual physiognomy of the time. We could keep on giving examples like this endlessly.

What these great portrayers of humanity have done in past times is still being done today by our authors and poets.

Here, for example, we Minnesotans have been going about for the last several years, carefree and nonchalant, thanking the good Lord that we are so much better than people elsewhere in the world. Then along comes this fellow Sinclair Lewis! He holds up a picture in front of our faces and bids us look at it. As we look at it we are mortally insulted! We see ourselves in this picture—just as this man has seen us; and our sinful image is so pitifully amusing. We stand there staring at the picture; we scold and we spit and we curse. Some do just like "S" in his piety: thank God there are so few who read books! But this thanks is rather misplaced, for there are many who are reading *Main Street* and *Babbitt*.

Now these books are not great works of literature. Nevertheless, they will live because they give a psychologically true portrayal of human society. This picture is of course strongly exaggerated and distorted, and yet the main lines of it are strikingly accurate. The self-righteous smugness and the dull inanity are easily recognizable. And see, here comes "S" in *Duluth Skandinav* and proves how strikingly true the portrait is for us and our people.

Let us go back and take another look at the thought I touched on a while ago, that literature has a powerful influence on a society in the making, on the society that will appear fully formed in the future. (Strangely enough, "S" seems to sense that this might be the case when he says: "Has the world been made better in these latter years with all this modern literature?—Has it not rather become worse?"—He seems to believe that it has become "worse."—But there has never been as much *preaching* as there is now, both from the pulpit and on the street corners. There has never before been such *extensive activity on the part of the church* as there is now, and even so the world has become "worse." What does "S" have to say about that?)

It is well known in the history of literature that both the minstrels and the troubadours contributed much toward keeping knighthood alive. In like manner, we cannot deny that right down to our own time literature has done its part toward making war seem desirable. The epic glorification of battle and war in literature has contributed strongly to keeping alive this most vile of all the destructive forces that have ever ravaged humanity. Those who are familiar with the period of the enlightenment also know what a powerful ally rationalism found in the literature of the day.

But let me present a few examples which are better known.

Sursum Corda!—Up with your hearts! sang Bjørnson to the youth of Norway in the 1850s, 60s and 70s, just as the romantic movement was growing rapidly in that country. The youth of Norway awoke and looked around in great wonder, and Bjørnson became their prophet. Over in England the prisons were in a wretched condition. The judicial system was old fashioned, out-of-date. But then Charles Dickens began shaking things up in his novels. Some of his works cast a garish light on both the prisons and the judicial system. Who can forget the famous case of *Jarndyce vs Jarndyce* in *Bleak House*? The tale of this case sounds completely comical to us; and we laugh heartily when we read it. But Englishmen in Dickens' time did not laugh. They looked at the picture he had drawn, and became angry and ashamed. And with that they went to work and corrected the situation. And finally I would like to remind you of Harriet Beecher Stowe's novel *Uncle Tom's Cabin*. It is far from being a great work of art; some knowledgeable people might not even classify it as literature. Nevertheless, this novel hastened the American Civil War more strongly than any other factor. (No doubt "S" knows that there were Norwegian pastors in America at that time who taught from the pulpit that the institution of slavery was established by God.)

The influence of literature on society works most strongly through the individual. Here again I will shed light on the matter by giving several examples.

When Fridtjof Nansen departed from his ship *Fram* up in the polar regions and set off toward the North Pole with only one companion, he went through hardships and suffering which we ordinary mortals can scarcely imagine. Nansen himself reported that on this memorable journey it was the admonishing and fiery words of Ibsen's *Brand* which gave him the ability to continue.

Here is testimony from Charles Darwin. Toward the end of his life he spoke these memorable words.

"If I had my life to live over again, I would have made it a rule to read some poetry and listen to some music at least once every week; for perhaps the parts of my brain now atrophied would thus have been kept active through use. The loss of these tastes is a loss of happiness, and may possibly be injurious to the intellect, and, more probably, to the moral character by enfeebling the emotional part of my nature."

Finally, I will include a confession by the English poet Coleridge. He says of the poets of his youth:

"For the writings of these mystics acted in no slight degree to prevent my mind from being imprisoned within the outline of any single dogmatic system. They contributed to keep alive the heart within the head.——If they were too often a moving cloud of smoke to me by day, yet they were always a pillar of fire throughout the night during my wanderings through the wilderness of doubt, and enabled me to skirt, without crossing, the sandy deserts of utter unbelief."[65]

5

Let's take a look at the qualities of literature that give it such a strong influence on life.

In order for a piece of writing to qualify as a work of literature it must affect the reader in one of three ways. It must either 1) awaken a sense of beauty in him, or 2) ignite his ethical consciousness—

either to enthusiasm or indignation. And 3) all great literature inspires the reader—though naturally only the reader with an open mind!

I will take the last quality first; that way I can say what I want to most easily and quickly.

Inspiration is hard to define. We can talk about it, but it is difficult to define it precisely. Inspiration is the magical power of a work—the sorcery in it. After we ordinary earthly mortals come in contact with it we are not the same people that we were before. A spark from above has entered into us. And even though our inert substance has a hard time catching fire, the spark still lives in us. The heat from it begins to work, in some people over a long period of time. The Norwegian poet Welhaven has immortalized the idea of inspiration in the poem *Ganymedes* (in *Digtets Aand* [The poetic spirit] it appears in a somewhat different form), and I am positive that this poem will live as long as the least shred of Norwegian language still exists. Readers often say of a particular book or poem that "it moved me." No one knows how this expression came about. It must have sprung out of the minds of the people themselves. And it is a splendid expression. What do we really mean by this picturesque speech? We imagine that the reader has touched something, or perhaps it would be more correct to say that an invisible power has touched the reader, has "stirred" something inside him. This is what we call inspiration.

And yet inspiration is not some special quality separate from the other two, rather, it is intimately connected to both.

Inspiration springs from clarity in the poet's mind, from greatness, from power, from majesty, from breadth. These are combined with the "magic" he uses to get us to see what he sees and feel what he feels.

Perhaps one could define inspiration as the first conception of the fundamental idea, the basic motif in a poem. But I think that is wrong. For the first conception is surely only the result of the poet's vision. He contemplated until he understood,—that is to say, until he thought he understood. Because he understood, he wasn't *able* to keep silent any longer. The true poet writes because he must write. A force drives him. He must communicate his emotions to others. It is the clarity in his vision and the emotion in his soul at the sight he has seen, and his way of telling it to us, that "stirs" us. This is what we call inspiration.

Some of us have felt a work of literature ignite a sense of beauty in us. We can be sitting reading a book in the poorest, the darkest, the most miserable surroundings and we forget time and place, hunger and misery. We are transported to another world, a world of supernatural beauty. Many of us have experienced this strange phenomenon. There is magic in words!

"A literary work must first and foremost be beautiful," said the romantics. Beauty above all! I cannot discuss this statement here, it would lead too far afield. I will only point out that no other branch of the arts contains so much beauty as literature. Indeed, no other branch of the arts, with the possible exception of music, is as widely cultivated.

The "good and kind gods" have granted to some poets a "divine gift," have equipped them with a supernatural ability. And this ability is such that no matter what they touch, no matter what they tell or sing about, the tale or the song is beautiful. Even the most ordinary things, yes, even the ugly and the loathsome become beautiful through their magic touch.

In order to convince the reader of what I am saying, I must have permission to present some evidence.

It seems as though Bjørnson must have said to himself one day: "Well, now it is time to expand the bounds of drama. We must see if we can't get it to have more effective repercussions on life than it has in the past!" And with that he sat down and wrote a play about the most prosaic, the most unpoetic theme under the sun: about money and business. This piece he wrote is unusually rich in beauty. With it, Bjørnson made history in world literature.[66]

The hero in Selma Lagerlöf's *Banlyst (The Outlaw)* is supposed to have eaten human flesh. For that he was excommunicated from human society. This is surely no lovely topic, yet you will have to search far and wide for a more beautiful novel.

The plot in Thomas Hardy's *Tess of the d'Urbervilles* is far from beautiful. Actually it is raw and brutal. But as we sit and listen to Hardy tell the story, we are bewitched by the beauty in the tale.

As another example, let's take the story in Edgar Allen Poe's poem "The Raven." If we analyze it, it is downright disgusting, even repulsive. But many readers shed tears over Poe's treatment of it.

Let me mention one more example (there are thousands upon thousands to choose from!). The English poet Thomas Hood has written a poem called "The Bridge of Sighs." The action in this poem in its bare form is this: a fallen woman has taken her own life by jumping from a bridge. Later her body is found, dirty and disgusting. It is hard to imagine an uglier or more abhorrent theme for a lyric poem. And yet from this story Hood has fashioned the most musical, the most melodic poem in the English language. Welhaven has treated a similar theme in his poem "Sjøfuglen" (The Sea Bird), but in a rather different manner. Welhaven's poem is also rich with beauty.

Now if all that I have said above is true—and I would like to see the person who could disprove it,—then I cannot understand how so many people can afford to go without books. I cannot understand how a human soul can live without beauty. I have the feeling that they are not really living, just vegetating. The wise man in the *Koran* once said: "If you have two loaves of bread, then you ought to sell one loaf and buy yourself a rose with the money, for your soul also needs nourishment." (This is cited from memory.)

The great realists, and the minor ones too, do not acknowledge this basic law of the romantics, that "a work of literature must first and foremost be beautiful." The realists have put another law in its place. They say: "A piece of literature must first and foremost be *true*." Truth to the realist is synonymous with morality. That which is untrue is immoral. The poet—the author—must tell the truth. Woe unto the one who lies about life! "A work of literature is just a slice of nature" (= a slice of life) "seen through a temperament," said Zola. According to the realist, what is untrue is always immoral, no matter how beautiful it is, and what is true is always moral, no matter how repulsive it is.

I cannot discuss this issue here now. It will just have to stand. I will only point out the fact that all works of literature have a moral essence, just like all human beings. Just by being around some people we are ennobled. They don't need to preach to us! We become good because they are good. And there are others whose company has the opposite effect. They don't preach either. Nevertheless they corrupt most of the people they come into close contact with.

And it is the same with books. I will give several examples. Read Boccaccio's *Decameron*, Balzac's *Short Stories*, Shakespeare's *Venus and Adonis*, and certain episodes in Hamsun's works and you will feel sensuality rising like an acrid odor from the pages of the book. On certain minds this odor has a titillating effect and wakens their sensuality. That is why some books can have a harmful effect on some people.

But then right afterward take the following series of works: Tolstoy's *Kreutzer Sonata*, Graham Phillips' *Susan Lenox*, Jonas Lie's *When the Sun Goes Down*, and Ibsen's *Ghosts*, and you will feel the difference.

And the remarkable thing is that both these series treat approximately the same sins. The major difference is that in the first series sin is not really sin. Especially to the uncritical reader it is first-class epic and lyrical material. And the result in the reader's mind can become comical, and for some readers even downright beautiful! But in the second series, sin is truly sin. Sin there is ugly, vile, and as fatal as pestilent air for all human life.

I could easily end this "observation" here. However, I would like to add just a few more words. The good and the beautiful is such a rich topic. So I would like to add a few remarks on these two forces—not in connection with books, but in the world around us.

The first thing I am compelled to say is that the world is full of beauty. We can question whether there is anything in nature that is not beautiful if only a sympathetic mind recognizes it and understands it. You see beauty wherever you turn your eye. In the form and color of the clouds, as well as in their swift course across the high vault of the heavens. You hear it in the singing of the wind through the branches of the trees, in its humming in the flowers and leaves of the meadow. And when the storm grows, tearing up trees by their roots and sweeping away people's homes, well, there is beauty in that storm too. Is not such might beautiful? Power can fascinate, "*Strength can bewitch.*"

And sun and sunlight! Look at it in the morning, look at in the evening, and in the strength of the day, when it gives of its abundance to all life! And then take the moon, that old scoundrel. He has inspired some of the most beautiful love poems in the world, even though the old fellow up there is just a big icicle beaming with borrowed glory. And yet how beautiful he is when he stands up there scattering his glittering silver haze down upon longing souls.

Look at the wide open expanses of the prairie in the fullness of summer and admire the bulging crops of autumn. Observe it when winter's desolation takes over!

What can one say about the forest lake when it hums its happiest song along the shore on a summer evening!

I have not yet mentioned flowers and animals and people—the loveliest of God's creatures! And the sea, "the mighty sea," and the mountains, and the high blue roof of the sky, which the longing mind so often seeks! Who can ever manage in song or tale to coax from these *all* their beauty? From the first morning of creation the poets have sung of them, and have not yet tired of doing so. And these songs are still just as beautiful and just as treasured.———No, let me stop; for it is impossible to *count* the beauty in nature, much less show it to others!

You can find beauty in life, perhaps to just as great a degree as in nature. There is beauty in sorrow as well as in happiness. Even pain can be beautiful. And joy? Yes, cannot joy be lovely? Have you heard a healthy child laugh!——And strength, and longing, and all the good in a human heart, yes, who can name all that is beautiful in people?

Now let us talk about the good! That too is as universal as beauty. And do you not always find the good where you find the beautiful? There is good in every child of man. Just reach out your hand in all earnestness and you will see that you will get a reply. It is harder to define the goodness in humans, for it varies in form and color with the children of each generation and nation.

You find goodness in other creatures too. Have you seen a cow licking its calf? And the little thrush giving food to its young? And the drop of dew quenching the thirst of the meadow flower?

Yes, even lifeless nature is filled with goodness. Is it not good of the night to sink its impenetrable veil over the strife of the day, and over all the wounds received in battle? And if night did not come, we would have no stars to twinkle over our lives!

And what about winter? Does it not bring rest to the fruitfulness of the earth?

Goodness is untiring and eternal!

Unfortunately, it is true that the sated mind, the lazy soul sees neither goodness nor beauty.

6

The job of a pastor is a difficult one, and perhaps more so now than in any previous time. If we really believe that the world is evil, that even from childhood people are evil, that there is an eternal battle for human souls, and that the pastor must be the guide to "the brighter pastures," then it is a given that his duty will be extremely difficult.

Our time is tragic, neurotic, preoccupied, doubting, frivolous in the extreme, extroverted, sick with self-indulgence such as no other time has ever been. Neuroses are common in all levels of society. This makes it so much more difficult for a pastor to capture the minds of his congregation. And capture them he must, if he is to have any chance of winning a hearing in their hearts for his message.

What kind of man is needed to preach the gospel in such a time? First and foremost, "a child of God," many will say.

Well, of course. This is so obvious that it would not even occur to me to mention it. For I assume that any truth-loving person believes in the cause he preaches. Otherwise that person is false. Naturally it is particularly important that a pastor be sincere. So I will not discuss this aspect of the matter. But not all children of God are suited to be pastors!

And now I will make the perverse claim that the pastor must also be something of a writer. I do not mean by this that he has to write poems and novels and plays. But it is no mere coincidence that so many of the leading pastors of our own and other nations have also had great literary talent. On the contrary, it is inevitable. And some of the greatest pastors from the time of Paul, to Luther, and to our own time have been great writers.

When we examine this more closely, it becomes clear at once why this must be so. I said earlier that a poet, in order to write, first had to learn to see, to look at life sympathetically and with a sense of wonder, so that he could understand what he saw. In addition, he must have the gift of words. If you think about this, you will immediately exclaim: "Yes, but these are precisely the gifts a pastor must have in order to be a good shepherd to his flock!" And I would reply: "That is correct. It precisely these gifts that a pastor *ought* to have. A pastor ought to *see* and *understand* life; and in addition, out of the secret essence of his personality, he ought to be able to speak about what he has seen and understood."

I see a great crowd running to attack me. I hear them coming at a quick march. For what I have just said is heresy to them. Well, "take it easy, good people; I wish to speak. Later we can do battle!" These dear zealous ones will attack me with their "one thing needful." Their fervor reveals tremendous spiritual poverty, and is completely misplaced. I am in complete agreement with them about "the one thing needful"; I believe in it with what little power of faith I possess. But I would like to pose a question. Who is the pastor supposed to preach "the one thing needful" to? Is it to the air? Or to the pews and the walls in the church? Or is it to God? No, it must be to life, to people, to tired minds, to weary hearts, to indifferent, hungering, longing souls, to the cheerful and to the world-weary, to the sinner and to the simple-minded person who is scarcely aware of sin.

Even a child can understand that for the pastor to speak so that people can understand, he must himself understand people. The deeper and more intimate his knowledge of humanity is, the greater chance he has of reaching into the minds he is addressing—not only in his preaching, but in all of his work as a pastor. That he himself possesses "the one thing needful" is not enough. If he is to make people understand, then he must also understand people. If possible, he ought to be able to say "Nothing human is foreign to me."

Yet this is no easy matter, to learn to know people. The only one in all of humankind who ever completely managed to do this was The Son of Man. He accomplished this perfectly.

But He, Jesus our Savior, is also the greatest poet of mankind, even though He Himself, as far as we know, never wrote a single line. No one has composed a line about life as beautifully as He has. No one has solved the mysteries and problems of life as perfectly as He has. No one has put so much meaning into human words as He has. Go "and see!"

The reason no one else has managed this to the extent that He did is no doubt that their compassion has not been great enough. They have not felt strongly enough about life; they lacked a great sense of wonder. It is remarkable what compassion Jesus had for the seeking, the hungry, the poor in spirit, for the really terrible sinners! And how mild His words were when He chastised them!

Remarkable too how strong His indignation was when He encountered the self-satisfied, the conceited, the handsome, the respectable, and even more, the yes-people and jolly good fellows! These He whipped until raw red stripes appeared. But His noble face was distorted in pain—so great was His compassion for these people. He pronounced the death penalty over the city that repudiated Him, but He wept over it!

As I have already pointed out, there is no mirror that reflects life with the clarity of poetry, of literature. Therefore it is a powerful aid to the pastor who uses it correctly. It is one of his most important allies in that it teaches him to understand the spirit of the time, in other words, the minds he is addressing. A pastor least of all can afford to cut himself off from literature, unless he himself is a great psychologist, that is, a poet. And if he is, he wouldn't attempt to cut himself off, he would accept with gratitude the help that literature offers him.

Let me tell of an experience I have had myself. It will illustrate clearly what I am trying to explain.

One Sunday morning here in the church in Northfield Pastor Kildahl came to the pulpit. After having read the text for the day and the prayer, he leaned forward on the pulpit and began telling Jonas Lie's magical tale "Jo i Sjøholmene." Calmly and at great length he recited the main points of this tale. And then he began preaching about what it means to sell your soul to the devil—a good theme for a sermon in our day and age! Kildahl analyzed the soul exactly as Jonas Lie had presented it in the tale. And you can well believe there was some preaching that day! Nor is this so remark-able either, for here two great minds were working to simplify and illustrate the same basic theme.

That is one of the few sermons I will never forget.

Now there is not even the slightest hint, not one iota of "the one thing needful" in this tale. It deals only with "worldly matters." Yet not only do I still remember this sermon, but I went straight home from church and reread "Jo i Sjøholmene." All because a great mind shed light on this story, made me understand it with much greater clarity than ever before. Because of Kildahl's sermon I will never for-get that story by Jonas Lie.

I am sure I will be misunderstood in what I now will be so bold as to say, but I will say it anyway. It is wrong that our pastors do not make greater use of literature than they do. Furthermore, it is dis-astrous for them and for our people that they know little or noth-ing of Norwegian-American literature. We get all the news about our people from coast to coast in our newspapers, reports about every quarrel and issue come from that same source. But we know nothing about those issues preying most deeply on the minds of our people. We hear nothing of those, and no wonder, for only lit-erature can portray the deep life of the soul.

Now I admit that the picture presented by literature can some-times be rather unclear. Yet even when the lines are distorted, the portrait may be completely convincing. Take for example many of Baumann's poems, or Buslett's story "Og de solgte ut" ["And they sold out"], or Ager's "Han saa liten og uanselig ut" ["He Looked Small and Insignificant"], "To tomme hænder" ["Two Empty Hands"], "Løst fra alt" ["Torn Loose from Everything"], "John McEstee's vuggesang" [. . . cradle song"], and others, Thor Helge-sen's "En begravelse i et norsk-amerikansk nybygge" ["A Funeral in a Norwegian-American Settlement"], Strømme's *Hvorledes Halvor blev prest [How Halvor Became a Minister]*, Simon Johnson's *Et nyt rike [In the New Kingdom]* and *Fire fortællinger* [Four stories], Dorthea Dahl's *Returning Home*, or Wist's *Jonasville*, or Ristad's poems, or cer-tain sections of [Jon] Norstog's dramas, those which are addressed to us, or some of [Sigurd] Folkestad's lyric and some of his epic poems. Take these as examples. Some draw moving, true pictures, some are very beautiful. Many would be well suited to use as illustrations in a sermon.

The majority of our pastors don't care about Norwegian-American literature. They know nothing about it. They feel no need to become familiar with it. But there are no other depictions of the people they seek to serve. This, in my opinion, is a part of our spiritual poverty.

To date, the clergy have been our largest and strongest cultural force precisely because they are just about the only educated people—or perhaps more correctly, the only people with a higher education—who come into intimate contact with our people.

It is natural that people will look to the pastors for guidance in determining what is valuable. One cannot expect people to be interested in anything that the pastors don't care in the least about.

This relationship between our pastors and our literature is quite inexplicable. Most of our authors are idealists of the first water. Some of them have devoted their whole lives to the temperance movement. Others have given that cause both time and money they could ill afford. To give this much to the welfare of the people is surely to "perceive the ideal behind the deed."

Our authors have always been in the vanguard in the work of enlightening the people. No others have spoken so warmly about the fourth commandment as they have. During the World War, some of them were in danger of being blacklisted because they were not *pro* this or that, but were so innocent that they believed war was fratricide. In short, you can go down the entire list from Buslett, who was the first, to Professor [Carl E.] Nordberg, who has spoken last, and you can scarcely accuse any of them of being self-serving. And every single one of them is as poor as a church mouse.

In their writing, without exception, they have championed that which according to their light was good and beautiful. They have preached against sin! In spite of this, the majority of our pastors have ignored them. And we must say that this is something of a phenomenon! One would have thought that our pastors, as educated people, would have had enough intellectual curiosity to become acquainted with what our literary men and women were

peddling, and for that reason alone would have familiarized themselves with it. But they have not done this. I repeat: this is a part of
our spiritual poverty!

While I am talking about the pastors, I have to beg their forgiveness: not for what I just said here, but for something I said in part 2
of this series. I made "S" into a pastor, and I now understand that
that is wrong, and an insult to the profession.

In a later issue of *Duluth Skandinav* "S" has an article about the
same matter, and there he makes several statements that are so remarkably unintelligent that no educated person could possibly
have written them. That is immediately apparent. I will quote a few
of them:

"And where have our Norwegian-American authors placed God
in their poems and stories? How beautifully they have sometimes
praised the seasons—fall, spring, summer, winter, Christmas and
other holidays, father and mother, sunrise and sunset,—the world
and the heavens; but which of them has praised Him who created
everything, who has given us all?"

No pastor could have written this. I am sure this statement will
live on in Norwegian-American newspaper polemics. It is too classic to die.

And now I must ask this person who calls himself "S" a question.
Not in any attempt at humor or arrogance, but as one who is seeking the answer to a clever riddle. What should a person praise God
for, if not for his works? Can one praise God for anything else?

Let me make this question clearer by way of a little anecdote.
Let's suppose that "S" really is a pastor. Let's further suppose that
one day he preached a sermon that really moved the congregation.
As people came out of church they said "That was a wonderful sermon! It did me so much good. I will never forget this Sunday!"

Who was the congregation actually praising? Would "S" rather
have them say "Yes, today 'S' was really something! Our pastor is a
first class fellow. No one can beat him." I don't know if "S" understands, but I can't make my meaning any clearer.

I have to take one more statement by "S" from the same issue.
There are others just as good, however: "We have seen that Professor Rølvaag has convinced himself that the Norwegian people in

America had a much different interest in reading and literature in earlier times—yes, that people who remember that time speak warmly of it whenever they think of it. And in contrast to that time—the spiritual poverty of today—nowadays people don't read literature and have no interest in it.—But I invite the reader to take the yearly reports from the Norwegian Church in America of 30-40-50 years ago and then compare them with the ones from the last years. Professor Rølvaag, what growth, what development!"

Well, I just bet that when "S" wrote that, he figured that now he had really struck a blow! And not surprisingly, for this statement bears the marks of immortality. Actually, it was this statement that convinced me that "S" is not a pastor, but rather a blacksmith or perhaps even a milkmaid. For by "growth" and "development" "S" means, according to his own mode of reasoning, "growth in the life of God" and the advancement of "the one thing needful." Yet it is an ingenious idea, to measure the progress of such things by the thickness of a yearly report! Suppose that the increased thickness of the report had to do with the way it was prepared by the secretary—that is certainly possible. Or that cheaper and thicker paper was used? Or larger type? And there have surely been a few newcomers drifting over the Atlantic Ocean these past fifty years. Occasionally several synods have gone together on one yearly report. But it is unthinkable that such little things as this have anything to do with the matter!

I really wonder if our good Lord saves up these yearly reports, and if it is the lists of names in *them* he will use?

"S"'s piece is so full of such statements that a saint could be tempted to take them out and hold them up for examination, but I won't do that. I wouldn't even have mentioned "S" again, except that I felt I had to beg the clergy nicely for forgiveness. Now I have done that, and I feel much relieved.

And now I will say, as did the great skald when he wrote his last line, "Thank you!"

SIMPLE REFLECTIONS ON
the Name Change

PREFACE

At the annual meeting of the Norwegian Lutheran Church in America in Fargo, North Dakota, in 1918, a motion was made to remove the word Norwegian from the name of the church. An intense debate about this issue soon broke out in our Norwegian-American newspapers.

In the course of the winter of 1919, *Lutheraneren* posed five questions that the editors believed would shed light on the whole issue. *Lutheraneren* invited Dr. J.N. Kildahl to write in favor of the change; I was appointed to present the opposition point of view.

The questions that were put forth were these:

1. How quickly ought the transition to happen, and what principles should determine the speed? ("Transition" here means the transition to the exclusive use of English as the language of the church.)
2. To what degree should the name of a church reflect its origins?
3. To what extent does the name of a church affect its health and well-being?
4. What does history teach us with regard to how quickly (in which generation) the Norwegian language ceases to be the language of the heart?
5. To what extent is the mission work of a church among people of other national origins harmful or beneficial to that church?

Below, I will repeat, for the most part in the same words, what I wrote in *Lutheraneren* at that time. Here and there I have made a few additions to make the meaning clearer, but most of what follows was published in issues 18, 19, and 20 of *Lutheraneren* for 1920. Instead of repeating the questions, I will refer to them by number in the same order as they are given above.

1

First and foremost I must state that the answers I give here do not represent any movement or any party line. They reflect only my own individual view of people and conditions, of problems and trends, and must therefore be charged entirely to me. Next I must bring to your attention the fact that at least two of these questions are impossible to treat exhaustively in a newspaper article, for they touch upon so many issues, have so many deep roots that it would take quite a different treatment to clarify them completely. These answers will therefore be somewhat incomplete, in spite of their apparent length.

The first question concerns the transition. And by "transition" the editor here means the gradual diminishing of the use of Norwegian as the language of preaching, and a gradual increase in the use of English until Norwegian is no longer heard either in the sermon or in the hymns. It must be made clear that here we are only discussing the language of the church. I know there are people among us who really believe that we ought to get away from all use of Norwegian as a means of communication at school and in the home; but fortunately we don't often meet such narrow-mindedness. Yet it is unbelievable what even educated people can come up with. For example, I am dismayed that someone could stand up in a public meeting and apologize for having been confirmed in Norwegian, for not having received all religious instruction in English, or for having learned Norwegian before learning English.

However, I am not accusing the editors of *Lutheraneren* of being reactionaries! I just want to take the opportunity here to say it is unthinkable that a time will come when Norwegian *is not* used as a vehicle of culture and education among a rather large number of Americans with Norwegian roots. Even the warmest supporters of a rapid transition in regard to the language of the church surely believe this and will work for it too.

The question is this: *How rapidly should the transition to English as a language of the church take place?* The answer seems to me to be quite straightforward and obvious: as long as it is possible to reach into the heart of a single person *better* by preaching in Norwegian, then it is the simple duty of the church to use Norwegian as a means of communication in so far as that person is concerned. Please don't misunderstand and accuse me of wanting all services in Norwegian just for the sake of this person! I did not say all of them, or half of them, or a third, or a fourth. I only maintained that Norwegian must be used for this one individual. Dividing church services between two languages is often a very difficult matter, and demands the greatest thought and understanding, and much Christian love—toward both English and Norwegian! But division there must be, whether within the same congregation or into two congregations.

Accordingly, the "transition" cannot be completed until at least one generation has grown up after the last immigrant has stepped ashore on our coast. Until such time the Gospel ought to be, and no doubt will be, preached in Norwegian in America.

I am assuming as a self-evident truth that the main task of our church in this country is first and foremost to take care of the people of Norwegian descent. There is no other church body in this country as well qualified to do this as ours. If our church does not care for our people, then what church will? In connection with another question I will attempt to show that the work of our church in the future will be for the most part restricted to this task.

It is painful to see how our church has neglected our own people in this country. And this is true not only of our church in this country, but also of the church in Norway. It is now almost 100 years since emigration from Norway began. During this time, a substantial number of Norwegians have found their way across the Atlantic Ocean. Most of them were young people. Most of them had been baptized and confirmed by Norwegian pastors. These pastors had blessed them with the sign of the cross in baptism and had instructed them in confirmation in order to strengthen them to service under the resplendent banner of the cross. This was beautifully done. Indeed, it was done so well that one would assume that these pastors in Norway would continue to care about these young people. But have they done so? Have they shown any interest in the young people they confirmed who later went out into the world to seek their fortune? No, they have not. One would think that pastors in Norway might continue to care for these young people whom they baptized and confirmed. If the pastor truly was a shepherd to this flock, he would have accompanied these young people as they went out into life. It would have been an easy matter for a pastor in Norway to accompany these young people to America! Almost all who left intended to come to one or another of the Norwegian settlements in America. And all such settlements have a congregation and a pastor. It would have been easy for the pastors in Norway to get lists of names and addresses of their colleagues in Norwegian America. If the pastors in Norway had had the slightest bit of initiative and love, they would have attempted to guide the young emigrants—and the older ones too—to the pastors in the Norwegian areas of America where the emigrant was heading anyway. The pastor in Norway could have informed the pastor in America, could have written and said "Here is a young man or a young woman who is traveling to your parish. I have baptized and confirmed him. Therefore he is dear to me. And now you must watch over him, for I no longer can. Now you must care for him so that he does not 'damage his soul!' " How many pastors have sent such letters across the Atlantic? Not very many. But if they were living the Gospel they preached, was it not their plain duty to do this? Were they not absolutely obliged to do this?

What is our church over here doing for the newcomer? One would think that our pastors would do what their colleagues in Norway have neglected. Most of the newcomers are from country districts in Norway and from the working class in the towns; that is exactly the type of people the church should have a good chance to recruit. We can assume that the annual normal emigration from Norway varies between twelve and fourteen thousand. That is about the number our government will allow into the country (spring of 1922). And the statisticians over in Norway think that this rate will soon be normal.

Now you would think that the church over here, our Norwegian Lutheran Church, would place special emphasis on recruiting new members from these twelve or fourteen thousand immigrants.

That would surely be a nice source of inflow. One can scarcely imagine a better mission field. But do they do it? No. They let this stream run wherever it will. Seemingly no one cares about the newcomer.

I know to the letter the arguments that "Brother Consideration" will make against this. He will say that since the newcomer, the immigrant, has been baptized and confirmed, he should himself seek out the church. Such talk is just as thoughtless and superficial as "Brother Consideration" himself. The newcomer has all the shyness towards strangers that is characteristic of Norwegians. He cannot help this, any more than the Irishman can help that it is natural for him to elbow his way in and easily adjust to all kinds of complex situations. And so the newcomer drifts about among us like a stranger among strangers. He doesn't know us, and we aren't so sure about him. Several of our pastors have stated as an article of faith that today's immigrants are impossible people. They have no interest in Christianity. How did this conviction arise? From the fact that the newcomer so seldom seeks out the church for himself. But why should he do that? He doesn't understand much of our language, nor do we understand his either, even though he is "our brother according to the flesh." Even when the preaching is in Norwegian, he listens in astonishment. The language sounds so foreign and strange, sometimes amusing, other times quite incomprehensible, even though it is a Norwegian church service and a Norwegian sermon. He doesn't know that he must talk to the pastor or a venerable deacon and apply for membership in the congregation. Most often nothing happens. He remains an outsider. But with the inexorability of a law of nature, a cold fog rolls in over the life of the newcomer's mind and heart, closing them up until the sects come along and open them again. The sects have discovered a rich fishing ground among our Norwegian newcomers. And this is our own fault. Furthermore, it is proof against the argument that the new immigrants are so terribly unChristian.

Now don't misunderstand me! I do not mean to say that taking care of Norwegian immigrants is the sole duty of our church! No, I do not think that. But what church will take on this task if we neglect it? Don't we have a greater duty here than others do? And aren't we better qualified to do this work than any other church in America?

What principles should determine the speed of the "transition?"

There are many. It will be determined, for example, by the influence of all the "followers of Governor Harding"[67] around in the Northwest; by the agitation and propaganda for more English by men within our own group who see no blessing in upholding the language of our own kin; by the language we use in our homes; by the language we use in our parochial schools; and not least by the fact that our urban congregations are struggling to stay alive. This latter especially has *frightened* us into using more and more English.

I must say a bit more about this last "principle."

It is easy to demonstrate that many of our urban congregations are having difficulty surviving. Anyone can find irrefutable evidence. But those who place the sole blame on the language only show that they do not understand the situation and cannot see the trend of the times. I will mention several things that play a much more important role than does language.

First we have the completely perfunctory manner in which many congregations admit new members. One would almost think that we were attempting as far as possible to avoid nurturing in our youth a sense of community and responsibility for the congregation.

Let us observe how this is done in many places.

A family moves into the town. If there is a Norwegian Lutheran congregation there, the pastor visits the family if he has time. And if the family have any interest in the church, they apply for membership. When the congregational meeting comes around, the pastor mentions that Mr. X and his family are applying to be members. The congregation votes, and the family in question become members. Probably no one even mentions how large the family is, and, if it happens to be mentioned, no information is given as to which children are confirmed and which are not. It is mere coincidence if all of the confirmed members of the family are present. Father is there. He is admitted together with his family, and with that the whole thing is taken care of. But as everyone knows, children seldom remain at home after they are grown up. First one leaves, then another. Therefore, in order for the congregation to survive, new members must be constantly moving to town. Unless the influence of the home has been quite unusual, how can we expect any feeling or sense of responsibility for the congregation in young people who have become members in such a careless fashion? In addition we have the bad habit in many families of having the father pay all expenses to the congregation for both the confirmed and the unconfirmed members of the family. In these cases, it is clear that the young people will not have any great sense of responsibility for the congregation they belong to and even less for the place they move to after leaving home. It is inexplicable that our clergy and church board have not tried to correct this bad practice. This *must* be corrected! There ought to be some kind of formal admission to the congregation for all adults, both men and women, and it ought to happen right after confirmation. Every confirmed person must be made to feel that he or she is an active member and has a responsibility for the growth of the congregation. From confirmation on, if not before, young people must also bear their portion of the congregation's expenses.

The next reason that so many of our urban congregations are declining lies in the very circumstances of urban life.

It has been many years since we first noticed that it is nearly impossible for an urban congregation to maintain itself. This was a cause for concern. And so we got together and consulted with each other, and then we fell into the nearest the trap. We blamed it on the language. Our young people were turning their backs on what we held dearest because they couldn't understand what we were saying. Then we went home from our meetings feeling a mixture of sorrow and joy. We were relieved to have found the cause, and concerned that what we held so dear should be just what drove the young people from us. So we started using English, and soon more English. And we will continue using it more and more, partly out of real need and partly as an experiment. But what have the results been as far as growth of the congregations goes? About the same as before!

If we really study the matter, not just hurriedly look at it in passing, then we will surely see that it is not just the language that is taking our young people from us. No, it is life itself, circumstances, acquaintances, friends from school and the street, social life, the process of assimilation, and not least the taste for amusement and entertainment which unconsciously takes possession of those who frequent moving picture theaters. And many many other things aid in drawing our young people away from the church. Look a bit more seriously at the matter! Our children enter school when they are six years old. They spend nine months of the year there until they are eighteen (in the case of those who continue up through high school). During all these long years the blessed light of Christianity is barred from the curriculum. That which should undergird all teaching, giving it light and warmth, that which should provide a context for the colorful multiplicity of life is excluded from the schools. It is banished!

For those who live in towns where the population is drawn from many nations, and that is true of nearly all towns in the Northwest, it is difficult for parents to control the child's circle of acquaintances. Our children will naturally come into contact with the children of other national backgrounds and find their friends there. In school our children and the others sit side by side, they work on the same things, they read and learn the same things, acquire the same interests, and have common joys and sorrows in play as well as in work. Should we be surprised that when our children reach more mature years they continue to associate with these others? This is only to be expected. Life's hidden forces spin and weave together even the most heterogeneous elements.

All this becomes even more natural when you look at the loose relationship between the home and the child. The short vacation from school may be spent mostly on the street. And then there are organizations and clubs and small gatherings of close friends in and out of school, during school and during vacations. And the children must belong if they are to count for anything in their circle of friends. Perhaps home isn't such a pleasant place to be either. Father is working hard and is so busy he can barely find time for meals. Mother too is busy with many things outside of the home.

For example, there is the music circle, the literary club, the social tea, the development league (of one sort or another), the child welfare league, in addition to the congregation's ladies aid, and a whole lot of other things that a town mother ought to be a part of if she is to count for anything within her circle of friends. She must join if she is even to *have* a circle of acquaintances. We even have a child welfare league, where mothers take care of other people's children! We are very good at looking after others. This business of the others has become almost a mania among us.

But mother is not almighty. Therefore the home often becomes just a boardinghouse and a lodging place, a place where tired, listless children droop over their lessons and are scolded. Or else mother is completely absorbed in caring for the children so they can go to school and take part in all the different activities both in and out of school. She cooks and bakes and takes care of everything, she washes and irons and waits on everyone. She is the only servant in the home, and the children are the masters.

When we look at this matter calmly and seriously it doesn't seem so strange that our children are in no mood to accompany us to church on a Sunday morning when we serve up such old-fashioned fare. Nor is it remarkable that in their more mature years they simply turn their backs on our old church. No doubt you remember that old saying about the mills of the gods? They grind slowly, but they grind well. That is the process so many of our town youth are undergoing. All the different kinds of grain in the world are being ground together into a homogeneous whole. This is the case even with respect to religion.

And so little by little our children necessarily begin to reason like this: If these other people, my friends and acquaintances, are good enough to associate with for six days of the week, then why not also on the seventh? If I can do just as they do day in and day out without getting scolded or punished for it, why should it be so different on Sunday? We can reason with them as much as we like, try to convince them with clear and irrefutable arguments, but they will not believe us. We might get them to accompany us for a while because their childish obedience makes them, but we will seldom succeed in completely convincing them. You see, something has been formed in their souls as they grew that tells them these proscriptions of ours are unreasonable. They know these others that they have grown up with through the years. They feel that they know them *better* than we do. Perhaps they also know that these others are just as morally pure as they are, have just as high ideals and aspirations. Therefore there can be nothing wrong with their churches. So when our children go out into life as adults it is easy for them to land in a non-Lutheran church, if they land in any church at all.

It is much more pleasant and far more entertaining in that church. There they don't have to listen to serious talk about sin and rebirth, about contrition and repentance and daily consecration, and about the unspeakably serious day of reckoning that waits beyond death and the grave. In these other churches the Gospel sounds so beautiful and interesting. It's all about *the fatherhood of God and the brotherhood of man*. And you get into this fatherhood and brotherhood through your own *actions*, by doing something. It goes something like this: "Go and seek out the prodigal son, and patch him up until you make him into a good citizen, into a useful member of society. For only that which is worthless here in our time will be lost for eternity. Look my friend, when you act this way, then you will become a citizen in the kingdom of God!" It is quite depressing, the way that words such as *faith, repentance, rebirth* (in the meaning we give to the word), and *judgment* have gone out of fashion in these churches.

Therefore we can be absolutely confident that, as things are going now, our urban congregations as a group will continue to lose members. This trend will continue until they have made themselves just as outwardly attractive as these other congregations. Even so they will continue to decline. They must unless they continually recruit new members from the rural congregations.

Let me add another thought here.

There are many among us who believe that the Lutheran Church has the qualities to make it the church of the people, the church of the masses in this country. This view reveals nothing more than naive optimism. In the first place, no church which stands firmly grounded on truth can become a church for the masses. The masses don't want anything to do with the truth! In the second place, the spirit and nature of the Lutheran Church is so remote from the popular American spirit. Our most conspicuous national character traits point in another direction entirely. The Lutheran church is *introspective, searching*. It so strongly emphasizes the *life of the heart*, the individual person's *relationship to God*, the life of *faith*. The nation, on the other hand, is *restless, rushing*. As a nation we demand first and foremost *action, deeds*. We live as extroverts, not introverts. We look forward, not inward. And we have this insatiable appetite for amusement whenever we take a pause in our rushing about! Because we are like this, our national religion has become the cloying and empty talk of Social Service. No, for the Lutheran Church to become a popular church in this country it would have to change completely in both spirit and tone, which is precisely what is happening in those places where it has switched over to English. In such places the church is so different that it is hard even to recognize it. Is this what those who are most eagerly pushing the "transition" truly want to happen?

I am sure that many will consider what I have said above to be narrow-minded. Perhaps. For myself, I believe it to be farsighted. Because our church is the way it is, it can become the salt of the nation. As long as we are faithful to our confession, not just formally, but in spirit and truth, the church will remain a refreshing, bubbling spring, providing a large measure of blessing for our entire people.

But the strongest principle hastening the "transition" is the law of inertia itself. It is our spiritual laziness and apathy, the spiritual poverty amongst us. We are too intellectually lazy to remain a bilingual people. We don't even want to. It is so much easier—superficially at least—to have only one language to deal with.

But what if we applied this same simplifying goal to other areas of life! For example, just one room in the house, that would be so much easier. And just one window, that would make less for mother to wash and fewer curtains to iron. And then just one dress and one suit, and one pair of shoes and one hat! That would be much simpler and easier. And one newspaper and one book. And one cow and only one child in the house. Surely life would be simpler and easier, but also just a little bit poorer.

No, we can see that this would never do. We would lose too much by it. Our fellow human beings would laugh at us. We might even lose money by it.

But what about our spiritual losses? Shouldn't we also fear spiritual poverty?

I gave a speech once about "We Young People and the Norwegian Language." I will repeat it here, because it fits into my argument:

"The Norwegian language is a good medium for education. It is the bearer of a great and rich culture. For that reason, it is suitable for all people. It is true that for Americans there is not much money to be earned by learning Norwegian. But if money is the only measure of value for various things in this life, then all existence will become extremely impoverished. Then life will become bankrupt, in spite of all the money in the world. Man does not live by bread alone, for life is more than just food. It is far less important to learn to earn a living than it is to learn the art of living. There is an ancient saying 'If you have two loaves of bread, then you should sell one and buy a rose with the money, for your soul is also in need of food.'

"The Norwegian language is so much closer to us Americans of Norwegian descent than any other foreign language. We have a special relationship to it. A large number of young Americans speak Norwegian just about as well as they speak English. And why shouldn't they? I have heard groups of young people here in this country sing Norwegian hymns and songs with a freshness and strength and understanding that you can scarcely find better in Norway. I have heard American young people recite and declaim Norwegian pieces in Norwegian so well and so authentically that I might have thought I was hearing educated school children from the best circles in Norway. Most young people of Norwegian background have a *little* acquaintance with the Norwegian language. Even for the minority who know nothing, it is easier to learn Norwegian than any other foreign language. That is because even those who have gotten completely away from the language have still not completely lost their national temperament. And there is an intimate relationship between language and national temperament.

"But we must pay attention to *economy* in the work of education as well as in the world of finance. When one already possesses something worth working at, it is only sensible and good management to develop that to the highest possible level. It is equally true as well that for the person seeking an education—and for others too—it is an economic waste not to make use of knowledge one already has. So there are clear economic reasons why we Americans of Norwegian descent ought to study the Norwegian language.

"But moving beyond that, Norwegian is a *beautiful* language. It carries with it a great treasury of beauty. Listen to it in our folk songs and our folktales. Feel how warmly and intimately it embraces our ideas. Hear it in our hymns. Listen to it in our prayers. Hear it speak of eternal matters. It is truly beautiful! We can read the great poets from the earliest saga period until today, and their language moves us with a strange power. It is resonant, powerful, and rich. Its music falls like the beautiful sonorous tones of a still evening on the mind of the person with an ear for the harmony of language.

"And the Norwegian language is *rich* for those of us who have sprung from Norwegian roots. So rich it is priceless. For it is the language of our people, and has been for a long, long time, for thousands of years. Whether your ancestors spoke the literary language or some rural dialect, it was still the Norwegian language. It all comes from the same source. Norwegian is the main portal through which you may enter the house of your forefathers. Do you think it is important to enter there and look around? Oh, yes, it must be. For whether that house is large and light and lovely or small and dark and poor, it is the house of your forefathers. Your own kin reside there! You must go there to become acquainted with them. All the great treasures of the spirit that your ancestors have piled up through many long years are gathered there, and you too can find them there. There you will learn to know your kin, and thereby to know yourself.

"For us, the Norwegian language is a rich language. By immersing ourselves in it, we can see wondrous sights from distant times. We see our people, how they struggled, how they triumphed through the years. With the help of the structure, the turns of phrase, the idioms, and the vocabulary of our language we can become a part of our own kin. 'We see the dust and sweat of their

work on their faces. It is as though we can see their breasts heave, as
if we hear their short, tired breaths.'

"Yes, for us the Norwegian language is richer than any other foreign tongue. It is foreign and yet it is our own. For many of us it is
still the language of our own mother and father, the language of
grandmother and grandfather. It was this language they first read
with childish smiles on their lips. In this language they whispered
the most difficult farewell of their lives, the last one. And it was in
these same tones that, in the long life that lay between, they expressed their feelings, their hopes and joys, their sorrows, and all
their hard work.

"Because the Norwegian language is so close to us and brings
such richness to our own lives, we young people ought to study it
and cultivate it in ourselves. In doing so we will harvest the greatest
of blessings."

That was what I said in my speech. But the man in the street
does not see this. Nor do our spiritual leaders. For if they saw it,
then ordinary people would also come to see it.

By this I do not mean that our pastors ought to insist on preaching in Norwegian solely in order to preserve the language. This
would not be a wise action, and, even if they tried it, it would not be
possible to preserve the language in this way. But all the same, we
have the right to expect that those among us with a higher education will acknowledge the fundamental values which are dearest to
us and furthermore will show by word and deed that they believe in
these values. That much we have the right to expect. One would
think that even people without much formal education would see
that the language of our forefathers, the language of our kin is of
priceless value to our children.

But as a people we do not see this, do not want to see it, do not
care to see it. We join one organization after another to work for
other people's children, trying to reform them. We run from meeting to meeting and basically don't accomplish anything other
than to wear ourselves out. And perhaps these other children
don't need reforming any more than our own do. We ought to
understand that the only children we can truly reform are our
own. One time I talked to a mother about this. I tried to convince

her that if she taught her own children Norwegian it would do more good for both them and the country than if she was a member of the child welfare league. This is the answer I got [in English]: *It takes too much energy to teach the youngsters Norwegian during these hot days.*

These matters presented above are the most powerful principles governing the "transition"!

2

I don't see any compelling reason why the name of a church body must indicate its origin. So we can't get any discussion going on that, even if we tried. There is no compelling reason for it, but fortunately, there is none *against* it either!

When there are so many different Lutheran church bodies in this country, one might think it would be quite practical if the name indicated who we were. I'd like to give our theological professors an examination on the topic: the Lutheran church bodies in America. It would be interesting to put the professors in a classroom, give them pen and paper, and then ask them to name all the Lutheran church bodies and synods in America, as well as to explain what kind of people belong to each one and finally to point out how each one is different from the others. I'll bet that some of them would flunk this test! If we tried the same experiment with our pastors, it would go very badly for them too. It would be easier for them to name all the different parts of a Ford. And this is hardly surprising. Even I would suffer a similar fate on this exam, though I have tried to keep up with the life of our church for the last twenty years.

This name of ours, The Norwegian Lutheran Church in America, is a good name. It is a beautiful and a suitable name. It points to the origin of our church in this country, and by doing so it honors those forefathers who founded it. It is also suitable because it shows who we really are. To all Americans of Norwegian background it ought to serve as a symbol of unity, a rallying point— a magnificent banner to fight under.

When we have once raised this banner, let us not lower it just to try to make people believe that we are something other than what we really are! If anyone joined our church in the belief that we were something other than what we are, that we had a different origin than we do, that person would feel terribly misled when he found out the truth. We do not want that to happen.

3

I find it self-evident that the name of an institution can have an impact on its health and growth. Both sides in this controversy agree on this point. Proponents of both Norwegian and English have forcefully put forth this claim.

Quite apart from the discussion of this past year, it is easy to imagine a name that would only cause laughter and derision in the wider world. What would we think about a name such as "Holy Rollers" or "Holy Jumpers" or whatever these ultramodern sects have hit upon. One can both laugh and cry over them at the same time.

Yet, why go to such crass extremes? It is certainly possible to think of a name that contains nothing offensive, but which at the same time is so colorless and lacking in content that its very emptiness would be frightening. For example, imagine that we decided to call our church body "The Union"? Such a name would certainly fit very well with the spirit of our time. But how many of our people would join so pale and insubstantial a creature?

Insofar as the actual name is concerned, I will not deny that the adjective Norwegian might possibly scare a few fainthearted people away from joining us, but it would not be very many. We may quite reasonably presume that anyone who asks to join a congregation knows a little bit about the people in that congregation, perhaps has been to some of the church services and other meetings and has gotten acquainted with some of the people. But then that person will also know that these people are not *foreigners*, and the congregation is not Norwegian in the sense that it belongs to Norway. It wouldn't take a person long to discover that.

In addition, I must remind you once again that it is first and foremost the imperative duty of our church to care for the people of Norwegian descent. And I have such great belief in the natural wholesomeness of our people and their souls that when this hysteria has passed and it is no longer fashionable to wave the flag of patriotism, then the great majority will be glad that they have retained the word Norwegian in the name of our church. It will continue to beckon to every member of our national group with a friendly atmosphere of home, welcoming them to join us in our fellowship. And this is still necessary, for altogether too many of them are still standing outside the door.

4

This business about the "language of the heart" is not so easy to grasp, and it is difficult to say anything precise. It would be most interesting to meet a person who could speak with scientific certainty on this topic.

"The language of the heart." What does this phrase actually mean? I have thought a bit about this expression in connection with my own experience and that of others, and have concluded that "language of the heart" is one of those poetical expressions that are almost impossible to define. There is something vague and ephemeral about it. This is easily explainable, for the expression means one thing to one person and something completely different to another.

If I were to attempt a definition that captures the way most people construe this phrase, it would have to go something like this: "The language of the heart is that language in which a person most easily thinks and feels and in which that person can most easily express those thoughts and feelings to others."

Yet this definition is quite obviously wrong. This definition describes the language a person speaks every day, the language a person uses most frequently. Yet that cannot be the meaning of "language of the heart." It must be something purer and finer, something more delicate than the language we use every day to do business and issue commands, to shout and to curse. "The language of the heart" cannot be the same as our everyday language, can it?

I will try another definition: "The language of the heart is that language which contains and conveys the best and the purest in a human being."

There lies a world of difference between these two definitions. That is clear without further explanation. The problem is that when most people speak about the language of the heart, they mean the first, they mean the everyday language. They talk as though they are speaking of Sunday clothes made of fine, expensive cloth, sewn with great care, but when you take a closer look, it is just an ordinary everyday suit.

According to the first definition, I, and many like me, have no language of the heart in which to express superficial daily life. Most of us who came to this country at a comparatively early age speak English just about as well as Norwegian when it comes to everyday matters. The same is true for many who were born and raised here. It might be more correct to say, such people have two languages of the heart.

But according to the second definition, I have had many languages of the heart. First of all, my Helgeland dialect, then Swedish, then formal Norwegian, and perhaps even English. There was really a time in my life when *Fritjof's Saga* (in Swedish)[68] along with some of the melancholy and emotionally rich Swedish folk songs represented for me the epitome of all that was great and noble. They concealed in their rich lyricism what seemed to me at the time all that was great and beautiful in the world. It still sometimes seems that way to me.

The truth is, there are as many languages of the heart for an individual as a person with multi-faceted culture and interests can acquire. There may be one language from the street, another from the circle of friends, a third from work, a fourth from recreational activities, a fifth from mother's arms, perhaps a sixth from those serious hours alone with father.

I could well imagine that even a Swede or an American who had studied chemistry in Germany for some years could express himself better in German than in any other language when it came to purely scientific and technical matters. Someone who has studied painting at the feet of one of the great masters in Italy would likewise prefer Italian when it came to expressing technicalities about painting. An opera singer would prefer to sing Wagnerian operas in German, but *Il Trovatore* in Italian. Such a person would feel instinctively that only German words can adequately express the feelings that his tones are trying to express in Wagner's operas. So it is also with other works of art where melody and words must fit together. A cultivated person has many such "relationships of the heart." I dare to assert that most of those to whom I have taught Norwegian literature will agree that Norwegian is the "language of their heart" when it comes to Norwegian poetry. And likewise, I would have to say for myself that English is the "language of my heart" when it comes to American and English literature.

It is foolish to expect that older people and others who have received their religious instruction in Norwegian, who have said their prayers and sung the old hymns in Norwegian—people whose religious lives have been nourished entirely through Norwegian words—can be completely satisfied with exclusively English services, even if they otherwise speak and understand English perfectly. Especially the elderly. Take for example hymns such as "O Jesus se min skam og ve" [Oh, Jesus see my shame and woe], or "Jesu din søte forening at smake" [Jesus, to taste thy sweet companionship], or "Sørg o kjære fader du" [Grieve thou dear father], just to name a few of many. The soul which is accustomed to seeking the highest through such phrases will search in vain for words to express the same meanings *for them* in the English language. The words will sound so strange and therefore will seem cold; they simply will not convey the deep need of the heart. An older person who tries to say them with trembling lips only stammers. It does not work.

Last summer I found this same idea expressed in an editorial in one of our large American newspapers. It said: "A person's language is part of his life. Without language a man is but an animal. After a certain early age men cannot adapt themselves perfectly to a new language. When old age has come, they can hardly at all gain even a fair use of a foreign tongue. To deny an old person his native language is next to taking his life. This is particularly true of the language of religion. The language of commerce and social intercourse can be translated. The language of religion cannot be, in any effective sense. The deep doors of religious feeling have words and phrases for their open sesame. Words of the same definition in another [language] cannot take their form to lifelong experience and association."[69]

Now, we can use exactly the same argument when it comes to our young people and the use of English as the language of the church. However, this conclusion is rather too hasty. Until recently, the majority of our young people have been confirmed in Norwegian. At least this is true of those who come to St. Olaf College. And nearly all of our young people have heard and participated in Norwegian church services. It is so much easier for young ears to catch and preserve the impression made by foreign sounds! What is nearly impossible for the older person can, in this respect, be the easiest matter in the world for a young person, *if only he will.*

I will repeat my first statement: an educated person with many interests has many languages of the heart. Therefore it is pathetically stupid to call a congregation where primarily Norwegian is used a *foreign colony.* But there are plenty of people who think and talk like that.

This kind of talk is a gross insult to those many rural congregations where Norwegian is still primarily used. Such talk is a great sin against an honest and law-abiding people! Can loyalty and love for our country and our people be nourished and expressed only in English? Is the congregation that sits in the Lord's house on a Sunday morning and prays in *Norwegian* for His richest blessings on the land and the people, prays for the highest wisdom for our president and his advisers and the government, the congregation gathered with but one purpose in mind, to gain wisdom and strength and mercy from on high—is that congregation really a *foreign colony?*

And when a rural congregation or an urban congregation hires a teacher for a month or two during the summer to teach the coming generation about God's extravagant greatness and power and love, to teach their children how we must live in order to become citizens of this unknown kingdom toward which we all are striving, to teach their children what the parents know has made them better human beings now and forever—to try to teach the children all these things in a language other than the official one of the country, is this *"insisting on the perpetuation of foreign colonies in America?"*

The father and son who go out into the fields in the spring and talk over—in *Norwegian*—how they can best manage to comply with the government's challenge to produce the greatest crop for themselves and their country, as well as for suffering mankind—are they truly *foreigners*?

Or the mother and daughter who at the same time are in the kitchen enthusiastically planning—in *Norwegian*—how they can divide the housework so that one of them is always available to help outdoors, now that the one brother is away in the war, and there is no other help to be had,—well, are these women *foreigners*, do you think? Or the father who takes his small son around with him on the farm, all the while explaining to the little one how they can best run this farm to make it truly a model farm, and how they should take care of things and plant and improve and build, and make it the most beautiful place in the world. As these two go along chatting in Norwegian, without knowing that they are in reality planning in miniature our country's greatness, building and planning and envisioning the future until their eyes glow and their hearts swell, well, are these two fellows *trying to perpetuate a foreign colony in America*? Well, good folk, a "torrent of empty phrases" is now flooding the country. "The language" has really become a "substitute for thought" and we won't need to look far for the result!

Let me again repeat my assertion. A person has as many languages of the heart as he has interests. Let me illustrate this with some examples from my own experience.

This year I have in my freshman class a girl who was born and raised on the prairie in western Minnesota. In spite of this, she can read pieces by Hans Seland in his dialect with such authentic pronunciation and intonation and understanding that she could well be his own daughter. Judging by the grades she got last semester, she is about equally good in formal Norwegian and in English; she has good grades in both subjects. But what is her "language of the heart?"

Once I heard a man who almost never speaks Norwegian, but rather speaks a pedantically perfect English, become furiously angry at another man and begin to "tell him a few home truths." Even though they had not been speaking Norwegian and what they were quarreling about had nothing to do with language, nevertheless the first man suddenly began using some choice Norwegian words and expressions! What was his "language of the heart?"

Recently a St. Olaf student won first prize in a Norwegian declamation contest. His theme was "St. Olaf and the Battle at Stiklestad." Out of the six judges, five awarded him top marks, the sixth placed him second. And this young man belongs to the third generation. His grandparents came to this country as young people. As far as this speech was concerned, there is no doubt that the language of his heart was Norwegian. On the other hand, if he had been speaking about Abraham Lincoln, the language of his heart would no doubt have been English. And quite naturally, for that is the language in which he gained his knowledge of that particular subject.

At St. Olaf we have a class in beginning Norwegian for those who take Norwegian as a completely foreign language. Only those who have been confirmed in English and who know no Norwegian are allowed to take this class. When we start, English is used as the sole medium of instruction. I taught this class for the first time in 1919. Here is what happened to me the first day of class, which happened to be the day after President Boe was installed as president of St. Olaf.

I came into the class, and after roll call I asked [in English]:
"Do any of you speak Norwegian?"
They all shook their heads.
"Do any of you understand Norwegian?"
Same answer.
Then I asked:
"How many of you were present at the installation yesterday?
They all held up their hands.
"Then none of you understood Dr. Stub's speech?"

"Oh, yes," was the answer from the class, "we understood that, it was a sermon!"

Now President Stub's speech on this occasion was beautiful and elegant, but certainly not linguistically easy for those who know little Norwegian, nor was it intended to be. And yet the fact is, this class had understood it quite well. And these students were all from the third and fourth generations.

The examples I have given above are taken from 1919 and earlier. But I have more recent proof that Norwegian is not disappearing as fast as we think.

On March 31, 1922, the famous Olson Sisters performed at St. Olaf.[70] The program consisted of songs and readings. Among the readings was a humorous anecdote in Sogn dialect about an old lady who had all kinds of illnesses. The applause was thunderous. I turned spontaneously to the person next to me and burst out "It is astonishing how many in the audience understand the Sogn dialect!" And it was truly astonishing.

5

So we finally come to the last question: Is working among other national groups beneficial or harmful to the church?

To this the great majority will give the clear and direct answer: "Certainly it is not *harmful*!" Well, I would give this same answer, but I must ask for permission to add something to it.

We are carrying on mission work among many heathen peoples now, and there surely is not a thoughtful person among us who does not wish this work to prosper and bear the most wonderful fruit.

And here in the homeland of our church we are carrying on home mission work too. First and foremost among our own people, and secondly among people of other nationalities to the extent that we have felt capable of it. And that is just fine. We can surely do much more in that direction than we have done so far.

But we must not exaggerate the importance of this enterprise to such a degree that it becomes primary, to the detriment of the work we do among our own people. If that happens, then the work we do among other nationalities will not strengthen the church but rather will weaken it.

In spite of my stubborn Norwegianness, I do believe that we need strong *English*-language congregations in all the towns where people of Norwegian descent live and where our people are streaming in from the countryside. But there must also be strong *Norwegian* congregations in all the towns where people of Norwegian descent have recently been moving in from the country and where Norwegian immigrants will most likely come in the future if Norwegian immigration does not dry up. These congregations must be so strongly Norwegian (I mean of course Norwegian in language!) that older people and newcomers, and people who have been here a comparatively short time, can feel at home as far as the language is concerned. *For it is the unavoidable duty of our church to take care of these people!* And in many towns in the Northwest there are great numbers of such people. Which church would take care of them if not ours?

Now there are actually among us some who believe that as far as our urban church work is concerned it would be better for us to switch immediately to English. For if we did that, we could just open our doors and invite everyone to come in and join us. This, I think, would be a mistake. In the first place, relatively few people of other national backgrounds will want to join us, that is, if their own people have a church in the town. And in the second place, if we do this many of our own people will be left standing outside the church. Those among us who are pushing the transition so hard really have a duty to demonstrate that they are not abandoning those who are not able to participate because the English worship service is and will remain foreign to them.

"Oh well," some may say, "there are not so many left among us who are not comfortable participating in an English worship service." Such a statement, from my experience, reveals great ignorance. It is true that most of our people speak English after a fashion. But it is often only after a fashion! Even older working people with only an elementary school education have acquired a vocabulary of two or three hundred words used in daily life.

However, this is hardly adequate for them to get much out of an English-language church service. When you speak to them in the street or about business, it sounds as if they know some English. And yet they don't know it! The vocabulary they have acquired consists mainly of nouns, names of objects around them, and a few basic verbs.

But aren't such older people most often the backbone of the congregation? Aren't they the ones you meet at the congregation's prayer meetings? Don't they bear their full share, and maybe even more, of the financial burdens of the church? Aren't they among the most enthusiastic contributors to the mission society? Aren't they also the most faithful churchgoers? And when there is a congregational meeting, aren't they among those most certain to attend? Yes, in most congregations don't they form the backbone?

Yes, this is the way it must be! For their need is greater, they are more strongly affected by the seriousness of life, they have experienced "the wealth of pain" to a greater extent than the young. That is why the "court of the tabernacle" is so dear to them. If we make our church services so foreign to them linguistically that it becomes more beneficial for them to sit at home with their devotional books than to attend worship, and therefore they remain sitting at home, will the church not suffer thereby? I think so.

The argument for more English and exclusively English seems so logical and natural. For the younger generation in the towns apparently understand little Norwegian, and it is especially for them and for the future that we are building and working.

If adopting the English language were the only remedy, then we would have to be quiet. But it is remarkable how theory and practice can work at cross purposes. I remember, for example, when our congregation adopted an equal division between the two languages. I voted for it, by the way. Then the main argument went like this: We can't bring the children with us to church, for they don't understand what is being sung and said.

So we divided our services in as brotherly a fashion as we could. For the first few Sundays, there was actually an improvement, with more children in attendance. But it only lasted for a short while; now it is about the same as it was before.

But say for the sake of argument that we do adopt the proposed new program. Who could we expect to join us? I mean which national groups? For the most part only those of Lutheran origin. We wouldn't get many people of English descent, for they would mostly seek out the Methodist or the Episcopal or the Congregational churches. The Scot would go mostly to the Presbyterian Church. And the Irish to the Catholic Church. Most of the Russians, Bohemians, and Southern Europeans would also go there, and many from Central Europe too. "Denominations" said Billy Sunday in one of his sermons, "represent different temperaments. A man with warm emotions would not make a good Episcopalian, but he would make a crackerjack Methodist." And there is a certain truth to this.

I wonder when the time will come that national traits in this country are so completely obliterated that the above will no longer be true? One thing I am certain of: in spite of the most intense Americanization efforts many generations of people quite naturally will continue to join the *church* of their group whenever this is possible.

And it is not just *our* church in this country that is carrying on home mission work. The non-Lutheran churches are also doing so. Some of them much more zealously than we are. They also work first and foremost among their own people, and in addition try to proselytize as many others as they can. It is therefore in the nature of the matter that we must first and foremost recruit from among people of Lutheran background.

But even among them, our work will quite naturally be limited to those of Norwegian descent. For each nationality group, even among the Lutherans, tries to take care of its own. We of our own, the Germans of their own, the Swedes of their own, the Danes of theirs. Lately complaints and friction have arisen when one Lutheran church has tried to recruit those who by ties of blood belong to another. We have complained and written protests, and others have too.

It is therefore much to be hoped that the National Lutheran Council will look into this matter and divide the fields of work between the various church bodies. I understand that this is one of the issues the council has on its agenda. In this way, our home mission field will be more limited, and we will naturally get those Americans of Norwegian descent, for they belong to us. It would not occur to anyone to assign them to a German church and to get the Germans to join our church, except in those places where there are too few of one group to form their own congregation. We can all acknowledge the unavoidable necessity for forming "mixed" congregations in some towns. But for a long time such congregations will be a small minority.

We don't know how many Americans of Norwegian descent there are now. Estimates based on wild guesses vary widely. Some say two million, others four, and yet others five million. The first number is the most plausible. This is the strength that immigration from Norway has brought to this country in the course of ninety-seven years! How many will come in the next hundred years? It is pointless even trying to guess!

But only half a million of those who are here now are members of our Norwegian-American Lutheran Church! What has become of the others? Where can they be? Each and every one of us ought to see that it is the primary duty of our church to bring the word of God to this large and steadily increasing number of our own kin. And the church must make use of the Norwegian language to solve this problem, is *forced* to use it, even if now and then a few fanatics insult it by stamping it as a *foreign church*.

We often hear people say that the only task of the church is to save souls. And rightly understood, we can all agree with this. But there are many activities which at least indirectly can assist in this task. In fact, the church can make use of almost all good and praiseworthy activities in addition to the strictly religious in carrying out this task. It is far from adequate merely to educate pastors and missionaries and gather people together into congregations. A church of the people needs to expand its range of activities well beyond this. It must be broad enough to include extensive and manifold charitable work. It must also include the work of education and culture, not just to provide the church with pastors and missionaries, but also to prepare teachers and all the other workers needed by both the church itself and its affiliated organizations. The church should serve the people, and the people the church. That is why the activities of a church of the people are so many and so varied.

Under the educational and cultural branch of the church comes that area which for lack of a better name we call our work for the preservation of Norwegian heritage. The phrase is entirely misleading. I would prefer to call it our *work for Americanization*. If we don't do this, then who will? And I am stubborn enough to insist that this work can be a great blessing to the church and contribute invaluable service toward furthering the primary task of the church. It is impossible to go deeper into this now, as I have already gone on much too long. But I must have permission to point to just one thing. That is *unity*. We Americans of Norwegian descent have a common root and a common heritage which we have acquired through our ancestry. What if we could get people to see this? Would that not strengthen our sense of unity, and would that not in turn be a blessing for the church? Would it not be much easier to gather people together where this feeling is strong and deep than where it is absent? Look also at the ethical importance of this work. The father and son who go forward together in intimate understanding of what is true and right are unconquerable. How wonderful it is to enter a household full of affection and complete solidarity! Such a family will accomplish great things in this world. The same is true in a wider sense for entire ethnic groups and nations. The truth in the saying about "a house divided against itself" holds here too.

"We are Americans, and nothing other than Americans." Yes, of course we are Americans, and nothing other than Americans, as citizens! Whatever else in the world would we be? We are not Russians or Japanese or Malabarians! And as citizens of this country we owe it everything we have and are, yes, even our lives. Also all of our heritage and all of our property, everything we brought with us when we came. What else do we have to give? We are Americans, and as citizens nothing else in the world. But by descent, by ancestry, by *kinship* we are Norwegians, and can never be anything else no matter how desperately some of us try. For my part I cannot imagine that it won't always be true that *our* people originally came here from Norway. Therefore we are Norwegians by descent. And I believe that it is the absolute duty of the church to use this fact to its advantage. In my opinion there are riches and possibilities here which we have scarcely touched upon yet.

This will have to be enough, though it is difficult to say stop when one first begins writing about such things. One is left with the feeling that one has barely scratched the surface of all the things that might be said. And there has never been so much confusion in our thinking as right now.

NOTES

Notes to the Introduction

1. D.G. Ristad to Rølvaag, 1922, in the archives of the Norwegian-American Historical Association (NAHA), St. Olaf College.

2. In a series of letters in the NAHA archives written from Rølvaag to Jennie Berdahl during the period of their engagement in the fall of 1904 and following years, he explains to her his family background, his ambitions, and his temperament. Portions of this introduction are adapted from previously published articles, "Introduction to Rølvaag: Life and Works" and "Rølvaag's Views on Immigration, Culture, and Heritage," in *". . . etter Rølvaag har problema han stridde med, vorte til verdsproblem . . . ,"* report from the Rølvaag conference in Sandnessjøen, August 7–8, 1995, 7–44.

3. Letter from Johan to Rølvaag, 1912. NAHA archives.

4. Rølvaag's notebooks and letters from this period are found in the NAHA archives.

5. *Landsmaal* (now known as *Nynorsk*) is one of the two official languages in Norway.

6. Letter to Jennie Berdahl, quoted in Jorgenson and Solum, *Ole Edvart Rølvaag: A Biography* (New York, 1939), 98.

7. See Per Fuglum, *Norge i støpeskjeen 1884–1919*, vol. 12 of *Norges Historie*, Knut Mykland, ed. (Oslo, 1978), 409–413, and Sigurd Aa. Aarnes, "Nasjonen finner seg selv" in *Norges kulturhistorie: Det gjenfødte Norge*, vol. 4, Ingrid Semmingsen et al, eds. (Oslo, 1983), 127–150.

8. Rev. B.E. Bergesen, editor of *Budbæreren* in Seattle threatened to remove his son from St. Olaf because he did not like the tone of Rølvaag's writing in his articles about language preservation. Letter to Rølvaag, January, 1920. NAHA archives.

9. In a letter to Waldemar Ager Rølvaag claims that N.N. Rønning had been trying to get him fired at St. Olaf. He quotes Rønning as saying that "it is strange that an institution which has fostered something with such high ideals as the St. Olaf choir has also fostered me, who writes so coarsely and nastily." NAHA archives.

10. Personal reminiscence, Ella Valborg Tweet.

11. See Kenneth Bjork, "The Unknown Rølvaag: Secretary in the Norwegian-American Historical Association," in *Norwegian-American Studies and Records*, 11 (1940), 114–149.

12. These and other Rølvaag letters and papers are found in the NAHA archives.

13. See letters in NAHA archives from Nini Roll Anker, Margaret Culkin Banning, Johan Bojer, Lincoln Colcord, Samuel Eliot Morison, Eugene Saxton, Carl Sandburg, and many others.

14. This novel was not translated until 1971, when it was published by Dillon Press in Minneapolis. It was subsequently reprinted in the Harper Perennial Library Series. The English title was chosen by the editor at Dillon.

15. This speech is quoted at length in *The Third Life of Per Smevik*, 117–128.

16. Letter from Rolvaag to O.C. Farseth, March 9, 1913. NAHA archives.

17. Einar Haugen, *Ole Edvart Rølvaag* (Boston, 1983), 40.

18. Letter to Pastor Peter A. Bjelde, 1925. NAHA archives.

19. Letter to Pastor Peter A. Bjelde, 1925. NAHA archives.

20. Haugen, *Ole Edvart Rølvaag*, 54.

21. Letter from Rolvaag to Grandfather Berdahl, 1921. NAHA archives.

22. Rolvaag to Birger Osland. November 13, 1925. NAHA archives.

23. Joseph Baker, "Western Man Against Nature: *Giants in the Earth*," in *College English*, 4 (1942), 19.

24. I am indebted to Matthew Dion, University of Minnesota, for discussion of these ideas.

25. Rolvaag to D.G. Ristad, August, 1928. NAHA archives.

26. Rølvaag to Percy Boynton, June 3, 1929. NAHA archives.

27. November 1, 1931, as quoted in Haugen, *Ole Edvart Rølvaag*, 109.

28. See Ingeborg Kongslien, *Draumen om fridom og jord* (Oslo, 1989), 190; and Erling Dittmann, "The Immigrant Mind: A Study of Rølvaag," in *Christian Liberty*, October, 1952, 42.

29. Orm Øverland, "2. opponent," *Edda*, 4 (1988), 301–302.

30. Rølvaag to Percy Boynton, June 3, 1929. NAHA archives.

31. John Higham, *Strangers in the Land: Patterns of American Nativism 1860–1925* (2nd. ed., New Brunswick, NJ, 1992, reprinted 1994), 133–134. See also Philip Gleason, *Speaking of Diversity: Language and Ethnicity in Twentieth-Century America* (Baltimore, 1992), 18–19.

32. Letter from Lars Boe to Nora Solum, December 10, 1931. NAHA archives. The letter is written in English except for the one word "mismodig."

33. Vincent N. Parrillo, *Strangers to These Shores: Race and Ethnic Relations in the United States* (2nd. ed., New York, 1980), 52.

34. Horace M. Kallen, *Culture and Democracy in the United States* (New York, 1924), 122–123.

35. Gleason, *Speaking of Diversity*, 19.

36. Kallen, *Culture and Democracy*, 124–125.

37. Rolvaag to Ager, undated. NAHA archives.

38. Lecture notes, written in English, for immigration history course. NAHA archives.

39. Undated ms. My translation. NAHA archives.

40. Manuscript of talk to Nordmands-Forbundet, Minneapolis, January 20, 1909. My translation. NAHA archives.

41. Haugen, *Ole Edvart Rølvaag*, 23-24.

42. Gleason, *Speaking of Diversity*, 245.

43. Higham, *Strangers in the Land*, 11.

44. For example, in a letter to Martin Hegland in 1911, Rølvaag states that he does not foresee that Norwegian will be preserved forever as a spoken language in America. He makes a similar statement in a 1918 letter to O.A. Buslett. NAHA archives.

45. Rølvaag to Andreas Ueland, 1931. NAHA archives. In addition to writing *The Minor Melting Pot*, Andreas Ueland was a prominent Norwegian-American lawyer and judge in Minneapolis. He was noted for his liberal political views.

46. Rolvaag to Birger Osland, November 13, 1925. NAHA archives.

47. For a thorough discussion of the outbreak of nativism and anti-immigrant hysteria of the late 1880s and into the 90s see Higham, *Strangers in the Land*, 35-105.

48. Higham, *Strangers in the Land*, 183.

49. Higham, *Strangers in the Land*, 198, 247.

50. Carl Chrislock, "Name Change and the Church, 1918-1920," in *Norwegian-American Studies*, 27 (Northfield, Minnesota, 1977), 208.

51. Carl Chrislock, *Ethnicity Challenged: The Upper Midwest Norwegian-American Experience in World War I* (Northfield, Minnesota, 1981), 63.

52. NAHA archives.

53. O.J. Bryn to Rølvaag, 1920. NAHA archives.

54. Chrislock, *Ethnicity Challenged*, 131.

55. Chrislock, *Ethnicity Challenged*, 144.

56. *Lutheraneren*, December 11, 1918, as quoted in Haugen, *Ole Edvart Rølvaag*, 44.

57. NAHA archives.

58. Elliott Barkan, *And Still They Come: Immigrants and American Society 1920 to the 1990s* (Wheeling, Illinois, 1996), 18-19.

59. Rasmus B. Anderson, *Life Story of Rasmus B. Anderson Written by Himself with the Assistance of Albert Barton* (Madison, Wisconsin, 1915), 146.

60. See, for example, Chrislock, *Ethnicity Challenged*, 67. Ager wrote, among other things, a bitterly polemical novel, *Paa veien til smeltepotten* (Eau Claire, Wisconsin, 1917), translated by Harry Cleven as *On the Way to the Melting Pot* (Madison, Wisconsin, 1995).

61. See, for example, Theodore C. Blegen, *Norwegian Migration to America: The American Transition* (Northfield, Minnesota, 1940), 553-581. The Anderson and Blegen remarks were brought to my attention in Victor R. Greene, *American Immigrant Leaders 1800-1910: Marginality and Identity* (Baltimore, 1987), 70.

62. Ingrid Semmingsen, "Emigration and the Image of America," in *Immigration and American History*, Henry Steele Commager, ed. (Minneapolis, 1961), 34-35.

63. Dorothy Burton Skårdal, "Opponent ex auditorio," in *Edda,* 6 (1966), 402.

64. Sigmund Skard, "1. opponent," in *Edda,* 6 (1966), 371.

65. Skard, *Edda,* 6 (1966), 380.

66. Greene, *American Immigrant Leaders,* 85–87.

67. Greene, *American Immigrant Leaders,* 29, 35. See also Gleason, *Speaking of Diversity,* 274–275.

68. Toua Thor, *Minneapolis Star Tribune,* March 29, 1997.

69. Richard Rodriguez, "Go North, Young Man" in *Mother Jones,* July/August 1995, 33.

70. Rølvaag to Pastor Peter A. Bjelde, 1925. NAHA archives.

71. A manuscript translation prepared by Brynhild Rowberg has been available in the NAHA archives.

72. For a discussion of the meaning and impact of the Centennial, see April Schultz, *Ethnicity on Parade: Inventing the Norwegian American Through Celebration* (Amherst, Massachusetts, 1994).

73. Bjork, "The Unknown Rølvaag," 149.

74. Notebook dated 1923. NAHA archives.

75. Orm Øverland, *The Western Home: A Literary History of Norwegian America* (Northfield, Minnesota, 1996), 71.

76. See Gleason, *Speaking of Diversity,* 19.

77. After reading *I de dage,* Rønning wrote in a letter to Rølvaag, "Dear Rolvaag, You have something to say. You say it. You say it strikingly. You will get something for saying it, when I review *I de Dage.*" 1924. NAHA archives.

78. Jorgenson and Solum, *Ole Edvart Rølvaag,* 310.

79. Øverland, *The Western Home,* 11.

80. An exciting contemporary development is the Longfellow Institute established at Harvard University by Werner Sollors and Marc Shell. This institute focuses its work on American literature written in languages other than English, and has launched a series of bilingual editions of this literature. The work of this institute may well lead to some long-overdue translations and recognition of Norwegian-American literature as well as literatures of other ethnic groups.

81. See articles in *Lutheraneren,* December 11, 1918; April 30, May 7, May 14, 1919.

82. For a more thorough discussion of the controversy, see Chrislock, "Name Change," 194–223.

83. *Norden,* December, 1931, quoted from a 1930 letter to Carl F. Berg (original letter in NAHA archives).

84. There are still unsold copies in storage at St. Olaf.

85. Rølvaag to Simon Johnson, December 1922. NAHA archives.

86. This letter, signed G.P.H. is probably from Rølvaag's college friend, lawyer George P. Homnes. NAHA archives.

87. Jersing Thompson to Boe, 1922. NAHA archives.

88. D. G. Ristad to Boe, 1922. NAHA archives.

89. President Boe to D.G. Ristad, 1922. NAHA archives.

90. D.G. Ristad to Rølvaag, 1922. NAHA archives.

91. For a discussion of these terms, see Gleason, *Speaking of Diversity*, 245, and Higham, *Strangers in the Land*, 11.

Notes to Simple Reflections on Our Heritage

1. *Brand*, Act 1, Scene 1. Translated by Miles Menander Dawson (Boston, 1916), 12.

2. Job 7:10.

3. Matthew 25: 14–20.

4. Hans Nielsen Hauge (1771–1824), Norwegian lay preacher and leader of pietistic religious movement; Henrik Wergeland (1808–1845), Norwegian poet; Svend Foyn (1809–1894), Norwegian whaler, businessman, and inventor; Fridtjof Nansen (1861–1930), Norwegian explorer, scientist, and humanitarian; Roald Amundsen (1872–1928), Norwegian polar explorer; Christian Skredsvig (1854–1924), Norwegian painter; Stephan Sinding (1846–1922), Norwegian sculptor.

5. The association For Fædrearven (For our ancestral heritage) was founded in Eau Claire, Wisconsin, in 1919 as a reaction to the xenophobia that swept the United States during World War I. Rølvaag was secretary of this society and one of its main leaders. When Rølvaag refers to "we heritage folks" or "those of us in the heritage movement" in this book he is referring mostly to this organization and its supporters.

6. Henrik Wergeland, "To an Illustrious Poet" (Henrik Steffens), in *Poems*, translated by I. Grondahl (Oslo, 1929), 169.

7. Probably Olai Aslagsson, author of *Under vestens himmel* (*Under Western Skies*) among others. Aslagsson returned to Norway where he continued his career as a writer.

8. J. Olafsen, "Her hjemme," first two verses translated by Auber Forestier, third verse my translation. *Sons of Norway Songbook* (Minneapolis, 1948), 126.

9. Cited freely from memory [Rølvaag's note].

10. Sigurd Folkestad, "Leif Eriksen." The entire poem may be found in O.E. Rølvaag, *Norsk Læsebok II* (Minneapolis, 1920), 12. My translation.

11. Cited from memory [Rølvaag's note].

12. This poem mentions many times how to treat one's guests [Rølvaag's note]. *Poems of the Vikings*, translated by Patricia Terry (Indianapolis, 1969), 13.

13. The law regarding prohibition is a deplorable exception to this in Norway. There are several reasons for this. This law plays such a large role in people's economic lives—especially the fishing populace. And among the higher classes it has been anything but popular. The largest newspapers in the country have made fun of the law and of the people who break it. The cruder the jokes, the better. This has influenced popular opinion and has broken down respect for the law. The newspapers don't seem to understand that they have done society a real disservice [Rølvaag's note].

14. Terry, *Poems of the Vikings,* 21.

15. My translation.

16. N. F. S. Grundtvig, *Højskolesangen,* July 25, 1856, in *Udvalgte skrifter* 10 (Copenhagen, 1909), 78. My translation.

17. In a great work, *Civilization in the United States,* recently put out by one of the largest publishers in the East, we read as follows:———Viewed materially, our colleges and universities are the grandest achievement of the age,————but spiritually they are a colossal failure [Rølvaag's note].

18. Chapters 35–39, rearranged and paraphrased.

19. Bjørnstjerne Bjørnson, 1903; Knut Hamsun, 1920; Sigrid Undset, 1928.

20. Theodore Huggenvik, later professor of religion at St.Olaf College. Letters regarding this incident are found in the NAHA archives.

21. Norwegian composers and musicians of the nineteenth and early twentieth centuries.

22. Norwegian painters, sculptors, and artists of the nineteenth and early twentieth centuries.

23. See my essay on "The forest that covered the mountain," in *Norsk Læsebok II* [Rølvaag's note].

24. Gjermund Hoyme (1847–1902), a prominent Norwegian-American pastor and church leader, was also president of the United Lutheran Church in America (1890–1902).

25. Hoyme chapel, built in 1906, was destroyed by fire in 1923. Hoyme Hall, a student dormitory, was dedicated in 1961.

26. The expression *Speckled English* is often heard from those who are quite sure they know the language. I don't know who made up this phrase; but is seems to me to be somewhat of a linguistic monstrosity. One speaks of *speckled trout* and thinks of the most beautiful fish in the water. Not all flecks of color are considered ugly and shameful! [Rølvaag's note].

27. Mark 4:25.

28. "Landsmaal," today called "Nynorsk," is one of Norway's two official written languages. It was essentially created by Ivar Aasen in the mid-19th century based on west Norwegian dialects.

29. Here is a short list to choose from. Rølvaag and Eikeland: *Norsk Læsebok* I and II. Rolfsen: *Barneliv i Norge (Norge i Amerika).* Rolfsen: *Verdenshistorie for barn.* Olaf Hall: *When I was a boy in Norway.* Asbjørnsen and Moe: *Norske folkeeventyr.* Fru Koren: *Fra Pionertiden.* Hans Aanrud: *Sidsel Sidserk; Sølve Solfeng; Storkarer.* Bernt Lie: *Sven Bidevind; Peter Napoleon; Guttedage.* Barbra Ring: *Tvillingerne; Peik; Da Peik skulde Gjøre sin lykke; Tertit; Vi Tre i Hytten; Billet merk. 286.* Gabriel Scott: *Sølvfaks; Hollænder-Jonas; Gutten i Røiken; Trip, Trap, Træsko; Boken om de fire dukker; Paaskeeggene.* Dikken Zwilgmeyer: *Vi Barn; Ungdom; Maja; De Fire Kusiner; Anniken Prestgara; Mægler Porsvold; Utenlands; Inger Johanne.* Falk Ytter: *Haakon Haakonsen.* Nora Thorstenson: *Vimsen.* Rølvaag: *Amerika-Breve.* From these and other books it will be easy to track down many more. Hjalmar Ruud Holand's *De Norske Settlementers Historie* as well

as Dr. Gjerset's work, *History of the Norwegian People*, ought to be found in all Norwegian homes [Rølvaag's note].

30. Matthew 25:25.

31. Pastor J. N. Kildahl, a leader in the United Norwegian Lutheran Church, was president of St. Olaf College (1903–1914).

32. A version of this story appeared under the title "The Sovereign Congregation" in the Sons of Norway *Viking* magazine, March 4, 1974. No translator was given nor any information as to where it might have been taken from. What appears here is my translation.

33. This date would be correct according to the Icelandic Saga accounts; modern historians place it closer to shortly before 900.

34. "Norway and the Norwegians," *Scribner's Magazine*, October and November, 1914 [Rølvaag's note].

35. "Drot er hver for Jorden, Præst er hver for Gud!" Henrik Wergeland, *Samlede Skrifter II: Digterverker*, 2 (Christiania, 1918), 592.

36. Bjørnson, *Sunny Hill, A Norwegian Idyll* (New York, 1932), 19 (no translator given).

37. In *Ibsen's Poems*, translated by John Northam (Oslo, 1986), 73.

38. Bjørnson, *A Happy Boy*, translated by Mrs. W. Archer (New York, 1931), 1.

39. "Draumkvedet" or "The Dream Ballad" is a Norwegian medieval mystical-religious ballad.

40. See the Book of Revelation.

41. Bjørnson, "The Mother's Song," from *Arne*. Translated by Arthur Hubbell Palmer in *Poems and Songs by Bjørnstjerne Bjornson* (New York, 1915), 8.

42. Bjørnson, "The Angels of Sleep," *Poems and Songs*, 43.

43. Henrik Ibsen, "Vuggevise," from *The Pretenders*. Translated by Northam in *Ibsen's Poems*, 45. Rølvaag includes two more songs which I have not translated: "Vuggesang" ["Cradle Song"] by H. A. Mo and "Med alle smaa blomster" ["With all the small flowers"] by M. B. Landstad.

44. My translation of the Norwegian lullaby "Bissam, bissam baadne."

45. The song has an interesting history. It is a rewriting of the old German hymn "Schönste herr Jesus." In English there is a word-for-word translation of some of the verses; it is the well-known "Beautiful Savior" [Rølvaag's note].

46. "There" refers here to the teaching about atonement and redemption [Rølvaag's note].

47. Bjørnson, *Arnljot Gelline*, translated by William Morton Payne (New York, 1917), 92–93.

48. "Ånders Herre du skal raade" by Welhaven.

49. "Gud signe vårt dyre fedreland" by Elias Blix.

50. "Siste Reis" by Wergeland.

51. "Jeg så ham som barn." Text by Danish pastor Vilhelm Birkedal, an important follower of Grundtvig.

52. *Den Burtkomne Faderen* by Arne Garborg, *Brand* by Ibsen, *Det gyldne Evangelium* by Gabriel Scott, and *Kirken* by Nini Roll Anker.

Notes to Simple Reflections on Our Literature

53. For further information on these and other Norwegian-American authors see Orm Øverland, *The Western Home: A Literary History of Norwegian America* (Northfield, Minnesota, 1996).

54. Rølvaag is mistaken in this assertion. Zangwill, a British Jew, wrote the play in English. There is, however, a bit of Yiddish in the dialogue.

55. And what should we say about Camilla Collett's *The District Governor's Daughters*? It is surely striking enough, but thirty years after the work was first published it still had not sold more than 700 copies! [Rølvaag's note].

56. Gerhard Gran (1856–1925), Norwegian literary historian and professor of Nordic literature in Oslo.

57. From "Follow the call!" translated by G. M. Gathorne-Hardy, in Henrik Wergeland, *Poems,* 156.

58. As an example, when my book *The Boat of Longing* came out last Christmas, one of our newspapers mentioned getting a copy from the publisher, but the editor hadn't read it. They promised a review later, but no review has come out yet! [Rølvaag's note].

59. The identity of "S" is not known. Rølvaag eventually concluded that he could not have been a pastor.

60. Gjermund Hoyme (1847–1902), a prominent pastor and church leader, was president of the United Norwegian Lutheran Church in America (1890–1902).

61. *Husmandsgutten* by H.A. Foss was an incredibly popular novel that was serialized in *Decorah Posten*.

62. As soon as I read this quotation, I became suspicious; but I didn't have time to look it up. After I wrote the above, I reread Hoyme's 1900 ordination speech,— it is printed in the book *Prest og Formand*. It showed that my suspicions were justified. The expression "to preach the gospel without the admixture of human learning" does not occur in the speech as it has been printed. This does not prove that "S" is outright lying; it might be that Hoyme did not follow his manuscript as he spoke, and in such a case he might have made the mistake of saying something that he never would have written. And Hoyme would never have written something like that. Linguistically the expression is monstrous. Hoyme was too sharp a logician and had too keen an ear for the sound of language to have written anything like that—I am sure of this, but I suppose "S" won't agree.

The whole speech demonstrates anyway that what I have said about Hoyme above is correct. If he had not dipped deeply into the well of literature he could never have written it.

Toward the end of the speech, he has even written a poem and included several verses, and it does not take any great critic to see that these two verses were inspired by Ibsen's *Brand*. The two last lines sound as though they came directly from the mouth of Pastor Brand himself!

Well, what does "S" himself think now of his proof! [Rølvaag's note]

63. Søren Kierkegaard, *Either/Or,* part 1, translated by Howard and Edna Hong (Princeton, NJ, 1987), 19.

64. I have been unable to discover who wrote this poem. My translation.

65. Rølvaag quotes Darwin and Coleridge in English.

66. Rølvaag is presumably referring to *En fallit.*

Notes to Simple Reflections on The Name Change

67. This is a reference to Governor William L. Harding of Iowa, who issued a proclamation in May of 1918 prohibiting the use of any language other than English as a medium of instruction, in conversations in public places, over the telephone, in public speeches, and at church services.

68. An epic poem by the Swedish poet Esaias Tegnér (1782–1846) based on an Old Norse saga. There are several English translations, including one by W. Strong (1933) and one by Ida Mauch (1960).

69. This excerpt is quoted in English. It is possible that some words were inadvertently omitted in the final sentence.

70. The Olson Sisters, Ethel and Eleanora, were popular performing and recording artists specializing in humorous dialect sketches.

INDEX